The Kuomintang and the Democratization of Taiwan

The Kuomintang and the Democratization of Taiwan

Steven J. Hood

Routledge
Taylor & Francis Group
NEW YORK AND LONDON

First published in paperback 2024

First published 1997 by Westview Press

Published 2019 by Routledge
605 Third Avenue, New York, NY 10158

and by Routledge
4 Park Square, Milton Park, Abingdon, Oxon OX14 4RN

Routledge is an imprint of the Taylor & Francis Group, an informa business

Copyright © 1997, 2019, 2024 Taylor & Francis

All rights reserved. No part of this book may be reprinted or reproduced or utilised in any form or by any electronic, mechanical, or other means, now known or hereafter invented, including photocopying and recording, or in any information storage or retrieval system, without permission in writing from the publishers.

Trademark notice: Product or corporate names may be trademarks or registered trademarks, and are used only for identification and explanation without intent to infringe.

Library of Congress Cataloging-in-Publication Data
Hood, Steven J.
  The Kuomintang and the democratization of Taiwan / by Steven J. Hood.
    p. cm.
  Includes bibliographical references and index.
  1. Chung-kuo kuo min tang. 2. Taiwan—Politics and govemment—1988– 3. Democracy—Taiwan. I. Title.
JQ1519.A5C645   1997
324.251 '083'09049—dc20
                                                                96-33346
                                                                CIP

Publisher's Note
The publisher has gone to great lengths to ensure the quality of this reprint but points out that some imperfections in the original copies may be apparent.

ISBN 13: 978-0-367-29341-3 (hbk)
ISBN 13: 978-0-367-30887-2 (pbk)
ISBN 13: 978-0-429-31216-8 (ebk)

DOI: 10.4324/9780429312168

To Mary

Contents

List of Tables and Figures	x
Preface	xi
Acknowledgments	xiv

1	**Theoretical Considerations**	1
	A Party Shrouded in Controversy	1
	Liberalization and Democracy	4
	The Kuomintang and Political Tutelage	5
	Lessons of Democracy's Third Wave	7
	A Framework for Analysis	11
	Notes	17

2	**Rebuilding the Party on Taiwan**	21
	The Reorganization of the Kuomintang	21
	Building a Credible Economic Record	29
	Local Level Political Reforms	32
	Testing the System	35
	An Effective Instrument of Control	38
	Notes	39

3	**Political Calm and Slow Change**	42
	A Modernization Plan for Taiwan	42
	The Party Moves Towards Inclusion	43
	Chiang Kai-shek's Final Years	48

The Kuomintang on Taiwan: The First Two Decades	50
Notes	55

4 Chiang Ching-kuo's Break from the Past — 57

Maintaining Political Calm	58
A Quasi Opposition Party Emerges	62
Diplomatic Setbacks and Liberalizing the System	64
At the Brink of Change	70
Notes	70

5 Liberalizing the Political System — 73

The Growing Pressure to Liberalize	74
The Emergence of an Opposition Party and an End to Martial Law	78
Opening the Party and Representative Institutions	83
Chiang Ching-kuo and the Politics of Reform	84
Notes	90

6 Inner-Party Conflict and the Emergence of Democracy — 93

Securing the Party Chairmanship	93
Extending Reforms and Lee's Fight for the Presidency	97
The Rise of Constitutional Questions	101
Liberalization, Elections, and Lingering Constitutional Issues	103
The Development of Party Factions	108
Facing an Uncertain Future	116
Notes	117

7 Testing Democratic Reforms in Taiwan — 119

Lee Teng-hui's Diplomatic Agenda	119
The Fourteenth Party Congress and a Splinter Party	121
The City/County Campaign and Election	127
A Year of Endless Campaigning	129
Run-up to the Presidential Elections	132
Taiwan's First Presidential Campaign and Election	133

	Conclusion	141
	Notes	147
8	**Concluding Analysis: The Kuomintang and Political Development on Taiwan**	150
	The Kuomintang Record on Taiwan	151
	The Kuomintang and Political Development	165
	Notes	168

Acronyms	170
Bibliography	171
Index	178
About the Book and Author	182

Tables and Figures

Tables

4.1	Taiwanese Composition in Party/Party Organs	60
4.2	Taiwanese Composition on CC, CSC, 1981	68
5.1	Electoral Support for the KMT and TW in Selected Elections	74
7.1	Membership in the KMT, CC, and CSC	125
7.2	Factional Composition of KMT Party Elite, 1993	126
7.3	Election Results, 1996 Race for President/Vice President	141
8.1	Political Parties and Percentage of Electoral Support	162

Figures

2.1	KMT Organizational Structure, 1924-1950	24
2.2	Kuomintang Organizational Structure, 1951-Present	27

Preface

In the last few years there have been several important political studies focusing on Taiwan. This has been a welcome development. Taiwan's lack of diplomatic relations with other countries and mainland China's relative prominence in the world contributed to the lack of attention given to Taiwan. Some scholars have had an aversion to studying Taiwan because of their dislike for Taiwan's political regime.

This book's general focus is on this regime. I consider the role of the Nationalist Party of China (Kuomintang, or KMT) in the democratization of Taiwan. The study has filled an interest I have had in determining to what degree the KMT was the villain it is sometimes portrayed to be, and the embodiment of the political and moral good partisans have claimed it to be. I have found the party to be a fascinating organization of contradictory purposes and achievements. Its reputation is marred by ineptitude and by brutal acts of repression. It nevertheless still managed an incredible feat of economic modernization on Taiwan and eventually became a proponent of democracy.

I focus on the role of KMT party elites in the democratization process, which I believe is the most neglected aspect of studies done on the political transformation of Taiwan. While I do not question the heroic struggles of the political opposition in Taiwan, my attempt is to direct attention to the significant effort Kuomintang leaders took to thwart democracy, and later, smooth the way for democratic reforms. It is important to understand the KMT's evolution from a Leninist party-state to a fractious party in a competitive political system. While Taiwan's experiment with democratization mirrors the experiences of studies done on countries in Latin America and Southern Europe, important differences exist.

Latin American and European case studies focus on conflict, decisions, compromises, and accidents that result from relatively short-term confrontations between elites in the opposition and softliners and hardliners within authoritarian regimes. These factors are important in the Taiwanese case as well, but other aspects are more important. Taiwan's democratization has been a long-term process of elites wrestling within the confines of political institutions. For this reason, democratization came about through reform of the KMT party-state, Taiwan's representative bodies, and political ideology. Driven by a subethnic split between Taiwanese and mainland-born Chinese and a desire for a liberal regime, the opposition was the catalyst for putting the reform agenda in motion. These reforms liberalized the Kuomintang and the state simultaneously. For this reason, understanding the democratization of Taiwan requires an in-depth study of the Kuomintang.

Those who have done research on Taiwan-related topics know of the difficulty in finding credible sources. While Western scholarship on Taiwan is available, Chinese language sources are limited and ofttimes lack credibility. Pre-1989 writings on the Kuomintang are mostly the products of prominent party figures or those sympathetic to the party. Many of these materials lack scholarly development and are most often idealized accounts rather than accurate portrayals of political life in Taiwan under KMT rule. Recent works are better. They reflect the political polarization that has driven the forces of democracy, though they still lack theoretical development. Press coverage on political events in Taiwan, though greatly improved, is often too speculative. The Kuomintang archives proved helpful in providing early party documents, though the KMT Historical Commission has kept nearly all party documents dealing with Taiwan closed.

For these reasons, I relied heavily on interviews of scholars, party leaders, government leaders, journalists, members of the opposition, and business owners to fill in gaps where I thought the literature was still incomplete. Most of the interviews were conducted during spring and summer 1993. I am grateful to the Council of International Exchange of Scholars and the Fulbright Committee for awarding a grant to conduct interviews and archival research in Taiwan.

Several individuals in Taiwan helped me set up interviews. Johnny (Jennan) Sand of the KMT Cultural Affairs Department and Li Yun-han of the KMT Historical Commission made many of the initial contacts with party officials for me. Susanna Su called upon personal acquaintances, giving me access to several top-level officials. Michael and Jennifer Chi arranged lunch meetings and other contacts with Democratic Progressive Party legislators and party officials. To each of these individuals I express my sincere thanks. Without their help, many of my interviews would not have been possible.

I am grateful to factional leaders and local party workers in the Taipei City, Ilan County, and Tao Yuan County party offices for their time in helping me understand local party organizations and their relationship to KMT party central. Several professors spent many hours with me discussing all aspects of Taiwanese politics. Professor Hu Fo, Chu Yun-han, and Lu Ya-li of National Taiwan University helped sort-out the intricacies of Kuomintang factions. Professor Yang Tai-shuenn met with me on several occasions. His analysis of the political culture of Taiwan and the strengths and weaknesses of Taiwan's political system helped me assess the strength of democratic reforms in Taiwan.

In writing the book, I benefitted immensely from the comments of prominent scholars who know Taiwan well. Professors Andrew Nathan,

Preface xiii

Robert Scalapino, and Tun-jen Cheng all read drafts of this book and offered timely criticisms and suggestions. Their efforts greatly improved the quality of my work. I also received help from Professors Alan P.L. Liu, Karl Fields, and Paul Stern on the theoretical development of the book. Their comments early in the writing of the manuscript were invaluable. An anonymous reader at Westview made some helpful comments that led to a clearer analysis. Finally, I am grateful to my wife, Mary, for her reading of drafts, painstaking efforts to sharpen my writing skills, and enthusiastic support of all my endeavors.

Steven J. Hood

Acknowledgments

A portion of chapter 6 was published under the title "Political Change in Taiwan: The Rise of Kuomintang Factions." It appeared in the May 1995 issue of *Asian Survey*. I am grateful to the University of California Press for granting permission to reprint a portion of that article here. I also thank M. E. Sharpe Inc. for granting permission to reprint material from several tables in Hung-mao Tien's book *Taiwan's Electoral Politics and Democratic Transition: Riding the Third Wave* (1996).

SJH

The Kuomintang and
the Democratization of Taiwan

1

Theoretical Considerations

A Party Shrouded in Controversy

In October 1986, President Chiang Ching-kuo announced that political parties would be allowed to organize and challenge the ruling Kuomintang (Nationalist Party or KMT) in national elections on Taiwan.[1] Unprecedented political openness in the months prior to October buoyed up the opposition's hope that the KMT would be relinquishing its monopoly of official power within the government. Chiang's announcement, therefore, seemed a logical step in Taiwan's painful journey towards democratic rule.[2] Since the 1986 declaration of party pluralism, factional gaps have widened within the KMT and party leaders have openly criticized one another. Old-guard party members born on China's mainland have fought against the rapid pace of liberalization within the party and have lamented losing their exclusive hold on political power. Younger mainlander party members have formed a new political party to challenge the Kuomintang, now dominated by Taiwan-born members. President Lee Teng-hui has publicly called for greater democracy for Taiwan's citizens though he has resisted calls to democratize the party. These disagreements have weakened the effectiveness of the KMT vis-a-vis newly established political parties. The conflict caused some within the party to wonder whether the Kuomintang would stay intact long enough to celebrate its one-hundredth birthday in 1995.[3] Yet for all its problems, the party has managed to maintain a high level of public support. Many observers believe, and recent elections attest, that the KMT can survive its current struggles and emerge as a democratic party stripped of its authoritarian past.[4] More importantly, there is every indication that democracy is taking hold in Taiwan. Representative institutions have survived the transformation process and continue to gain strength. An open presidential election has been held. The people are free to express their opinions on policies, politicians, and the Taiwan's future. Political debates have been moderated by mostly centrist positions taken by government leaders, opposition leaders, the media, and members of the business community. Thus Taiwan has so far been spared the dangerous influences of extremism that has plagued so many democratizing countries.

The clash of authoritarian and democratic tenets within Taiwan's political system and the Kuomintang, and the party elite's handling of this contradiction is the focus of this book. The Kuomintang's role in the democratization process on Taiwan has been largely overlooked, though there are a number of good studies that have appeared in recent years that consider the emergence of democracy in Taiwan. Cheng and Haggard's *Political Change in Taiwan* and Tien's *The Great Transition: Political and Social Change in the Republic of China* are two excellent volumes that consider many important aspects of democratization, including economic and social development, the rise of opposition parties, Taiwan's relations with mainland China, and electoral politics.[5] The latter is also a focus of Tien's recent book *Taiwan's Electoral Politics and Democratic Transition* and Yun-han Chu's *Crafting Democracy in Taiwan*.[6] Alan Wachman has considered the important role of subethnic differences in Taiwan and how the national identity question has influenced the democracy movement, and Murray Rubenstein has written a fine study of politics and society in Taiwan generally.[7] But all of these books fail to focus exclusively on the role of the Kuomintang in the democratization process.

Peter R. Moody's *Political Change in Taiwan: A Study of Ruling Party Adaptability*, does focus on the role of the KMT.[8] Like Moody, I will analyze the Kuomintang both as an independent actor and as an institution that was acted upon by a variety of economic, social, and political agents. Moody downplays the role of Leninism, however, and he does not document political change in Taiwan or within the KMT chronologically. I suggest these are important elements that have been overlooked by Moody and others in the recent studies that consider Taiwan's democratization. They are the real keys to understanding Taiwan's evolution from an authoritarian regime to a democratic one.

There has always been widely divergent views of the KMT. Praised by some, despised by others, the KMT has always been a focus of controversy. During the Nationalist era in China (1927-37), the KMT was opposed by industrialists who colluded with foreigners the KMT deemed imperialists. Warlords took advantage of KMT appeasement while offering little in return. Japan's invasion of China in 1937 dealt yet another blow to the Kuomintang barely twenty years after individual Japanese had assisted in Sun Yat-sen's early efforts to build the KMT into an effective revolutionary party. The communists weakened the Kuomintang by offering attractive alternatives to the often contradictory and ineffective policies of Chiang Kai-shek. After fleeing to Taiwan in 1949, the KMT government initially won only mixed support. A successful land reform program and rapid economic modernization stood in stark contrast to political repression characterized by fraudulent elections and organized brutality.

But by the late 1980's, Taiwan was in the midst of a political transformation that mirrored the island's much heralded economic achievements. Though the transformation seemed to have sparked suddenly, it had in reality been a gradual and complicated process spanning over four decades. That process is continuing and democracy is taking hold on Taiwan. A consideration of the forces of liberalization that has fueled democratic expectations on Taiwan gives rise to several important questions. How did the process of political liberalization begin? Did the KMT leadership employ a plan to create a "democratic miracle" to coincide with the "economic miracle?" What role has the party rank-and-file played in this process? What non-KMT forces played an important part in planting the seeds of democracy in Taiwan? Are there lessons in the Taiwan case for other authoritarian states facing liberalizing pressures? More particularly, since the regime in Taiwan was a Leninist party-state, does it provide a blueprint for other Leninist states to follow? Lastly, what is the quality of Taiwan's political system now and what can we expect in the future?

This book seeks to answer these questions. In order to do so, a focused study of the Kuomintang on Taiwan is essential because the Kuomintang regime has been both an opponent and proponent of democratic change on Taiwan. We consider the contradictory mission of the KMT on Taiwan as a party organized along Leninist lines that promised democracy to its people. For decades that promise seemed empty--mere words spoken to buy time for a paranoid and repressive regime obsessed with a dream to reunite all of China under Nationalist rule. Under pressure of a patient but persistent opposition that was driven by subethnic rivalry and the hope of democracy, the Kuomintang gradually came to accept the legitimacy of democratic rule. This transformation warrants close examination.

This chapter begins with a consideration of what is meant by the terms liberalization and democracy. We then turn to a discussion of Sun Yat-sen's notion of KMT democratic tutelage and how the KMT came to adopt a Leninist organization. Next we review what contemporary scholars have learned about the democratization process and how this relates to the KMT's claims of having democratized Taiwan. Then we introduce the framework that will be used to analyze the party and the emergence of the democratic movement on Taiwan. This will be followed by some general conclusions of this study.

Liberalization and Democracy

Some argue there exists a distinct style of democracy in East Asian states.[9] While particular arguments relating to the cultural aspects of democracy in Taiwan will be discussed later in this book, this study rejects the democratic uniqueness argument and accepts a more traditional concept of democracy as forwarded by Joseph Schumpeter, Philippe Schmitter, and Terry Lynn Karl. Democracy is "...a system of governance in which rulers are held accountable for their actions in the public realm by citizens, acting indirectly through the competition and cooperation of their elected representatives."[10] The expectation in this definition is that citizenship matters in a democracy. Citizens are able to vote in competitive, fair elections, run for public office, demand accountability from elected officials, have political rights and values respected in the political system, and be ensured of majority rule. While the above definition speaks in a general sense of what democracy entails it is by no means exhaustive. This study also seeks to analyze the staying power and quality of democratic principles in Taiwan. This necessitates considering some aspects of democratization in the consolidation phase of democracy.[11] Democratic consolidation occurs when the democratic regime is reasonably secure from reverting back to authoritarian or pre-democratic rule. Rules are established, democratic procedures are made secure by the cooperation of competing political parties, groups, and the masses. Democratic uncertainty is replaced by a general sense of fair play, trust, tolerance, and moderation.[12]

Many regimes caught up in the most recent wave of democratization are not yet democratic, though they are in the process of liberalizing.[13] Liberalization is done by degrees: loosening press restrictions, legalizing political parties, freeing political prisoners, tolerating free speech, etc.[14] It is the process of opening up the political system, but ruling elites may not necessarily have in mind democratization when liberalizing a system. A regime that liberalizes may be trying to begin a process of democratization, or it may be trying to gain legitimacy to maintain its exclusive control of the system. It is argued in this study that until late 1986, KMT leaders found it necessary to liberalize the political system in degrees without having immediate intentions of moving towards democracy. In 1986, they found it was no longer possible to liberalize without beginning a democratic transition because further resistance would risk political chaos.

While the political system in Taiwan has gone through considerable liberalization, it is only now becoming fully democratic. The power of the executive remains great even though the legislature has been popularly elected and has become a powerful body in recent years. The office of president was contested in direct elections for the first time in 1996, and incumbent Lee Teng-hui won by a large margin. But uncertainty will continue to exist over the role of the president in regards to both law making and the extraordinary privileges the KMT executive has enjoyed in controlling the government bureaucracy.

The Kuomintang and Political Tutelage

The Kuomintang contends democracy is emerging in Taiwan because of its political tutelage plan. This plan was created by Sun Yat-sen on mainland China between 1910 and his death in 1925. Under Chiang Kai-shek's rule the Kuomintang paid scant attention to Sun's plan. Disastrous social, economic, and political policies, coupled with war and foreign encroachment shattered the KMT's hopes of ruling mainland China. Chiang Kai-shek planned to use Taiwan as a temporary capital and base to launch a subsequent invasion of the mainland. But after retreating to Taiwan, Chiang realized he needed a tighter political organization to not only gain the strength needed to confront the communists, but to save his unpopular regime on Taiwan as well. A reorganization committee of the Kuomintang used parts of the plan authored by Sun Yat-sen in its blueprint for reorganizing the Kuomintang party-state. A brief description of Sun's ideas are essential for understanding the Kuomintang's claims that it introduced democracy to Taiwan.

By 1912, Sun's ideas of political development were taking shape in a theory he referred to as the *San Min Chu I (Three Principles of the People)*.[15] The three principles Sun espoused were nationalism, democracy, and livelihood--the latter being a type of socialism. He believed nationalism had to be developed first to restore a great Chinese state. The development of nationalism would help the Chinese defeat its Manchu rulers as well as foreign powers who had encroached on China. Once China's sovereignty had been established, the livelihood principle could be introduced which would develop the country economically and pave the way for the realization of democracy. But Sun Yat-sen's idea of democracy was based more on organizing an efficient state apparatus and less on democratic principles. In addition, the socialism of Sun Yat-sen was a plan to have the state take control of the major sectors of a modern economy--transportation, industry, construction, utilities, and finance. Because the *San Min Chu I* encouraged a strong role for a central authority in implementing its goals, the idea of a broad-based democratic system characterized by party competition did not always interest Sun. He did maintain, however, that he eventually wanted the Kuomintang to compete as a democratic party in a parliamentary system but felt it would be best for the KMT to be an authoritarian party until the country was prepared for democracy. Sun attempted to control the party by himself, but he believed further steps were needed to strengthen his role. A Leninist organization seemed to fit that need.

Although he originally stayed clear of Russian help, by 1924 Sun had come to see advantages of allowing Comintern agents to help reorganize the party. With a Leninist organization, the Kuomintang would enjoy exclusive political power in implementing the tenets of the *San Min Chu I*. Sun's position as party chairman would be unchallenged, and he would be able to send down directives to subordinates in the party. The party would then become the efficient power behind the state (a hallmark of the Leninist party-state system). Without the party chairman's blessing, the state would be powerless to enact policy. The party would be better disciplined and trained. Improved efficiency and clarity of purpose in the party would increase the chances of success in realizing Sun's goals for China.

Sun believed a Leninist organization could help him reach his goals of political tutelage. He had for some time favored a strong role for him personally as party president, and therefore believed a Leninist party gave him the tight organization the KMT lacked. It also reflected Sun's belief that a premature attempt to establish democracy would invite chaos and result in revolutionary failure. What he did not understand was that a Leninist party-state attempts to totally remake society by manipulating the way people think, the way they relate to one another, and the way they think about political authority. The adoption of a Leninist structure would temporarily transform society in a way that was antithetical to democracy. Sun felt the contradiction was not a significant one, however. Thus there was not an immediate concern for democracy within China or within the Kuomintang.[16]

Sun's hope that a complete reorganization of the party along Leninist lines would enable him to use "the power of the political party to reconstruct the nation," or to "place the party above the nation in order to rebuild the nation."[17] It became apparent, however, that more was needed than a Leninist organization. While a new organization gave strength to the party, it did not provide a political plan for accomplishing Sun's goals. Similarly, the *San Min Chu I* was largely a statement of political ideology, and did not present a clear agenda. In response to this need, Sun introduced his *Fundamentals of National Reconstruction* containing a blueprint for realizing the goals introduced in the *San Min Chu I*.[18] To establish nationalism Sun called for the party to conduct a period of military rule to subdue China's enemies so the party could construct a strong state apparatus. He then wanted the party to institute a period of political tutelage that first instituted economic reforms to improve the physical well being of people's lives and then begin training citizens in the practices of local self rule. He believed people would be better prepared for democracy at the national level after practicing democratic tenets in their own locales. Finally, the Kuomintang would replace tutelage with constitutional law, allowing all Chinese to realize their full rights as democratic citizens.

Sun's goals, to develop nationalism, a strong economic system, and a viable democracy, were extremely ambitious. Difficulties were likely to arise creating a need to adjust, abandon, or initiate new development strategies. But in addition to the ambition of these goals, the role the Kuomintang was supposed to take as military commander, economic czar, democratic tutor, and founder of constitutional law--all under the direction of a single powerful party chairman--was unrealistic given the realities of political struggle in developing countries. Development is not a neat linear process where nation-states go from traditional societies to democratic nations possessing mature economies. There is great uncertainty as political paths taken sometimes reap success, sometimes failure. Status-quo leaders are replaced by reformers, who are in turn replaced by more liberal reformers, or by conservatives trying to roll-back reforms.[19]

Until recently, the KMT viewed itself as the only party capable of saving China from foreign oppression and establishing prerequisites to democratic development. Now the KMT sees itself as a competitive political party that is to be thanked for building democracy on Taiwan according to the goals elaborated in the *San Min Chu I*. Is this self congratulation warranted? Can political parties develop a country by authoritarian means only to shift priorities at a certain juncture and establish democracy? While there is no question this was precisely Sun Yat-sen's goal, there is reason to doubt the Kuomintang's claim that it successfully fulfilled this promise by following Sun's plan. The KMT's use of Sun's plan to justify its rule is important, however. As we will see in this book, tenets of Dr. Sun's *San Min Chu I* and his tutelage ideas generally were used to justify authoritarian rule by couching party policies as tutelary or temporary measures on Taiwan's road to democracy--even though the party actually resisted democratization. All in all, Sun's ideas gave the KMT its Leninist organization and its control of the political system. Ironically, the Kuomintang's use of Sun's tenets on political development also gave the ruling party's detractors ammunition in their battle against exclusive KMT political control. In this respect, the challenge to KMT rule mirrors the experiences of other authoritarian regimes have faced in dealing with demands to democratize. This can be better understood by turning to a consideration of recent scholarship on democratization.

Lessons of Democracy's Third Wave

When analyzing the development of democratic regimes, Western political philosophers have traditionally pointed to two prerequisites to democracy: the existence of a middle class, and the acceptance of democratic mores.[20] This concern for prerequisites had long been important to comparativists as well.

Scholars determined that a country's level of economic development, its cultural attitudes and constraints, historical conditions, and external influences were the major factors inhibiting or encouraging democratic development.[21] But by the mid 1980s, research increasingly questioned the direct relation of these factors to the establishment of democracy. Scholars suggested more could be learned about democratization by focusing on the structural constraints to democracy and how elites react to and deal with these limitations.[22] Indeed, most comparative theorists emphasize the pivotal role elites play in the democratization process and discount that played by the masses.[23] Elites make democratic change from above. They compete, bargain, compromise, and negotiate with each other in ways the masses cannot. The burden of keeping people up to pace with political liberalization and democratization falls upon the shoulders of elites. In short, democratic transitions are brought about by elites who hold political power, both hardliners and softliners, and by elites who oppose those who have the power. This study finds elites who fit neatly into each of these categories, and others who fall somewhere in between. While most of the attention will focus on party chairmen and their control of the KMT organization, there are generally four groups of elites that are considered in this study:

1. *Party Chairmen.* Since Taiwan had a Leninist system for the better part of four and a half decades, party chairmen held the lion's share of power. This is particularly true of Chiang Kai-shek's and Chiang Ching-kuo's respective tenures as party chairmen. Lee Teng-hui eventually came to share power with elected leaders and other party elites as the system became increasingly open. Now the office of president has replaced the office of KMT chairman as the most important focus of power in Taiwan. By focusing on party chairmen, we can see how leaders learn from their political environment and gauge the liberalization process from authoritarianism to democracy.

2. *Other Top Party Leaders.* Other top party leaders, namely those serving on the Central Standing Committee of the KMT Central Committee came to have greater significance as the system became more liberalized and required technical expertise in government. Some of these leaders supported ongoing reforms, others resisted reform. Those party leaders who were "mainlander" usually had more influence, and older mainlander leaders were more likely to resist change than younger mainlanders.

3. *Other Party and Government Leaders.* Rank and file administrators, managers, and technocrats gained importance as the party and government called upon the expertise of college-trained experts to implement development plans and government policy. Though most were loyal to the Kuomintang, many became erstwhile critics of the KMT party-state by the early '90s. Their

support for democratization helped stabilize reform measures.

4. *Opposition Leaders*. Leading opponents of the KMT were usually college educated, and in recent decades, Taiwanese. They resented rule by the mainlander-dominated KMT and primarily used the weak national legislature, provincial assembly, and local representative bodies to gain a foothold. Evidence of their success is demonstrated in the newly established strength of Taiwan's elected bodies, and the enthusiasm for the Taiwan dialect and local culture--previous targets of the mainlander-controlled KMT.

The emphasis on studying the role of elites in democracy, although not a new one, has come about in part because elites have changed their attitudes about democracy. This change has been described by Nancy Bermeo as "political learning." By this she means authoritarians come to realize the benefits, or in some cases their only option for survival, is to move towards a democratic solution.[24] Part of political learning comes from witnessing the successful transitions to democracy in other countries, or conversely, the undesirable results of violent conflict if efforts to liberalize are resisted. Thus even standpatter leaders can liberalize a system either intending to democratize, or in attempting to partially open-up their regimes.[25]

Though Chiang Ching-kuo supported the status quo, he eventually found it reasonable to move towards democracy, even though many senior leaders in the party failed to support this transition. But Chiang realized the KMT could benefit from a democratic solution, and would face violent conflict if the system were not liberalized.

Research indicates gradual change is far more desirable than rapid change in the transition to democracy. Samuel Huntington and others have pointed out that in nearly every case, political systems are better off if they have experienced a transition from authoritarian rule to democracy with the cooperation of the old guard rather than an abrupt replacement of the authoritarian regime because replacement regimes usually fail as democracies.[26] The consensus is that the revolution-approach to democracy is dangerous and seldom successful. Incremental transitions allow rules to be established in a climate of moderation rather than one of political turmoil. Institutions have time to develop, thus making each liberalization phase seem normal rather than extraordinary. This is especially true in the development of electoral institutions. Elections are risky things in liberalizing or newly democratized countries. In countries where gradual transitions occur, oligarchs realize they have an advantage over the opposition in winning first-time elections because they retain some support from the masses and can maintain limits to institutional openness that favor their election.[27] They are also more likely to recognize their future success in electoral politics depends in part on their ability to solve problems while the country is still under authoritarian rule.[28] Similarly, oppositions increase the survivability of democratic movements if they are seen as cooperative and tolerant of gradual change. The prospects for a successful democratic transition in Taiwan was aided by every advantage mentioned here. In fact, while the transition in Taiwan has been long in coming, it has nevertheless been one of the smoothest transitions among newly democratized countries.

Recent scholarship also suggests the factors previously considered necessary for the establishment of democracy are vitally important in the consolidation of democracy. In fact, some scholars argue these factors are more often the product of democracy rather than prerequisites to democracy. If a country has a reasonable degree of economic development resulting in a large middle class, is not torn by ideological extremes, is given to measured political change, enjoys high levels of literacy, has a strong system of political parties that tend to lean to the political center of the country, and develops a parliamentary rather than presidential type of system, democracy is more likely to consolidate and mature.[29] Democratic institutions, therefore, bear the immediate imprint of elite efforts while consolidation requires a favorable political, economic, and social climate to nurture a sense of fair play, trust, tolerance, moderation, and obedience to the law.

But while the importance of elites is readily apparent, the Taiwan case also suggests traditional requisites to democracy--favorable economic, educational, international, and cultural conditions--were all important factors leading to the Kuomintang's decisions to liberalize. At the same time these elements have increased Taiwan's chances to consolidate its democratic institutions and encourage further democratization to occur. This study, therefore, finds a more direct link between prerequisites in the democratization of Taiwan than what some scholars have found in other countries.[30] This accounts in part for the long-term liberalization of the regime compared to the more rapid transformations that occurred in Latin America and Southern Europe.

There is a striking similarity between the plan Sun Yat-sen laid out in his blueprint of political tutelage and the things scholars have pointed to in studies done in the West. Indeed factors can be identified in both Sun's work and the work of contemporary theorists to explain the democratization process in Taiwan. But while there exists common ground between Sun and Western theorists, this book does not suggest that Sun's tutelage plan is the reason for Taiwan's experiment with democracy. Sun correctly identified some important factors in the democratization process, but KMT leaders came to realize the importance of these elements from a political perspective quite removed from Sun's theories. This study suggests that the KMT was never serious about Sun's plan. The Kuomintang used Sun's thought primarily as a way to build an ideological base for the party. The primary goal of the party was to reclaim mainland China. As opposition forces in Taiwan grew, and as the political balance in the subethnic cleavage between Taiwanese and mainlanders began to shift in the Taiwanese' favor, the party found it necessary to give in to demands for greater inclusion. As long as the KMT could maintain power, the party's leadership had little intention of extending political rights to the people. But when they could no longer exclude others from political participation, they realized the necessity of leaving behind its authoritarian ways and find new life as a democratic party.

A Framework for Analysis

Sun Yat-sen put together a political organization that was authoritarian and revolutionary. But his plan also called for the party to establish democracy. The Kuomintang failed to realize this goal on mainland China. But in Taiwan the forces of political liberalization have steadily increased the chances of Taiwan being able to reach democratic maturity. Because of the Kuomintang's contradictory purposes, it can claim to have played a significant role in the democratization of Taiwan, though the role it played was, until the late 1980s, also one of democratic resistance. In order to fully understand how the KMT both helped and hindered the emergence of democracy on Taiwan, it is necessary to look at the party in detail to see how the forces for democratization emerged in Taiwan. The Kuomintang's ability to build a stable state on Taiwan, coupled with socio-economic development and a patient opposition, raised the prospects of political contest. By 1990, calls for political liberalization were commonplace, even within the party.

This book is primarily interested in the role of KMT elites in the democratization process. Because the KMT was a Leninist party, Taiwan's leaders took a long view to their political prospects. They found it necessary to pay particular attention to party organization, ideology, their policy agenda, practical problems of governance, and the relationship between the party and government. So while the specific focus is on Kuomintang leaders and the democratization of Taiwan, these other points will help us understand the leadership's role in greater detail. In addition, they are useful categories for helping us look at the forces of democratization at work in and out of the party over time.

They suggest elites in Taiwan were engaged in a long-term process of give-and-take that eased the political system into a path of liberalization, then democracy. Long-term change took place in party and government institutions and in political ideology. These changes came about within the tangled web of a subethnic rift between Taiwanese and mainlanders that provided a political issue with far reaching significance thereby keeping the political struggle focused. A detailed explanation of why these criteria have been selected and what they entail reaffirms the importance of these points.

1. Leadership

Recent scholarship suggests focusing on the role of elites as a starting point for studying the emergence of democracy. This study concurs with this assessment. Understanding the role party leaders play is vital for comprehending the complexity of the KMT, the liberalization of the political system, and the prospects for democratic consolidation in Taiwan. For this reason we look at how Kuomintang leaders have ruled, and how they have responded to challenges from within the party and from the political opposition. The KMT leadership played a key role in easing the system gradually towards democracy. This slow-track transition stands in contrast to the military, political, and economic "moments" of compromise and collaboration identified by O'Donnell and Schmitter and others.[31] While recognizing the benefits of gradualism and moderation in the transition process, these scholars suggest authoritarians and opposition leaders decide on a democratic compromise at critical junctures resulting from political crises. While there have been political crises in Taiwan, they have not been as acute as the cases the authors of the *Transitions From Authoritarian Rule* series comment on. This is because KMT leaders learned from their mistakes on the mainland and from their experiences of four decades of rule on Taiwan. Bermeo's comments on political learning is important here. Leaders determine limited compromise is necessary to avoid having to take more extreme forms of political control such as military rule.[32] The Kuomintang's compromises along the way eased the system into a process of liberalization that eventually led to real democratic reforms that defy identification of a political moment. This study will show that the gradual movement towards democracy in Taiwan was dependent on political elites transforming political institutions and political ideology, sometimes willingly, at other times with great reluctance.

The role of party leaders has changed within the KMT. As ideological fervor and hopes for mainland recovery diminished, the conditions that facilitated the existence of a strong central leader began to disappear. We consider the quality of leadership generally and the conflict between party leaders driven by ideological concerns and leaders influenced by pragmatism. Ideological adherents can be either authoritarian or democratic.[33] In some cases they may be the former while claiming or believing to be the latter. Pragmatists can also be given to either authoritarianism or democracy.

While most contemporary theorists suggests the role of elites over prerequisites in the democratization process, the view in the late 1960s was somewhat different. Huntington argued that the "primary problem of politics is the lag in the development of political institutions behind social and economic change."[34] This study suggests Taiwan's political institutions did lag at times behind social and economic change, but more recently were considerably easier to democratize than public opinion. Democratic requisites are, therefore, also important in understanding democratic development in Taiwan. Elite conflict in Taiwan was in part an outgrowth of a steady improvement in Taiwan's physical quality of life and increased literacy, and continued subethnic conflict. For this reason, party leaders realized they risked too much in maintaining exclusive control of the political system.

The Taiwan case suggests prerequisites were helpful but not sufficient conditions for democracy. But democracy's failure to emerge in individual countries does not rest solely on the inadequacy or adequacy of socio-economic requisites.[35] Elites ultimately move a system towards democracy after believing democracy to be inevitable. So while Taiwan was blessed with a high level of socio-economic development, it is enough for leaders in other countries to observe the correlation between higher standards of living and democracy. For this reason, socio-economic development may lag in some newly democratized states.

2. Organization

Because of the KMT's Leninist tradition of leadership, it is necessary to expand our examination of party elites and consider the role of the party organization generally. We will see how the party organization has had to change to meet new political challenges. Indeed, the organizational function of the KMT has changed drastically since its reorganization on Taiwan. Through the years, the party has been promoted as the embodiment of the state's unified interests.[36] As Bermeo points out, studying party organizations is important because party leaders are the key players during the transition period. Political parties may moderate the transition process and increase the likelihood that elections will be held.[37]

Many one-party systems exist because of a strong central leader but have little or no real purpose of their own. Others possess a bureaucratic function, but lack cohesiveness and administrative ability. It is important to see at what point the Kuomintang began to liberalize the system and embrace democratic principles. Can democracy be introduced by a Leninist party and not lead to the dissolution of that party after democratic institutions have been established?

3. Ideology

Unlike many authoritarian regimes, KMT leaders have espoused a political ideology. Juan Linz suggests authoritarian regimes generally lack an elaborate or guiding ideology.[38] The role of ideology has been important in KMT history. At times certain ideological tenets have been emphasized too heavily in order to bolster party support.[39] Eventually the Kuomintang found it had to practice moderation to maintain mass support. This meant abandoning much in terms of recovering mainland China, and practicing exclusive rule generally. So while the *San Min Chu I* served as the official ideology of the party, the leadership's pragmatic view of the political situation in Taiwan led to moderation and abandonment of certain ideological tenets.[40] The party's attention to ideology, therefore, is a key to understanding what party leaders have deemed essential for their survival, the party's survival, and the survival of the nationalist government. At what point does the espousal of mainland recovery and Leninist tenets lead to policies that harm the chances for establishing democracy? Are ideologies meant to support authoritarian actions justifiable if a stable political climate is maintained and eventually leads to democracy? Are the goals of Sun Yat-sen's *San Min Chu I* compatible with KMT practice on Taiwan? How do Sun's theories and KMT practice compare with the conclusions scholars have reached in regards to democratization?

4. Agenda Setting

Political expediency and ideological orientation determine a great deal of a regime's policy agenda. Though some one-party systems can exist with little attention to goal setting, most need an agenda for purposes of legitimizing party rule and giving meaning to policies within the system.[41] The scope and ambition involved in setting the political agenda has both helped and harmed the KMT over the years. KMT leaders have embarked on impressive economic development plans in lieu of political freedoms, though in doing so, created a climate of political expectation. At the same time, the KMT's abilities to tackle many socio-economic problems improved the prospects for a smoother transition to democracy in Taiwan and its survival as a democratic party in the new climate of partisan politics.[42] It is important to consider who has been involved in agenda setting, and what purposes the agenda seeks to fulfill. Is the agenda primarily based on repression and control or on democratic development? Can short term policies that are strong-armed in character improve the chances for democracy later?[43] These too are important questions for this study.

5. Quality of Governance

One of the basic tensions running through every political system is the fragile balance of the means and ends of power on the one hand, and respect for political rights and social welfare on the other. As in most one-party systems the KMT's record is mixed, but specific attention to how the party has dealt with these issues is essential for understanding the Nationalist regime and how democratizers have gone about challenging the Kuomintang. The degree of attention the Kuomintang has given these issues suggests a great deal about the intentions and priorities of the party in maintaining authoritarian rule, liberalizing the system, and in allowing for the emergence of democracy.[44] In considering these matters we will look at the role of intellectuals, business people, interest groups, and the opposition generally who all sought redress or tried to build a power base of their own to challenge KMT rule. These are the politically aware recipients of an improved standard of living, higher education, and an awareness of functioning liberal democracies abroad and they are anxious to see democracy work at home.[45] A good deal of the concern for the quality of governance is associated with socio-economic conditions mentioned earlier that give rise to democracy and aid in the consolidation process by drawing attention to individual rights.

6. Party-Government Relations

Since the KMT's reorganization on Taiwan (in fact since the first party congress in 1924) and until recently, the party has considered the government to be a tool or extension of the party. The party claimed this to be justified under the principle of tutelage established by Sun Yat-sen. Yet the party and government have not always functioned harmoniously despite the fact that key government posts were held by top KMT officials. In addition, administrative realities and party directives have diverged from what the party leadership intended. For these reasons it is imperative to consider the relationship between the party and government in the party's attempts to rule Taiwan. Can a party that has been the power behind government separate itself from the government and behave as just another party in a democratic system? Can government institutions that have been liberated from Leninist control undergo a transformation that will enable them to operate democratically?

There are, of course, many other factors that could be employed to analyze the Kuomintang. The above six criteria are suitable and constitute a framework that both general comparativists and Asian specialists will find useful. By using these criteria in conjunction with theories and case studies of other comparative studies, some general conclusions about the Kuomintang and the democratization of Taiwan emerge:

1. The role elites have played are crucial in understanding the burgeoning democratic movement on Taiwan. While the KMT has been a Leninist party that has dominated the political scene in Taiwan, the party's leaders have developed the island economically, socially, and politically. While the Kuomintang embraced a Leninist power structure, its rhetoric (albeit often insincere) called for a democratic solution. This gave party leaders room to liberalize the system gradually, thus increasing the chances of a peaceful political transition to democracy.

2. The importance of an initially weak but persistent opposition has been important. Had the opposition been more imposing, extreme demands may have been made that would have given the KMT reason to resist all calls for liberalization. The opposition realized the people of Taiwan were supportive of many Kuomintang policies even though they desired expanded political freedoms. This tempered the opposition's positions on many policies and helped keep debates closer to the political center.

3. Factors such as economic growth, increased education levels, the emergence of a middle class, policies of external actors, and the demonstration effects of other regimes having made successful transitions to democracy were important in the liberalization of the KMT regime. At the same time these factors have aided in the consolidation process now underway in Taiwan and in rooting-out the remaining authoritarian habits of the past. Remaining doubts of democratic uncertainty will diminish only with the acceptance of democratic rules, and a with a growing sense of trust, moderation, and tolerance.

4. The passive nature of Taiwan's people has been a boon to liberal reform even though the rift between Taiwanese and mainlanders has been great at times. Taiwan's people have been patient in their wait for democracy and have even expressed ambivalence over the rapid pace of liberal reform. Although demonstrations have occurred on a regular basis in recent years, they have not been as violent or broad-based as they have tended to be in some other countries. This has been a result of the Kuomintang's legacy of repression, but it is also a cultural trait of Taiwan's people. At the same time Confucianism has proven not to be the obstacle to reform as argued by some. The influence of Confucianism encourages support for government leaders, which gave the KMT some room to liberalize the system at a safe pace.

5. The stability of the KMT's Leninist structure was important for introducing economic and social reforms useful for the growth of democracy. At the same time Kuomintang rule was also an obstacle to political change and the emergence of democracy. For the better part of three decades, the KMT's Leninist organization prohibited penetration by the opposition. Thus while the economy grew, political power remained in the hands of KMT leaders born on the mainland. This set the stage for "quasi-ethnic" conflict between mainlanders and native Taiwanese. But the KMT's acceptance of a

free market economy and other freedoms gave the party room to adapt to political circumstances in ways that Leninist parties in communist states cannot. This suggests that the kind of authoritarianism matters significantly in the liberalization/democratization process. Though there are no guarantees, exclusionary regimes that allow other outlets for participation in society besides politics can increase the likelihood that the liberalization process will go more smoothly than regimes that control all public aspects of the people's lives.

6. The future success of the Kuomintang relies on the party's ability to become a typical competitive party. This will require the party to become more democratic in its operation and will ultimately require a fundamental reorganization of its structure and operations. It will also require greater success in resolving the mainlander-Taiwanese conflict on Taiwan, and the related issue of Taiwan independence.

The chapters that follow are arranged chronologically. Chapter two examines the reorganization and establishment of the Kuomintang on Taiwan and looks at the KMT as a personal instrument of Chiang Kai-shek (1949-1960). Chapter three considers Chiang's modest efforts to make the political system more inclusive (1960-1975). Chapter four turns to an evaluation of the KMT under Chiang Ching-kuo. In particular it considers the "Taiwanization" of the Kuomintang and its reaction to the struggles of an infant opposition movement (1975-1982). Chapter five looks at the important final years of Chiang Ching-kuo, the rise of a significant opposition movement, and Chiang's decision to end martial law (1983-1989). Chapter six documents Lee Teng-hui's rise to power and his battles with the opposition and within the party (1989 to 1993). Chapter seven follows Lee's efforts to keep the party unified amid lingering questions of Taiwan's political identity and the rough-and-tumble world of electoral politics. The framework for analysis introduced above will be used at the end of chapters three, five, and seven to analyze the era of each KMT chairman in the Taiwan political scene. Chapter eight summarizes the general conclusions of this study, and suggests several important lessons of the Kuomintang's experience in regards to democracy and transitions from authoritarianism to democracy.

Notes

1. *Washington Post*, October 7, 1986, p. A18.
2. Andrew J. Nathan and Helena V.S. Ho, "Chiang Ching-kuo's Decision for Political Reform," in Shao-chuan Leng's *Chiang Ching-kuo's Leadership in the Development of the Republic of China on Taiwan* (Lanham, Maryland: University Press of America, 1993).

3. Chiang Yung-chin. *Pai-nien Lau Tien: Kuomintang Ts'an-sang Shih* (One Hundred Year-Old Store: The Kuomintang's Turbulent History). Taipei: Ch'uan Chi Wen Hsueh Ch'u-pan She, 1993.

4. See for example the views expressed by several prominent politicians and scholars in Taiwan after 1993 year-end county elections in the *Chung-Kuo Shih-Pao* (China Times), November 29, 1993.

5. Tun-Jen Cheng and Stephan Haggard, eds., *Political Change In Taiwan* (Boulder: Lynne Reinner, 1992); Hung-mao Tien, *The Great Transition: Political and Social Change in the Republic of China* (Stanford: Hoover Institution Press, 1989). Jaushieh Joseph Wu's *Taiwan's Democratization: Forces Behind the New Momentum* (Oxford: Oxford University Press, 1995), is also a good approach in considering the forces behind Taiwan's democratization process.

6. Hung-mao Tien, ed., *Taiwan's Electoral Politics and Democratic Transition: Riding the Third Wave* (Armonk, New York: M.E. Sharpe, 1996); Yun-han Chu, *Crafting Democracy in Taiwan* (Taipei: Institute For National Policy Research, 1992).

7. Alan Wachman, *Taiwan: National Identity and Democratization* (Armonk, New York: M.E. Sharpe, 1994); Murray A. Rubenstein, *The Other Taiwan: 1945 to the Present* (Armonk, New York: M.E. Sharpe, 1994). Another good source on the Taiwan democratization process in Chinese is Yang T'ai-schuuen's *Cheng-tang Cheng-chih yu Taiwan Min-chu Hua* (Party Politics and Taiwan's Democratic Culture) (Taipei: Democracy Foundation, 1991).

8. Peter R. Moody Jr., *Political Change in Taiwan: A Study of Ruling Party Adaptability* (New York: Praeger, 1992).

9. Clark D. Neher, "Asian Style Democracy," *Asian Survey* (November 1994), pp. 949-961.

10. Philippe C. Schmitter and Terry Lynn Karl, "What Democracy Is...And Is Not," *Journal of Democracy* (Summer 1991), p. 76. This definition is actually adopted from Joseph A. Schumpeter's classic work *Capitalism, Socialism, and Democracy* (New York: Harper and Row, 1942), p. 250.

11. Dankwart A. Rustow, "Transitions to Democracy: Toward a Dynamic Model," *Comparative Politics* (April 1970), p. 350.

12. Schmitter and Karl, "What Democracy Is," p. 83. Terry Lynn Karl, "Dilemmas of Democratization in Latin America," *Comparative Politics* (October 1990), p. 6.

13. Samuel P. Huntington, *The Third Wave: Democratization in the Late Twentieth Century* (Norman, Oklahoma: University of Oklahoma Press, 1991).

14. Rustow, "Transitions to Democracy," pp. 352-3; Nancy Bermeo, "Democracy and the Lessons of Dictatorship," *Comparative Politics* (April 1992); Karl, "Dilemmas of Democratization," pp. 6-11.

15. Sun Yat-sen, *San Min Chu I: The Three Principles of the People* (Chungking: Ministry of Information of the Republic of China, 1943).

16. Ts'ao Chun-han, "Su-tsao Chung-kuo Kuomintang Wei Kung-kung Cheng-tse Cheng-tang Tse-yi ("Molding China's Kuomintang into a Responsive Public Party"), in Yang T'ai-shuuen's *Cheng-tang Cheng-chih Yu Taiwan Min-chu Hua*, p. 56.

17. Li Chien-nung, *The Political History of China, 1840-1928*, Translated and edited by Teng Ssu-yu and Jeremy Ingalls (Stanford: Stanford University Press, 1956), pp. 444-5.

18. Sun Yat-sen, *Fundamentals of National Reconstruction for the Nationalist Government of China* (China, April 24, 1924).

19. Huntington, *The Third Wave*.

20. Aristotle, *The Politics*, translated by Carnes Lord (Chicago: University of Chicago Press, 1984); Montesquieu, *The Spirit of the Laws*, edited by Anne Cohler, Basia Miller, and Harold Stone (Cambridge: Cambridge University Press, 1989); Alexis De Toqueville, *Democracy in America*, Henry Reeve text (New York: Alfred A. Knopf, 1980).

21. Samuel P. Huntington, "Will More Countries Become Democratic?" *Political Science Quarterly* (Summer 1984).

22. Terry Lynn Karl, "Dilemmas of Democratization in Latin America," *Comparative Politics* (October 1990), p. 1. Some similar objections to the prerequisites approach were forwarded by Dankwart A. Rustow, "Transitions to Democracy: Toward a Dynamic Model," *Comparative Politics* (April 1970). Arend Lijphart has long emphasized the importance of elites in democratic consolidation. See his "Consociational Democracy," *World Politics* (January 1969), p. 212.

23. Guillermo O'Donnell and Philippe C. Schmitter, *Transitions from Authoritarian Rule: Tentative Conclusions About Uncertain Democracies* (Baltimore: Johns Hopkins University Press, 1986); Larry Diamond and Juan J. Linz, "Politics, Society, and Democracy in Latin America," in the authors' *Democracy in Developing Countries, Volume Four: Latin America* (Boulder: Lynne Reinner, 1989); Doh Chull Shin, "On the Third Wave of Democratization: A Synthesis and Evaluation of Recent Theory and Research," *World Politics* (October 1994). Although Samuel Huntington focuses on the role of elites, he still finds more use for the prerequisites studies than many others in this regard. See *The Third Wave*, chapter two.

24. Nancy Bermeo, "Democracy and the Lessons of Dictatorship," *Comparative Politics* (April 1992). See also Robert A. Dahl, *Polyarchy: Participation and Opposition* (New Haven: Yale University Press, 1971), p. 15.

25. Nancy Bermeo, "Rethinking Regime Change," *Comparative Politics*, April 1990, p. 372; Huntington, *The Third Wave*, chapters three and four.

26. Huntington, *The Third Wave*, p. 142; O'Donnell, Schmitter, and Whitehead, *Transitions From Authoritarian Rule*.

27. Philippe C. Schmitter, "Danger and Dilemmas of Democracy," *Journal of Democracy* (April 1994), p. 59.

28. Juan J. Linz and Alfred Stepan, eds., *The Breakdown of Democratic Regimes, Part I: Crisis, Breakdown, and Reequilibration* (Baltimore: Johns Hopkins University Press, 1978) pp. 41-46.

29. Guillermo O'Donnell, "Delegative Democracy," *Journal of Democracy* (January 1994), p. 56; Larry Diamond, "Rethinking Civil Society: Toward Democratic Consolidation," *Journal of Democracy* (July 1994), pp. 4-17; Francis Fukuyama, "Democracy's Future: The Primacy of Culture," *Journal of Democracy* (January 1995), pp. 7-8.

30. While the case studies presented by Schmitter, Whitehead, and O'Donnell, and Linz, Diamond, and Lipset deemphasize prerequisites in comparative studies, Huntington sees continued importance in looking to these factors.

31. O'Donnell and Schmitter, *Tentative Conclusions*, pp. 40-41.

32. Bermeo, "Democracy and the Lessons of Dictatorship," and "Rethinking Regime Change," pp. 372-3.

33. O'Donnell and Schmitter, *Tentative Conclusions*, Chapter 3.

34. Samuel P. Huntington, *Political Order in Changing Societies* (New Haven: Yale University Press, 1968), p. 5.

35. See Terry Lynn Karl's critique of the preconditions to democracy in "Dilemmas of Democratization in Latin America," pp. 3-5. See also Guillermo A. O'Donnell's *Modernization and Bureaucratic-Authoritarianism: Studies in South American Politics* (Berkeley: Institute of International Studies, 1979), p. xiii.

36. Stephanie Lawson, "Conceptual Issues in the Comparative Study of Regime Change and Democratization," *Comparative Politics* (January 1993), pp. 196-8.

37. Nancy Bermeo, "Rethinking Regime Change," p. 370.

38. Juan J. Linz, "Totalitarian and Authoritarian Regimes," *Handbook of Political Science, Volume III*, p. 264, Fred Greenstein and Nelson Polsby, eds. (Reading Mass: Addison Wesley, 1975).

39. A frequent problem according to Clement Moore. Clement H. Moore, "The Single Party as Source of Legitimacy," in Samuel P. Huntington and Clement H. Moore, eds., *Authoritarian Politics in Modern Society: The Dynamics of Established One-Party Systems* (New York: Basic Books, 1970), p. 53.

40. Tun-Jen Cheng, "Democratizing the Quasi-Leninist Regime in Taiwan," *World Politics* (July 1989).

41. John W. Kingdon, *Agendas, Alternatives, and Public Policies* (Boston: Little, Brown, 1984); also Cheng, "Democratizing the Quasi-Leninist Regime in Taiwan," p. 491.

42. Linz and Stepan, *The Breakdown of Democratic Regimes: Part One*, p. 41.

43. Sidney Verba, "Sequences and Development," pp. 302-3, in James S. Coleman, Joseph LaPalombara, Lucian W. Pye, Sidney Verba, and Myron Weiner, *Crises and Sequences in Political Development* (Princeton: Princeton University Press, 1971).

44. Huntington, "Social and Institutional Dynamics of One-Party Systems," in Huntington and Moore's *Authoritarian Politics in Modern Society*, pp. 32-40.

45. Cheng, "Democratizing the Quasi-Leninist Regime In Taiwan," p. 483; also Richard Bendix, *Kings or People?* (Berkeley: University of California Press, 1978) pp. 11-14.

2

Rebuilding the Party on Taiwan

The nationalist move to Taiwan was a last attempt to avert total defeat at the hands of the communists. Nationalist army remnants were routed in their few remaining holdouts on the mainland, and the KMT was reeling from mass defections and internal conflict. Indeed, Chiang's KMT-controlled government was being criticized from every corner. The U.S. was considering ending its support for the regime and establishing official relations with Beijing. Several Western nations had already forged ties with the communists, further tarnishing Chiang Kai-shek's prestige as the leader of modern China. It was clear drastic measures needed to be taken to stop the demise of the Kuomintang. If the party collapsed, the communist-domination of Taiwan would be inevitable.

The Reorganization of the Kuomintang

In the first few months of 1950 nearly every KMT member of significance had a theory explaining the reasons for the party's defeat on the mainland. Some pressured Chiang to purge rival factions. A few bold individuals created their own plans suggesting which direction the party should take. Chiang paid little attention to specific recommendations at first. Instead he acted on his own distrust toward many of the party leaders who had gained prominence on the mainland. Numerous officials were asked to resign. Many felt the heat and voluntarily left their posts. Among those leaving office were such notables as T.V. Soong, H.H. Kung, Sun Fo, and members of the CC Clique.[1] Li Tsung-jen, provisional president of the Republic of China, had taken medical leave to the United States, and became a primary target of Chiang's attacks. The generalissimo accused Li of being soft on communism, attempting to assert unconstitutional authority over the government, and not properly sustaining the goals of the party. For his part, Li complained that

Chiang never allowed him to fulfill his responsibilities as provisional president because Chiang used the party as a personal instrument at his disposal to thwart government policies. Most observers knew as long as Chiang ran the party Li would not have a chance to run the government as he desired. Theoretically, the KMT was to end its tutelage of the national government when Chiang "retired" from the government in early 1949. Some even hoped he would leave the country for a while and not interfere in politics. But the party continued its leading role. Chiang took steps to firm-up his control of the Standing Committee of the CEC--then the most powerful organ of Kuomintang central authority, thereby ensuring his ability to run the most important organs of the government.[2] Chiang's control over the party and government no doubt helped convince Li Tsung-jen to leave China in order to avoid Chiang's reprisals. For a time Li had the sympathetic ear of some journalists and members of the overseas Chinese community. But his continuous complaining, and his decision to join the communists in Beijing stripped him of his legitimacy to claim the presidency.

Other leaders were also critical of Chiang's strong role within the party. Carsun Chang was a key figure in writing the 1947 constitution. He complained that Chiang did not understand constitutional government. While the constitution clearly outlined the duties and powers of the various branches of government, and the responsibilities and limitations on leaders running the government, Chiang only gave lip service to tutelage and democracy and could not break away from his desire for autocratic rule. While still on the mainland, Chiang saw to it that the "Temporary Provisions Effective During the Period of Communist Rebellion," became law. This gave the president emergency powers and personal discretion in determining what articles of the constitution were relevant. The Temporary Provisions would serve as a defacto constitutional amendment until rescinded by Chiang Ching-kuo in 1989. The existence of the Temporary Provisions formalized Chiang Kai-shek's arbitrary rule and by-passed relevant agencies. Orders sent down through the ranks were often handwritten and made without any consultation from relevant parties within the government.[3] Many officials complained that Chiang's habit of

> pushing his interests as far as possible and exacting every ounce of advantage in any situation rendered it difficult for others to work with him. His unbounded confidence in his political and military judgment, his faith in his infallibility, and his mystic sense of identity with the nation made him arrogant and unsusceptible to advice and argument.[4]

Other party leaders accused Chiang and other significant KMT leaders of neglecting the doctrines of the San Min Chu I. Evidence of this neglect was the party's ignoring social problems while relying on the landed elite and lawless individuals for support.[5]

Chiang accepted some of the criticisms lodged against him. In a number of public speeches made during the first years on Taiwan, Chiang admitted the party had spent too much time on political and military matters, while not devoting enough time to social and economic reform. He acknowledged the KMT's lack of success on the mainland:

> All our past successes and victories were possible due to opportune occasions. They were granted us by history, not due to any real strength or solid footing of ourselves.[6]

At the same time, Chiang was not about to take personal blame for the nationalist defeat on the mainland. Until his death, he argued the KMT's greatest mistakes on the mainland were a weak organization, a lack of initiative and ideological substance, and a failure to take drastic actions against the communists.[7]

Amidst the confusion of laying blame and resettling the government in Taipei, Chiang Kai-shek took the first real steps towards giving the KMT a new beginning. Chiang organized the Central Advisory Council to retire older KMT officials so younger party members could be free of rigid thinking and habits that had limited party success. At the same time, a reform commission was set up to consider ways to reorganize the party. The basic party organization had not changed since 1924 (see figure 2.1). Several influential leaders within the party had been encouraging Chiang to set up the commission so the KMT could take the lead in implementing the livelihood principle of the San Min Chu I, particularly land reform.[8] The reorganization commission studied communist successes in rural China and in turn used the lessons learned for organizing reform in rural Taiwan.[9] Chiang also saw the reform commission as an instrument to weed out elements he deemed unfit to fill party posts and to improve the work habits of party and government leaders. Members of the reform commission were mainlanders, younger and better trained than most of the old guard KMT leaders. Commission members were highly educated and had a genuine desire to see party policy succeed.[10]

They reviewed communist literature as a guide in their deliberations because the CCP proved Leninism could be a success if it was organized properly.[11] This led to one of their first significant recommendations--the abolishment of the Central Executive Committee--an organ originally intended to coordinate the efforts of the party's top committees. This left the Standing Committee of the Central Committee as the most powerful decision making body of the party and greatly increased the Standing Committee's ability to

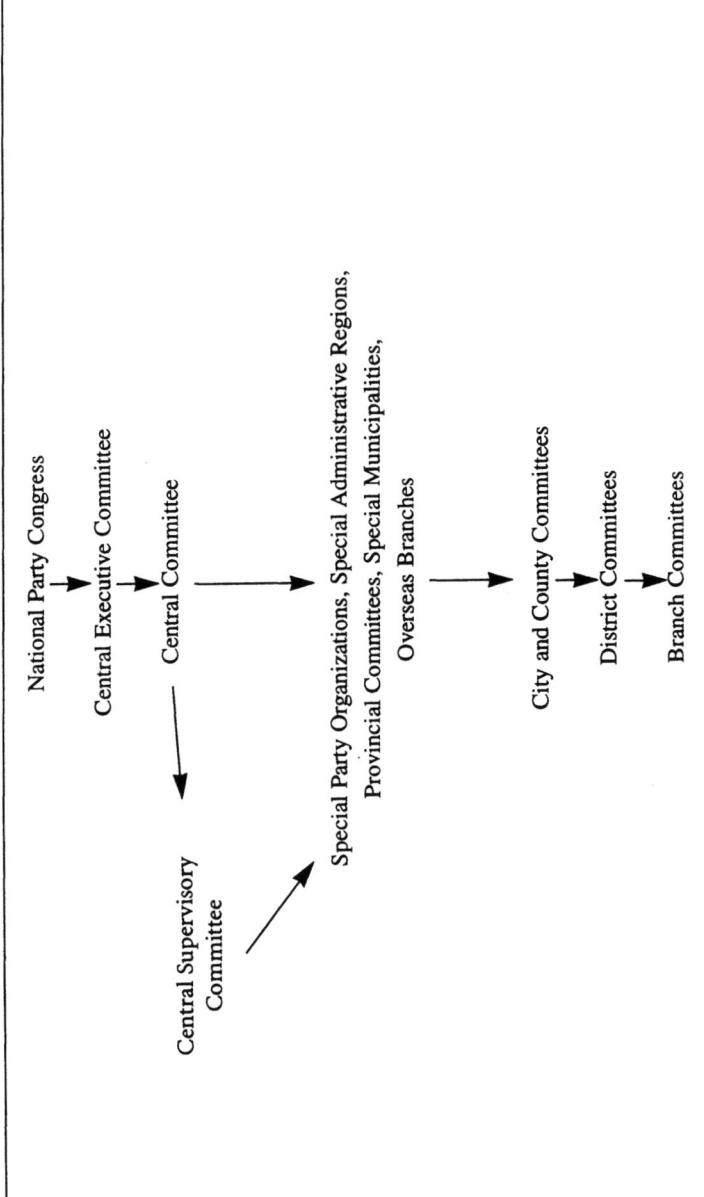

Figure 2.1   KMT Organizational Structure, 1924–1950*

National Party Congress → Central Executive Committee → Central Committee → Special Party Organizations, Special Administrative Regions, Provincial Committees, Special Municipalities, Overseas Branches → City and County Committees → District Committees → Branch Committees

Central Committee → Central Supervisory Committee → Special Party Organizations, Special Administrative Regions, Provincial Committees, Special Municipalities, Overseas Branches

*Adapted from Tsou Lu, *Chungkuo Kuomintang Shihlueh*, (China: Hsiang-wu Press, 1945), pp. 118-9.

articulate policy without duplication by the CEC.[12] The reform commission identified six goals in reorganizing the party:

1. The KMT was to be a revolutionary democratic party.

2. Party membership should be enlarged to include youth, intellectuals, farmers, and workers.

3. The party structure should continue to be based on the concept of democratic centralism.

4. Party cells would serve as the fundamental organizational units of the party.

5. The KMT would maintain strict standards of leadership throughout all sectors of society. All important decisions would be made by the party.11

6. The San Min Chu I would provide the basis for ideology.[13]

From the broad guidelines established above, the Reorganization Committee worked on details that had been neglected on the mainland. Wherever possible, a college diploma became a prerequisite for service as a cadre. This would take several decades to realize fully as many important cadres held leadership positions in the party having only completed high school.[14] Professional cadres (those receiving wages) and volunteer cadres were both expected to be held to the same standards of party loyalty. They were to demonstrate their love for the party by working tirelessly for the revolution. They had to demonstrate practical qualifications before being appointed to a particular responsibility. They were to live clean lives and be public minded. They had to be willing to learn from party members under their responsibility and demonstrate enthusiasm for national reconstruction.[15]

More was expected of the rank and file membership as well. A party member had to demonstrate greater loyalty to the party than in the past. Party members had to know the purpose of the party, know party principles, and perform service for the party. Dues were to be paid by party members. Two kinds of dues collection were established. Party members who demonstrated significant promise were encouraged to commit to a certain amount of dues to be paid monthly. Other party members were encouraged to pay dues as they were financially able.[16] The Reorganization Committee emphasized that the party headquarters needed to take greater care in nurturing local party members and strengthening local organizations. The committee stressed the need for party members to focus on the needs of society first. This helped the party create a clearer political agenda and a purpose for its existence that was missing in KMT efforts on the mainland. The party was encouraged to bring prosperity to the people and build a secure republic. This meant that the party was to build good relations with business leaders, educators, and other representatives of society. Although the intent was not to create a democratic society, it has been argued that these initial efforts did much to plant the seeds of democratic culture as the KMT learned to depend on society's strengths in its task of national development.[17]

There was a great consistency that the Kuomintang of the mainland years shared with the Kuomintang on Taiwan. This consistency was the contradictory purposes established by the party during both periods. Can a political party be both Leninist and democratic? Once again the party espoused democracy as a part of national reconstruction, yet it was clear that the structure of the party on Taiwan was still Leninist, in fact more Leninist than the party was on the mainland. As indicated in Figure 2.2, power was meant to flow from the top downwards to the local levels.[18] Membership on the Central Committee was to be cleared by the chairman of the party before formal nomination. This assured mainlander control of the most important organs of power. The Central Committee began meeting once a week to ratify decisions made by the Standing Committee. Theoretically, members were supposed to be able to report and forward their own ideas. But the size of the committee and time allotted for meetings made it possible for only the chairman and the Standing Committee to suggest the agenda of the meetings. The Central Committee reorganized working committees which were charged with expertise in party organization, cultural affairs, society affairs, youth affairs, mainland affairs, overseas affairs, women's issues, and training. Policies approved by the Central Committee were handed over to the Central Policy Committee which was the body in charge of implementing the policies into the government structure. This was facilitated by the fact that the Policy Committee's membership was comprised of significant legislators, ministers, secretaries, and other notables, thus securing the party's role as policy maker. Local organs of importance were county (hsien), city, and district organizations. They were charged with implementing party policy at the grassroots levels by sending directives to the branch and cell units. A notable aspect of these organizations is the fact that cell units have maintained no formal reporting structure back up the party apparatus, thus limiting their abilities to report successes or failures to the party hierarchy.[19] Thus the party, though supposedly an advocate of democracy, was in fact more tightly controlled in its organizational structure and operation than it had been on the mainland. In addition, Chiang Kai-shek ordered most of the larger county and city party posts to be filled by mainlanders, thus leaving less significant positions for Taiwanese party cadres.

Figure 2.2 Kuomintang Organizational Structure, 1951–Present*

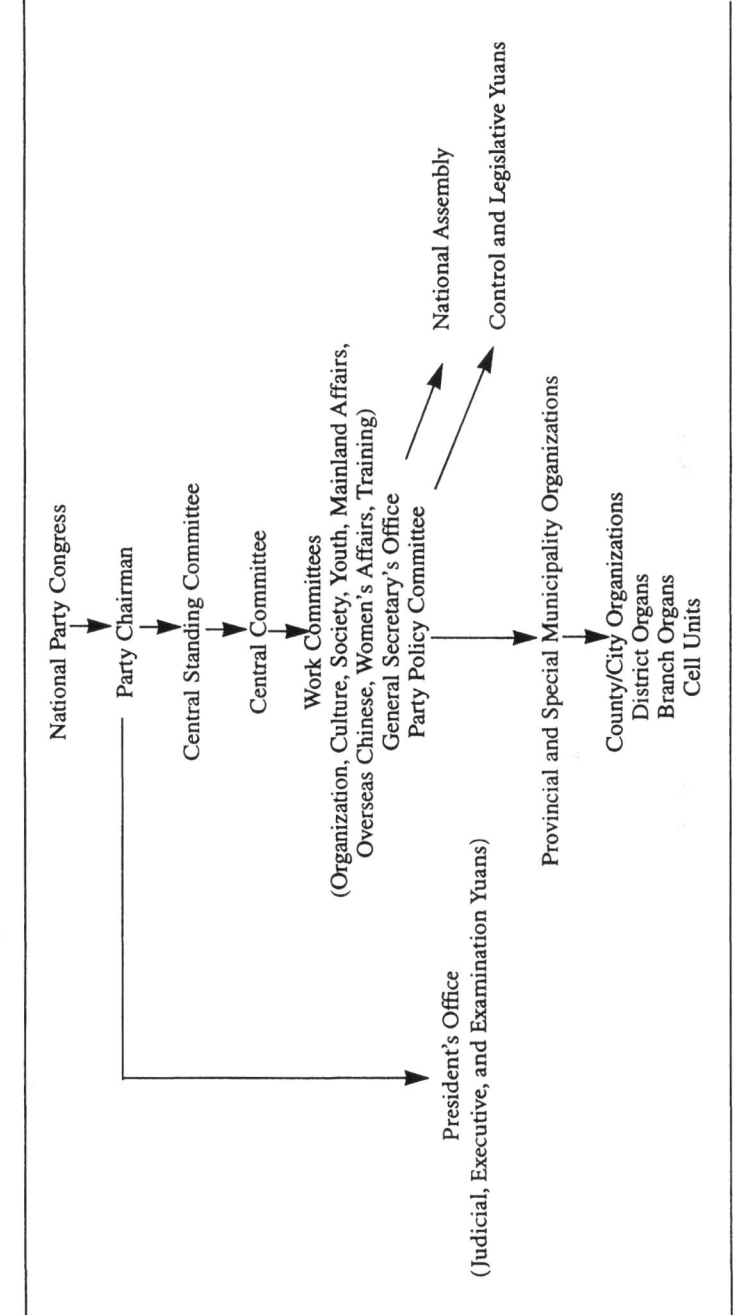

National Party Congress
→ Party Chairman
→ Central Standing Committee
→ Central Committee
   Work Committees
   (Organization, Culture, Society, Youth, Mainland Affairs,
   Overseas Chinese, Women's Affairs, Training)
   General Secretary's Office
   Party Policy Committee → National Assembly
                          → Control and Legislative Yuans
→ Provincial and Special Municipality Organizations
→ County/City Organizations
   District Organs
   Branch Organs
   Cell Units

Party Chairman → President's Office
(Judicial, Executive, and Examination Yuans)

*Adapted from Tsao Chun-han, "Kai-tsao Chungkuo Kuomintang," figures 1 and 4 (pages 61–2, 83).

The risks this contradiction posed to the party's mission were readily apparent. If the KMT devoted too much attention to the revolutionary aspects of its mission, then inner-party democracy would be sacrificed in favor of a strong role played by Chiang Kai-shek as director-general. If the party was to be truly democratic, challenges would arise from the ranks over how best to carry-on the revolution, and pressures to share leadership responsibilities would multiply. This would lead to a questioning of what Chiang Kai-shek's proper role in the party should be. While the KMT wanted broader representation, it is clear the reform commission wanted to steer clear of a democratic-structured party.

In his work *What Is To Be Done?*, Lenin outlines the basis of a party organization that is controlled by the party leadership.[20] He argued that only the top leaders (primarily he himself) knew the genuine needs of the country and how best to apply revolutionary principles. Party orthodoxy, therefore, would center on the role of Lenin and others who went along with the party leader's will would formulate policy and "send down" directives to national and local party organs for implementation. Thus democratic centralism, has always meant the party leader held the lion's share of power. Chiang wanted to maintain that characteristic in the Kuomintang.

Some scholars have questioned whether Chiang Kai-shek and Chiang Ching-kuo were in fact Leninist leaders. Edwin Winckler suggests the KMT was a "leaderist" dictatorship because the head of the party-state primarily relied on the security sector rather than the party apparatus to ensure obedience.[21] In a similar vein Peter Moody argues the party did not usurp state functions, Chiang Kai-shek and Chiang Ching-kuo did, thus making the two Chiangs dictators rather than Leninists.[22] But as Robert Tucker notes, Lenin's leadership style and Lenin's successors' styles were unique in one party-state systems because of the way they held ultimate authority as supreme leader in the party:

> Officially he was merely one of the members of the higher party organs....There was great discrepancy, however, between the formality and the reality of his position in the policy making bodies....He was a strong-willed and self-confident leader who repeatedly set himself against he main current of party opinion....[23]

Hannah Arendt similarly argues that the Leninist ruler is "not tied to any hierarchy, not even the one he might have established himself."[24] She further notes the independent role Stalin and others have played vis-a-vis the party in totalitarian systems.

But the Kuomintang was not totalitarian. It adopted a Leninist organization but did not try to remake human beings according to a political blueprint in the way fascism or Marxism attempted to.[25] As party leaders, Chiang Kai-shek and Chiang Ching-kuo used this Leninist organization to run the party, state, and the security apparatus just as Mao Zedong and Deng Xiaoping have done in China, and Lenin, Stalin and their successors did in the Soviet Union.

While the KMT wanted broader representation, it is clear the reform commission wanted to steer clear of a party patterned after Western political parties. Truly democratic parties value local representation and solicit feedback from local party leaders. They also accept the legitimacy of rule of law, competitive elections, and the need to gain a popular following at the polls.[26] Democratic centralism, the key Leninist instrument of organization, would continue to be the standard by which the Kuomintang would carry out its process of decision making and policy implementation. It was the intention of the party to allow voices of dissent to be heard at the upper levels of party leadership, as long as they were not direct attacks on Chiang Kai-shek's authority or threatening to the party's strategies of mainland recovery and development of Taiwan's economy.

The reform guidelines were intended to strengthen the authority of the KMT and put together a well-disciplined party that would be far more unified and well managed than the mainland Kuomintang. The revised party platform that followed reorganization emphasized recovery of the mainland and the obligation of the Kuomintang and country to fight communism. It did highlight the need to establish democracy, but these democratic ideals were identified as self-government at the local level, stamping-out corruption, educating the masses, and respecting academic and religious freedom. Little attention was paid to other constitutional provisions laid out in the 1947 constitution of the Republic of China.[27] And while the role of Chiang Kai-shek remained unquestioned, reorganization did allow younger mainlander party leaders to use their expertise and skills in implementing policies. This would result in greater government efficiency. It was also a key to the KMT's first shining success--the highly acclaimed economic development of Taiwan.

Building a Credible Economic Record

When the nationalist government came to Taiwan, some island residents preferred to form an independent republic with no political association with mainland China. Others opposed the harsh tactics of the Kuomintang but had not strong feelings on the independence issue.[28] Some claim the KMT was welcomed to the island as the legitimate government over all of China including Taiwan.[29] But there is widespread agreement that the KMT governor of Taiwan, Chen Yi, was neither a help to the people of Taiwan nor to the Kuomintang. Chen Yi managed to illegally confiscate properties and establish arbitrary laws that favored him and his cronies. Chen considered the residents of Taiwan to be a sub class of Chinese. At times he referred to them as Japanese collaborators because of a widespread belief held by some mainlanders that the people of Taiwan were too willing to cooperate with their Japanese colonial masters. Some mainlanders felt Taiwan was a frontier outpost that was more barbarian than Chinese. Yet a significant number of mainlanders were surprised at the high living standard on Taiwan compared to the war-ravaged mainland. In turn, many Taiwan residents were shocked at the backwardness of some of the mainlanders that first came to the island in the late 1940s.[30] But poor political rule turned many Taiwanese against the mainlander-dominated KMT. The residents of Taipei, Keelung, and Tainan launched an uprising on February 27, 1947. It stemmed in part from the beating of a woman in a Taipei park at the hands of government agents who took it upon themselves to punish the woman for selling tobacco without a license. But the riot was also a response to the KMT's mistreatment of the people and the party's failure to address nagging social problems. In the weeks that followed, thousands of people died in a vain attempt to depose of Chen Yi and Kuomintang rule. Chiang Kai-shek had to send troops from the mainland to reinforce those already stationed in Taiwan.

Chen Yi was removed from office and the seat was eventually filled by Ch'en Ch'eng, a capable administrator with a desire to restore calm and KMT prestige. Ch'en understood the KMT needed legitimacy in Taiwan to be successful. He believed economic reform, in particular land reform, was a necessary prerequisite to build support for the KMT. In preparing Taiwan to become a possible seat of government, Chiang Kai-shek gave Ch'en the go ahead to begin land reform in early 1949. Under the direction of the Taiwan Land Bureau, Ch'en began the reform with a 37.5% ceiling on rents, in preparation for land redistribution.[31] It was a first stage in Sun Yat-sen's land reform program. Land assessments and agriculture extension offices were established by the land bureau. The bureau oversaw the establishment of farmers associations and irrigation associations. There were quasi-governmental organizations to empower local farmers economically and enforce government guidelines.

The land reform program was popular and successful. Not only did it help pacify Taiwan's farmers, it built support for the Kuomintang as well. In summarizing the success of the program, Ch'en Ch'eng pointed out that under the old system of tenancy

> the life of ease and happiness enjoyed by the landlord was built entirely on the miseries of the tenant. This led to irreconcilable opposition between the two and created internal unrest in the rural districts and made them susceptible to external propaganda. This provided the communist agitators with an opportunity to infiltrate the villages. It was

one of the main reasons the Chinese mainland fell to the communists....
With the implementation of rent reduction, the livelihood of the
masses...was immediately improved. The communists were effectively
deprived of propagandistic weapons by a new social order that had
arisen in the rural areas.[32]

The KMT found advantages on Taiwan that did not exist on mainland
China. Taiwan provided an opportunity to implement economic policies
without resistance from competing political parties, warlords, and foreign
powers. Japanese colonization left working industries, roads, and other
infrastructure making continued economic growth possible.[33] The party elite
held no significant land holdings. For this reason there was no resistance to
land reform from government elites as there had been in the Philippines and
to a lesser degree in Korea.[34] The island was small, the population limited,
and the KMT had adequate power to enforce policies and evaluate them
properly. Government relocation and KMT reorganization reduced corruption
so urgent reforms could be implemented.[35] The people of Taiwan believed
it was in their best interest to support the KMT reforms, especially as success
with land reform became evident. The KMT realized it needed popular
support as well. Despite having a tarnished reputation in the United States,
the KMT regime received generous amounts of U.S. aid as Washington
wanted to strengthen Taiwan economically and militarily so it could serve as
a credible line of defense against the Chinese communists.[36]

After the reorganization of the Kuomintang, a new political program was
announced on September 1, 1950, that emphasized economic development.
The KMT dedicated itself to encouraging private enterprise while transferring
some operations to government ownership such as mining, petroleum
extraction and refinement, and steel production. Other industries such as
electric power, sugar, fertilizer, cement, pulp, paper, and shipbuilding were
also nationalized. Smaller industries such as the alcohol and tobacco
monopolies, and forestry were delegated to the provincial government, giving
local government its own source of revenues.[37] The Kuomintang promised
greater involvement of workers in management and ownership of enterprises,
and promised to attract foreign investment to supply a steady cash flow for
Taiwan's industrial development.

The emphasis on economic development was important not only to meet
the economic needs of the people, but as Sun Yat-sen had realized at the turn
of the century, it was essential for laying the groundwork for a democratic
republic. While the KMT proclaimed its devotion to democracy, there was no
earnest effort to introduce democratic reforms. Democracy was at best a
long-term goal, secondarily important to recovery of the mainland and
economic development. Economic success gave the KMT legitimacy that

bought the party time to plan its strategy for retaking the mainland. Some forms of political development were important, however.

Local Level Political Reforms

The Kuomintang believed that reorganization of the party was a vital part of introducing democracy into the system. But as suggested above, the reorganization of the KMT allowed for top level scrutiny of policies only, and uncompromising obedience to these ideals from subordinates. Party leaders were sensitive to the fact that political tutelage had been botched on the mainland and that the Kuomintang had to do something to bring substance to its platform of instituting local self-rule. In April 1950, the government announced that plans were being made to institute local rule in Taiwan. No particulars were elaborated on until September, however, as the Kuomintang had to finish its reorganization efforts. The September program of political reform included not only a schedule of upcoming elections, it also paid more attention to constitutional principles than the party had previously acknowledged.

Promulgated in 1947, few articles of the constitution of the Republic of China were considered for implementation until the nationalist retreat to Taiwan. Some scholars have argued the writers of the constitution had a good grasp of the Western concepts of individual rights and constitutionalism. Carsun Chang, considered to be the primary author of the document, was deeply influenced by the American founders' thoughts on political rights. Chang was also influenced by the constitution of the Weimer republic and its emphasis on basic needs for the people including food, clothing, housing, communications, education, and recreation.[38] The similarities between the principles Chang supported and Sun Yat-sen's livelihood principle in this respect are striking.

The main problem with the constitution as far as the Kuomintang was concerned was that it did not represent the immediate goals of party leaders. Nagging redundancies existed between the Legislative Yuan and the National Assembly, as well as between the Judiciary, Executive, Examination, and Control Yuans. These problems of overlapping authority were not able to be remedied, however, because the documents that outlined real political authority were Kuomintang documents that emphasized democratic centralism. There was also a problem of understanding what democracy meant. As mentioned above, the KMT platform and manifesto specified democracy as the establishment of an efficient and graft-free government. But democracies are not efficient in the sense that Chiang Kai-shek had in mind. Chiang was authoritarian and saw government policy flowing down from the top levels of the party. In some cases he was more given to the ancient Chinese belief that the government should be based on ethical and expedient considerations rather than laws. He failed to see the long-term value of rule of law and the high standards that were possible from following constitutional principles established in the West. In fact, it is not evident that he understood the principles of Western liberalism to any great extent.

This was true of other Kuomintang officials as well. Speaking in 1950, Chang Chi-yun, a member of the KMT reorganization committee and a famous Chinese scholar, spoke of the role of the Kuomintang to be principally the same as that of government in ancient China. He explained that the party was the focus of political activity and that the KMT had responsibility for the well-being of the people--a Confucianist ideal. But he failed to make the connection between the KMT's goals and democracy.[39] Chang called Mengtze, Confucius most famous student, China's greatest advocate of democracy because of Mengtze's insistence that government had the obligation to protect the property and physical well being of individuals. This is only partially what is mean by democracy in the West. He also saw the Kuomintang's goals of revolution to be loftier than those in the West. Chang suggested the primary purpose of America's revolution was independence, an ideal he felt was compatible with the nationalism principle of the San Min Chu I. He saw the primary purpose of the French revolution to have been the establishment of freedom.

In contrast, China's revolution sought to establish the San Min Chu I, which would take much longer to accomplish because the principles are an accumulation of ancient Chinese principles and modern political thought.[40] Chang's statements reflected the belief that the Kuomintang's goals were superior to those in the West and therefore justified the length of time necessary to realize these goals. More important, Chang's views were representative of many in the Kuomintang when it came to understanding democracy and democratic development. Similar statements were made by other high ranking KMT officials at the time and are still made today by conservative KMT officials who have objected to the rapid pace of reform the party has adopted. In short, the KMT paid more attention to the constitution on Taiwan than it did on the mainland, but the principles contained in the document were not greatly understood and were therefore not viewed to be as vital as the day-to-day politics the Kuomintang involved itself in. In addition, the greatest obstacle to constitutional law remained Chiang Kai-shek's call for unquestioned loyalty to him and party orthodoxy. This contrasted with efforts made by South Korean officials in the early 1950s. Seoul introduced a program to educate the population in democratic ideas and procedures. While democracy was abruptly abandoned in Korea, the education movement laid a groundwork for future liberalization efforts in the 1980s, as the democratic seeds sprouted in the generation that had been schooled in democracy three decades earlier.[41]

In January 1951, the much awaited elections for county and city council seats were held. The KMT candidates won handily as the only political party represented in the elections.[42] A few independent candidates did run for office, but they lacked the financial resources and access to the KMT-controlled media organs to run successful campaigns. For this reason, only a few independents were successful in gaining office. In April, county magistrate offices and city mayoral offices were contested. The Taiwan Provisional Provincial Assembly was organized in December, though the original members of this body were appointed. Local elections could not threaten Kuomintang rule because efficient power was in the hands of party leaders serving in the national government, and due to the fact that local leaders had few resources at their disposal. Furthermore, their responsibilities mirrored those of the national government, though local officials were obligated to follow the lead of the national government.

The establishment of local elections coupled with the Kuomintang's desire to recruit loyal local followers to represent the party as cadres resulted in the growth of factions. Holding local elections and recruiting local party leaders (mostly Taiwanese) was important to the KMT's claim to be a legitimate representative of the people. With the exception of county chiefs who were almost always from areas other than the county they represented, local party leaders at the branch and district levels were very often interested in personal economic gain in addition to developing their local areas. The KMT monopoly of political power gave them significant power locally. Although party headquarters set national policy and demanded unquestioned obedience to party directives, local leaders did have some say in how money was to be spent, and which areas were to be developed first. This factor more than any other led to the growth of local party factions.

Businessmen realized that good contacts with the party could enhance their chances to make gains as Taiwan's economy grew under the watchful eye of government and KMT planners. Significant contacts were made with local businessmen and with those who were interested in starting businesses. While businesses no doubt prospered legally during this period, some grew rich through illegal means as well. Without opposition leaders to keep an eye on local KMT officials, graft became commonplace as soon as the Kuomintang began to recruit local leaders and those leaders in turn were elected to office. Government contracts brought money to local businesses and into the pockets of some KMT officials in the form of payoffs. In some cases, village and town chiefs with little or no affiliation with the party would court KMT leaders for political favors and offer monetary rewards for satisfactory results. The growth of these factions, and the monied interests they represented, became a major reason why local KMT leaders would loose elections when democracy began to evolve as opposition leaders exposed their corrupt ways.

Chiang Kai-shek believed party reorganization, economic reforms, local elections, and a somewhat greater emphasis on constitutionalism, were sufficient to claim the establishment of democracy on Taiwan. While admitting that more democracy would be needed in the future, Chiang felt enough liberalization had taken place for the time being. Party leaders emphasized the temporary provisions surrounding martial law were still necessary. This extraconstitutional provision limited the kinds of political reforms that could be instituted. But economic reforms and the increased efficiency of the KMT were enough to provide the party with a base of support. For the first time in its history, the KMT had developed and followed through with a plan, and seemed to have learned from its mistakes.

Testing the System

In spite of the Kuomintang's successes, serious problems remained. The Taiwan Garrison Command, a military organization charged with enforcing martial law, had quickly become the most feared instrument of Kuomintang power. The Garrison Command maintained an extensive network of informants. Political officers in the military enforced loyalty there, and campus cells of the youth organizations watched over students at colleges and universities. Basic cell units throughout Taiwan watched over members of their communities.[43]

Former provincial governor and central committee standing member Wu Kuo-cheng (K.C. Wu) believed the garrison command and other security agencies were executing far too many people. Wu believed many arrests were made under the auspices of rooting out communist agents even though many of those arrested and executed were known to be anti-communists who were critical of the Kuomintang. He accused Chiang Kai-shek's son Ching-kuo of creating a spy network that created fear not only throughout society, but within the Kuomintang as well. Wu claimed only 18 out of 998 arrests made by secret police in 1952 were for crimes of misconduct. The rest were made to intimidate and root-out opposition to party directives and government policy.[44] Similar allegations were familiar to American officials in Washington, causing many to question the close relationship that had developed between the U.S. and Taiwan since the outbreak of the Korean War in 1950. Nationalist officials admitted the tactics used by the Garrison Command in Taiwan were extreme but were nevertheless warranted because it was trying to keep Taiwan free of communist infiltration. At the same time, party officials quickly pointed out that the KMT had expanded rights in Taiwan since 1949 and that local government was operating well in Taiwan.[45]

In spite of these claims, officials like K.C. Wu became more dissatisfied with the reluctance of top party leaders to extend greater rights to the people.

Wu met with Chiang in 1950 and encouraged the president to allow the organization of an opposition party. In trying to convince Chiang, Wu argued that without serious political rights, the people of Taiwan would continue to feel like a conquered people. Years later, Wu reported that while Chiang did agree to allow independent candidates to run for local office, he personally believed the party had the best men and therefore saw no need for another party.[46] The issue was not pursued further.

Chiang's brash ways bothered many KMT supporters. In speaking to a group in New York, the respected scholar Hu Shih tried to downplay Chiang's weaknesses while calling for continued support for the ROC government. Hu referred to Chiang as a prodigal son who had learned his lesson. He also argued the KMT defeat on the mainland was not merely a result of corruption, but of factors that the rest of the world was not always willing to consider such as prolonged war and difficult domestic circumstances.[47] But Hu nevertheless had reservations over the KMT's strong-armed tactics that would surface later.

The Seventh National Congress of the Kuomintang reaffirmed goals established two years earlier at the time of the party's reorganization. The manifesto of the congress made it clear that no other political parties were necessary and restated the KMT's role as a revolutionary party. At the same time, the reliance on Sun Yat-sen as a popular symbol began to fade in favor of the cultification of Chiang Kai-shek. Party rhetoric referred to Chiang in more reverential language than in previous congresses. The party maintained its need to launch a counterattack on the mainland and promoted Chiang as the spiritual force behind that effort.[48] The party's platform failed to make specific references to democracy. Some attention was placed on military matters, foreign policy, economics, education, and social services, but only the anti-communist tenets of the platform contained any specificity.[49]

The cultification of Chiang Kai-shek was in part made possible by successes in economic growth and in the establishment of some local self-rule. It allowed the party to ignore further calls for liberalization and focus on the goal of recapturing the mainland. Democratic development could not take precedence in the minds of top party leaders if a successful recovery were to take place. Taipei was the temporary seat of the Chinese government, not the permanent capital of a Taiwan republic.

At the second session of the national assembly in 1954, assembly member Hu Shih challenged the platform of the Kuomintang. He stated his agreement with the Kuomintang that there were essentially two forces in the world, communism and anti-communism. He also verified that despite his disagreements with party policy, he believed the KMT deserved support. At the same time, he believed the Kuomintang had not gone far enough to understand the people who were anti-communist, but also critical of KMT rule. He stated his belief that the KMT placed too much emphasis on unconditional obedience to the leader, and needed to establish greater freedoms for individuals and the press on Taiwan.[50]

Hu Shih's criticisms were followed by an announcement by K.C. Wu in the United States that he was leaving his post in the ROC government because the Kuomintang organization contradicted Sun Yat-sen's principles. Sun Li-jen, commander-in-chief of the army was similarly forced out of office for calling on the KMT to adopt principles of Western liberalism. Wu cited military intervention in politics, and the importance placed on secret police units as the real source of enforcement power in the Kuomintang, and charged that no serious efforts had been made to secure individual rights and freedom of the press. He called for an investigation into the finances of the KMT, an abolition of the security apparatus linked to the Chiang family, the creation of opposition parties, an end to illegal detentions and prosecutions by the government, and an abolition of the political commissar system run by Chiang Ching-kuo.[51]

While his allegations hurt Chiang's and the Kuomintang's reputation in the U.S., much of Wu's complaints were kept from the public eye in Taiwan. Similarly, the contents of Hu Shih's remarks were better known outside of Taiwan than they were on Taiwan. The complaints underscored the KMT's obsession with controlling dissent. But the party did make a modest effort to ease some restrictions. The press called for greater Taiwanese representation in government.[52] By 1956, newspapers began to print some stories the KMT previously considered dangerous for public consumption.[53] Some reports alleged government officials had been obstructed in their jobs by party officials. Some officials claimed they had to bribe other officials to provide services necessary to make their cities and counties run properly. In some cases school teachers had to buy their jobs, and police officials involved themselves in illegal enterprises in order to earn handsome salaries. Newspapers in Taiwan called on the government to reform the system and pay decent wages to promote efficiency and to relieve the temptation for official corruption.[54] Intellectuals also called on the government to loosen control over the academic establishment and be more open to Western liberalism.[55]

The first election for the Taiwan Provincial Assembly was held in early 1957. Although it provided a way for local Taiwanese to enter politics, the party still controlled the agenda and dominated the assembly because of the number of members it was able to get elected. Some idea of this advantage can be understood by considering an important study done on campaigns and elections for seats on the Taiwan Provincial Assembly. KMT candidates were brought under intense scrutiny by both the party hierarchy and security units. The secret police cleared the slate of candidates, and the party's organization department in consultation with top KMT leaders approved the applications of specific candidates to run for office. Approved candidates could rely on the party to get the vote out from soldiers, government workers, and family members, and by buying votes. Votes were bought twice in the process. The first in bribing to get nominated for office, the second in paying to get elected.[56] Finally, the KMT-controlled press assured party candidates were reported on in a more positive light than their challengers.

Despite these advantages the Provincial Assembly did provide a forum for political discussion. Independent assembly members used this forum to pressure the KMT to give the representative body real power. The Kuomintang was careful to not delegate too much power to the provincial assembly for fear of it usurping some of the authority of the national bodies.

An Effective Instrument of Control

Chiang Kai-shek had succeeded in establishing a political party that was both directly answerable to him and firmly in control of the political system. The Kuomintang survived its relocation to Taiwan. The party organization was solid. Representative bodies, though not democratic, had been established. Bureaucratic expertise had grown under KMT guidance. In spite of the horrendous KMT mistakes made in 1947, the people of Taiwan had gained a sense of respect and toleration for KMT rule. And unlike many authoritarian regimes, the KMT had a political ideology and the residents of Taiwan knew what the primary goals of the KMT were.

Still after nine years on Taiwan, the KMT seemed no closer to realizing its primary goal of liberating the mainland of communist control. For Chiang and other senior party leaders, this goal could not be compromised. Political opponents had to be swept away if they detracted in any way from the KMT's efforts to overthrow the communist regime in China. But other KMT leaders were worried that mainland recovery offered little for the people of Taiwan. They believed some policy development was needed in other areas. If the KMT failed to show concern for Taiwan's needs, political threats could arise that would call the KMT's legitimacy into question.

Chiang Kai-shek came to appreciate these concerns. In the last years of his life, he would augment his goal to rule all of China with a subtle but significant step towards addressing the needs of Taiwan's people. In doing so, he would call upon younger leaders, including his son, to formulate more ambitious plans to speed up the modernization of the Taiwan economy. The much heralded Taiwan economic miracle was about to begin. Unbeknownst to many, these modernization attempts would also sow the seeds of political contestation that would grow with the passing of Chiang Kai-shek.

Notes

1. In the late 1920s, two brothers, Ch'en Li-fu and Ch'en Kuo-fu were charged with reorganizing the Kuomintang's local organizations. Their group also dominated the feared Central Bureau of Investigation and Statistics, a secret police organ Chiang Kai-shek relied on to maintain loyalty to him and the party. Though the bureau was disbanded before the KMT retreated to Taiwan, the CC Clique's influence, under the guidance of Ch'en Li-fu, continued to be felt in KMT politics until the mid 1980s.

2. See "The Reminiscences of Li Han-Hun," pp. 188-205, Chinese Oral History Project, Columbia University Library, Rare Books and Manuscript Division (Columbia University, New York).

3. Carsun Chang, "Chiang Kai-shek and Kuomintang Dictatorship," in Pinchon P.U. Loh's *The Kuomintang Debacle of 1949: Conquest or Collapse?* (Boston: D.C. Heath, 1965). It should be noted that Carsun Chang was not a member of the KMT.

4. Tang Tsou, *America's Failure in China, 1941-1950* (Chicago: University of Chicago Press, 1963, pp. 122-3.

5. Ping-chia Kuo, *China: New Age and New Outlook* (New York: Alfred A. Knopf, 1956), pp. 27-30.

6. Chiang speech segment quoted by Alan P.L. Liu in *Phoenix and the Lame Lion: Modernization in Taiwan and Mainland China, 1950-1980* (Stanford: Hoover Institution, 1987), p. 30.

7. Chiang Kai-shek, *Soviet Russia in China: A Summing Up at Seventy* (Taipei: China Publishing, 1969), pp. 223-33.

8. These leaders included Yu yu-jen, Chu Cheng and Tsou Lu. See Republic of China, Ministry of Information, *China Handbook, 1951* (Taipei: China Publishing, 1951), pp. 319-25.

9. Bruce J. Dickson, "The Lessons of Defeat: The Reorganization of the Kuomintang on Taiwan, 1950-52," *China Quarterly* (March 1993), p. 63.

10. Members of the commission included Ch'en Ch'eng, Chang Ch'i-yun, Chang Tao-fan, Ku Cheng-kang, Cheng Yen-fen, Chen Hsueh-p'ing, Hu Chien-chung, Yuan Shou-Ch'ien, Tsui Shih-ch'in, Ku Feng-Hsiang, Tseng Hsi-pai, Chiang Ching-kuo, Hsiao Chih-ch'eng, Shen Ch'ang-huan, Wu Kuo-ch'eng, and Lien Chen-tung. See *New York Times*, July 27, 1950.

11. Dickson, "The Lessons of Defeat," pp. 61-3.

12. "Pen Tang Kai-tsao Kang-yao" (Reorganization Platform of the Party), *Ke-ming Wen-hsien*, Volume 43, KMT Central Committee, Taipei, 1966, pp. 171-179.

13. See "Outline of the Reform Program of the Kuomintang," 1950, in Shieh, *Kuomintang: Documents*, pp. 217-224. See also Hung-mao Tien's *The Great Transition*, pp. 64-5.

14. Interview with members of the Taoyuan County Party Headquarters, June 22, 1993.

15. "Pen Tang Kai-tsao Kang-yao," pp. 171-179.

16. Interview with members of the I-lan County Party Headquarters, June 15, 1993.

17. Ts'ao Chun-han, "Su-tsao Chung-kuo Kuomintang," pp. 57-9.

18. Ibid., p. 59.

19. Ibid., pp. 60-76, and interview with cadres of the I-lan County Party Headquarters, June 15, 1993.

20. Vladimir Lenin, *What Is To Be Done?: Burning Questions of Our Movement*, in *The Collected Works of V.I. Lenin, Volume II* (New York: International Publishers, 1934).

21. Edwin A. Winckler, "Taiwan Transition?", in Tun-jen Cheng and Stephan Haggard, *Political Change in Taiwan* (Boulder, Colorado: Lynne Reinner, 1992), p. 225.

22. Moody, *Political Change on Taiwan*, pp. 65-6.

23. Robert C. Tucker, ed., *The Lenin Anthology* (New York: W.W. Norton, 1975), pp. lv-lvi.

24. Hannah Arendt, *Totalitarianism: Part Three of the Origins of Totalitarianism* (New York: Harcourt, Brace, Jovanovich, 1951), p. 103.

25. There were attempts made by Chiang Kai-shek to incorporate fascist principles into the party-state during the 1930s, however. See William C. Kerby's *Germany and Republican China* (Stanford: Stanford University Press, 1984); and Hung-mao Tien's *Government and Politics in Kuomintang China, 1927-1937* (Stanford: Stanford University Press, 1972), pp. 54-64.

26. Joseph LaPalombara and Myron Weiner, eds., *Political Parties and Political Development* (Princeton: Princeton University Press, 1966), pp. 3-6.

27. "Current Platform of the Kuomintang," September 1, 1950, in Shieh, *Kuomintang: Documents*, pp. 225-236.

28. See Douglas Mendel, *The Politics of Formosan Nationalism* (Berkeley: University of California Press, 1970), p. 27.

29. See Joseph W. Ballantyne, *Formosa: A Problem for United States Foreign Policy* (Washington: Brookings Institution, 1952), p. 59.

30. Interview with Chiang Ch'un-nan (Antonio Chang), Editor, *Hsin Hsin Wen* (The Journalist), Taipei, May 19, 1993.

31. In some cases, the 37.5% ceiling for land rents was a fraction of what tenant farmers had been forced to pay. Reliable sources indicate land rents had in some cases cost as much as 70% of crop production per year. See Tai Hung-chao, *Land Reform and Politics: A Comparative Analysis* (Berkeley: University of California Press, 1974), p. 72.

32. Ch'en Ch'eng, *Land Reform in Taiwan* (Taipei: China Publishing Company, 1961), pp. 47-8.

33. See Thomas Gold, *State and Society in the Taiwan Miracle* (Armonk, New York: M.E. Sharpe, 1986).

34. Karl D. Jackson, "The Philippines: The Search for a Suitable Democratic Solution, 1946-1986," in *Democracy in Developing Countries: Asia, Volume III*, edited by Larry Diamond, Juan J. Linz, and Seymour Martin Lipset (Boulder, Colorado: Lynne Reinner, 1989), p. 239.

35. See Y. Dolly Hwang, *The Rise of a New World Economic Power: Postwar Taiwan* (Westport, Connecticut: Greenwood, 1991), pp. 34-5.

36. See Neil H. Jacoby, *U.S. Aid to Taiwan: A Study of Foreign Aid* (New York: Praeger, 1966), p. 170.

38. See Jyh-pin Ra, "The Introduction of American and European Constitutionalism to China," in *The U.S. Constitution and the Development of Constitutionalism in China*, edited by Ray S. Cline and Hungdah Chiu (United States Global Strategy Council, 1988, pp. 13-20.

39. See *Chang Ch'i-yun Hsien Sheng Wen Chi* (The Writings of Mr. Chang Chi-yun), (Taipei: Chinese Culture University, 1989), Volume 14, pp. 7079-7080.

40. Ibid., Volume 15, pp. 7881-2.

41. Sung-Joo Han, "South Korea: Politics in Transition," in Diamond, Linz, and Lipset, *Democracy in Developing Countries: Asia*, p. 269.

42. The China Youth Party and the Democratic Socialist Party also fielded a few candidates, but they were only partially independent parties. The Kuomintang has historically restricted these parties by forcing them to pledge allegiance to the principles and authority of the KMT.

43. Ralph Clough, *Island China* (Cambridge: Harvard University Press, 1978), p. 42.

44. See "The Reminiscences of Wu Kuo-cheng," pp. 207-225. Chinese Oral History Project, Rare Books and Manuscripts Division, Columbia University Library, New York.

45. See Han Lih-wu, *Taiwan Today* (Taipei: Hwa Kuo Publishing, 1951).

46. "Reminiscences of Wu Kuo-cheng," pp. 165-186.

47. *New York Times*, January 15, 1951.

48. "The Manifesto of the Seventh National Congress of the Kuomintang," October 20, 1952, in Shieh, *Kuomintang: Documents*, pp. 237-47.

49. "Platform of the Party as Adopted by the Seventh National Congress of the Kuomintang," October 20, 1952, in Shieh, *Kuomintang: Documents*, pp. 249-254.

50. *New York Times*, February 24, 1954.

51. *New York Times*, March 15, 1954. It is important to note that Wu claimed that Chiang Kai-shek had plotted his murder prior to his escape to the U.S. At the time of his escape to the United States, Wu's son was arrested by security officials and held for several days under interrogation and beaten before being allowed to join his father in the U.S. See his "Reminiscences," p. 36.

52. See John Israel, "Politics on Formosa," in Mark Mancall, ed., *Formosa Today* (New York: Praeger, 1964) p. 61.

53. It is possible that the Kuomintang's willingness to accept greater public scrutiny came in part as a result of the Chinese Communists institution of the Hundred Flowers Blooming campaign.

54. *New York Times*, September 16, 1956.

55. Mei Wen-li, "The Intellectuals on Formosa," in Mancall's *Formosa Today*, pp. 121-129.

56. Arthur J. Lerman, *Taiwan's Politics: The Provincial Assemblyman's World* (Washington, D.C.: University Press of America, 1978), pp. 30-36.

3

Political Calm and Slow Change

At its Eighth National Congress in October 1957, the Kuomintang showed signs of having been influenced by calls for greater openness. The party presented its mission of mainland recovery in terms of democracy against totalitarianism, though the reliance on the military in forwarding KMT goals was still paramount.[1] But the political platform paid less attention to the communist threat than ever before by stressing constitutionalism, economics, and foreign affairs. The party saw the need to streamline government operations and define party/government functions more carefully. The attention to economic goals on Taiwan was unprecedented.[2]

A Modernization Plan for Taiwan

Although no promises had been made to extend democracy, the KMT made an important step in shifting its mainland recovery strategy from a military emphasis to a political one. Though top party leaders did not intend to abandon the military option or even make it secondarily important, the attention to economic and political issues was a turning point in the party's acknowledgment that it still had a long way to go in providing political leadership to the people of Taiwan.[3] Economic development was always important to the KMT on Taiwan, though recovering the mainland was Chiang's top priority. He realized an economically strong Taiwan was an essential component for mainland recovery, both for industrial support of the military, and to prove the Kuomintang development worked. In addition, the KMT had to prove it could reverse its spotty economic showing on the mainland with real success on Taiwan.

Economists called for import substitution policies and export oriented growth strategies to build the Taiwan economy. Secondary education programs were geared to facilitate expertise in manufactures for export and the production of consumer durables for purchase at home. The benefits of Taiwan's ambitious economic policies were apparent to all. People realized their standard of living would improve under the economic guidance of the KMT party-government. This legitimized the Kuomintang's monopoly of power, though improved living standard would eventually result in calls for political modernization as well.

Despite the party's progress in being more public minded, some leaders came to see Chiang Kai-shek as an obstacle to party progress. In 1958 the premier was called before the control yuan to testify on corruption charges. Chiang intervened and allowed the premier to reject the control yuan's order.[4] Some party officials complained that members of the Chiang family were intervening in ways that were damaging to the party and to the government. The complaints were made privately, however, as criticism against Chiang was considered a seditious act.

For a period of time in 1958 and 1959, the government stepped-up security measures in response to the armed conflict with communist forces in the Taiwan Straits. Special effort was exerted to contain expressions of dissent. The legislative yuan did pass the Law of Compensation for Wrongful Detentions and Convictions, another step towards admitting that mistakes had been made in the government's haste to rid the island of critics. But independent political thinking remained a dangerous thing in Taiwan.

The Party Moves Towards Inclusion

An attempt was made in early 1960 to prevent Chiang Kai-shek from taking a third term as president of the Republic. According to the constitution, a president may serve for only two terms. Chiang and his immediate supporters felt it necessary for him to hold on to the top party post and serve concurrently as president, even though the real power behind the presidency came from Chiang's position as director-general of the Kuomintang. Pro-KMT scholars opposed a third term fearing it would erode overseas Chinese support for the regime, and lessen the chances of Taiwan becoming democratic.[5] Their desires were turned aside, however, as the Central Standing Committee of the Kuomintang sent a proposal to the national assembly, the body charged with both electing the president and amending the constitution. The CSC wanted approval of a temporary provision allowing Chiang to run for more than two terms as president. Because of the power of the CSC, the proposal passed without serious opposition. But younger KMT members had come to view some older KMT leaders as out of step with the needs of Taiwan and democratic success on the island and its connection to mainland recovery. They believed it was time for the KMT to turn to a younger generation of leaders, still mostly mainlanders, to guide the development of Taiwan.

Chiang's reelection as president increased opposition towards the regime. Native Taiwanese politicians called for an end to one-party rule and charged the KMT with rigging local elections.[6] The KMT refused to seriously consider any request to allow an opposition party to be organized, though it pledged to honor all anti-communist forces whether in or out of the party. On one occasion, Ch'en Ch'eng assured critics that a serious opposition party would be accepted providing it was not a party of warlords, hoodlums, or rascals.[7] But the Kuomintang ridiculed any group it deemed as undesirable or as a threat to be one of the above three groups, thus squelching any serious talk of allowing an opposition party to organize.

One group of individuals nevertheless decided to test the Kuomintang and declared their intention to form the China Democratic Party. The announcement took many by surprise. While admitting that the individuals forming the party were not affiliated with the communists, the KMT accused the party of being comprised of underworld figures, thus rejecting their proposed party.[8] The leader of the party, Lei Chen, was a well known KMT critique who published *The Free China Fortnightly*, a journal originally started by Hu Shih. He was arrested in early September, 1960, not on charges that he had illegally started a political party, but that he had conducted communist activities, a reversal from the KMT's earlier claim.[9] A few days later the government announced that Lei Chen's partner, Liu Tzu-ying, had confessed to being a communist united front element dispatched by the CPC. The government claimed Liu used Lei's influence to make contacts for the communists. Chiang Kai-shek personally involved himself in the incident, arguing that in his magazine, Lei Chen called for a coup d'etat and made verbal attacks against Chiang Kai-shek. Chiang's involvement in the case made it difficult for defenders of Lei to fight the case solely on legal grounds for fear of contradicting the president. In careful fashion, individuals closely connected with Lei argued the magazine had firmly established an anti-communist line, but did call for an end to KMT dominance, an audit of KMT finances, reduced military expenditures, and increased civil liberties. They also renounced the policy of reclaiming the mainland by military means and advocated replacing it with the political goal of developing Taiwan democratically, thereby providing a blueprint for the peaceful recovery of the mainland.[10]

The formal indictment against Lei and Liu was a document that could never have been used in a court of law in a Western democracy. The document establishes Lei Chen's and Liu Tzu-ying's acquaintance, and specifies articles published by the journal and other circumstantial information, but nothing that established a communist plot or direct threat to

Kuomintang rule.[11] It is clear the KMT's case against Lei Chen had been for the formation of an opposition party. legislative yuan member Fei Hsing accused the government of building a case against Lei and Liu that was based on false charges. He argued that trying the two in a military court was illegal and that a civil court should hear the case to insure a fair evaluation of the evidence. At the same time he suggested that the KMT should not be so paranoid and allow opposition parties to be organized.[12] Other opposition leaders accused the KMT of going back on its word of allowing many political voices to be heard as long as they were anti-communist. They demanded greater rights for minority candidates in local elections, and called on the KMT to turn away from extra-constitutional behavior.[13]

Despite the unusual pressure from opposition leaders, the KMT refused to budge. Lei Chen and Liu Tzu-ying were convicted and sent to prison for ten years. Chiang Kai-shek refused the petition of 46 prominent citizens to pardon Lei Chen.[14] Despite the KMT's willingness to allow some opposition voices, the Lei Chen affair was to stand as a warning against those who had a desire to advocate a political position that could challenge Kuomintang authority.

The secret police continued wiretapping suspected KMT enemies and set-up surveillance units overseas to watch college students. Some students were punished for the views they expressed while studying in the United States or in other countries.[15] In addition to this harassment, military and surveillance operations bled the government of needed funds. Local officials complained that with security expenditures so high, they hadn't the financial resources to govern their cities adequately.[16]

The gradual pace of change continued, however. Anti-communist propaganda was no longer used to justify mundane government policies. The party realized continued support depended on successes at home. At its Ninth Party Congress, the Kuomintang recounted land reform success and the establishment of local government rule. At the same time, the communists' blunder with the Great Leap Forward and the stagnation of China's communes gave the KMT old guard hope that their ultimate goal of mainland recovery would soon be realized.[17] The party promised the central government would be reorganized and the constitution would be followed fully after the mainland was recovered. In the meantime, the KMT would devote itself to urban reforms, foreign trade, improving health care, providing insurance and welfare, and extending other services to society.[18]

Out of necessity, the Kuomintang paid more attention to domestic conditions on Taiwan. At the same time, the volatile and yet unfailing footing of the communist government on mainland China, and the ever-increasing number of countries switching diplomatic representation from Taipei to Beijing fueled the formation of factions within the party. The United States announced its intention to end foreign aid to Taiwan. This seriously damaged

Chiang Kai-shek's hope of someday launching an invasion of the mainland with U.S. assistance. In addition, repression and lack of opportunity at home was adding to a growing brain drain problem in Taiwan. This prompted younger KMT leaders to seek new policies to step-up the development of Taiwan.[19] Some of these younger KMT leaders saw hope in Chiang's son Chiang Ching-kuo and supported his efforts to succeed his father as leader of the party and government.

The younger Chiang was something of a curiosity. Like his father, he was not interested in financial power and surrounding himself with opulent things. He respected his father's wishes on political matters, but was disliked by Madame Chiang and some of the elder Chiang's closest associates. His longtime association with the security establishment made him one of the most feared officials in Taiwan. But he was an early advocate of giving Taiwanese positions in the party and government, and relied on them as an important base of future support.

There were fears of creating a Chiang dynasty if Chiang Ching-kuo succeeded his father. Some wondered what would happen to the party if the younger Chiang took over. There were also younger Taiwanese KMT members who favored the introduction of Taiwan natives into significant posts and felt Chiang Ching-kuo would in the end, block Taiwanese from gaining key political positions in favor of mainlanders. The opposite view was held by many older KMT leaders who worried Ching-kuo was not as concerned about mainland affairs as his father and was too willing to allow Taiwanese to gain significant posts in the party and government. Almost everyone agreed, however, that the younger Chiang was a progressive force supporting the economic development of Taiwan. By the late 1960's, Chiang Ching-kuo was busy building his own support base--something his father fully encouraged.

Chiang Kai-shek continued to be the key player throughout the 1960's. Under his direction the party kept an ever-vigilant watch over college campuses. A case in point was the arrest of Professor Peng Ming-min and several of his students. The group organized a reading group to read and study communist literature. The government had forbidden such activities and made no exception especially in academic circles. Peng and his students were arrested in late September 1964, but were not tried by military court until April 1965. The trial lasted one day, with the conviction being handed down at the same time. In addition to his sentence, Peng's sister, a professor at a college in suburban Taipei was fired from her job because of her relation to her brother and the possible threat that posed, not because of any actual dissident behavior on her part.[20]

The Communist authorities' Cultural Revolution prompted a KMT campaign spearheaded by Chiang Kai-shek to celebrate the virtues of China's classical tradition. Chiang wanted to preserve what he saw as a natural connection between the Kuomintang and ancient China's ethical and philosophical values. The media was organized and students mobilized to celebrate these ideals through art and literature.[21] The movement was reminiscent of Chiang's New Life Movement introduced during his mainland years and was intended to add to the cultification of Chiang.

By 1968, a calm settled over the Taiwan political scene. Opposition candidates continued to function within their limits, economic success continued, and the government and KMT were generally viewed in positive terms.[22] Chiang Ching-kuo began to have his people moved into significant government and party posts prior to the party's tenth congress, attesting to the strength of his support base of younger mainlanders and the blessing of his father.[23] C.K. Yen became premier and concurrent vice president. Li Huan was appointed head of the Taiwan party organization. Chang Pao-shu was appointed secretary-general of the Central Committee on recommendation of Chiang Kai-shek. Some talented government employees who were not KMT members were promised high ranking positions if they joined the party. Many students who were brought in to the party had either been sent to the United States or Japan to acquire graduate degrees, or were promised they would have such opportunities if they joined the party.[24] 500 generals and 2000 colonels were retired because of age. Overall, the average age of the 250,000 government employees dropped to 40.[25]

Changes initiated in 1968 resumed at the Tenth Party Congress in Spring 1969. Gaining membership on the Central Committee were many technocrats, most serving as heads of managerial and technical posts in and out of government. Ten percent of these significant posts went to Native Taiwanese.[26] These adjustments during 1968 and 1969 in the party and government constituted the greatest changes to party power since the reorganization in 1950. The party pledged itself to specific improvements in economic infrastructure, especially in transportation and communications. A renewed pledge was made to recruit better trained government officials and to develop a tenure system for civil servants.[27] The usual goal of liberating the mainland was restated, though it became more evident that the dream was fading and the goal was used more as an excuse to maintain the Kuomintang's extraordinary powers over the constitution.

With reunification being a distant hope, party leaders felt it necessary to extend political rights in order to maintain its support. It was decided to hold elections for the national assembly, legislative yuan, and control yuan--the first since 1947. The party kept tight control over the election, allowing only those seats that had been vacated by retirement or death to be contested. In total, this meant only five percent of the seats in these representative bodies were up for election. Even if all the KMT candidates were defeated they still would have maintained a clear majority. Despite this, the people of Taiwan followed the campaigns closely. And the KMT took the elections seriously. Candidates argued the issues with unprecedented openness. Some candidates accused the

KMT of discrimination against the Taiwanese but only received minor rebuffs from the government. In the end, the KMT won 23 of the 26 contested seats.[28] The election itself was considered by most to be fair in terms of the vote count. But there were complaints about the unfair advantage the KMT had in campaigning because of the vast financial resources at the party's disposal, the KMT's control of the media, and party's ability to mobilize significant sectors of society to support KMT candidates.

The sharp limitations on the elections kept the KMT from having to consider what to do in the event the opposition made significant electoral gains. But the supplementary election reemphasized that a gradual political shift was underway and that the KMT had given this shift its blessing. These developments, coupled with changes in the upper level of party and government leadership, solidified Chiang Ching-kuo's position as heir to his father, and brought about a new way of doing party and government work. The younger Chiang was more willing to listen to criticisms and ideas previously shunned by his father. His primary limitation was the will of Chiang Kai-shek to maintain his own dominance in politics.

Chiang Kai-shek's Final Years

The Kuomintang's slow but continuous move towards openness brought more calls from politicians, intellectuals, and the media to bring about real pluralism. Members of the control and legislative yuans called for competitive elections. The press quickly endorsed the appeal for freer elections, though the government did not respond directly to the demands.[29] The government's lack of involvement in the issue reflected its desire to show some tolerance for dissent providing it did not threaten public order. But it also reflected the difficulty the government was facing internationally. In addition to the steady stream of countries shifting their diplomatic offices from Taipei to Beijing, United Nations recognition of Beijing seemed inevitable. The prospect of loosing UN support worried the KMT because it would weaken Taipei's claim as the legitimate government of all of China. This could in turn undermine one of the Kuomintang's main reasons for insisting on monopolizing power--completing the revolution by becoming defacto government of all of China.

In preparation for a UN vote against the ROC, Chiang Ching-kuo had 5000 prisoners released from prison, of which about 40 were political prisoners. It was a gesture intended to show tolerance and the government's willingness to work with the people of Taiwan in the event of further diplomatic setbacks. One month later, in late November 1971, the UN did vote to replace the Taipei mission for representatives from Beijing. The shock of the UN vote prompted the Kuomintang to pay more attention to domestic demands for change. The party announced elections would be held in the next year for the national assembly, legislative yuan, and control yuan. The elections would not replace representatives elected on the mainland, but they would fill vacancies left on the bodies and add additional seats.[30]

There was no violence in Taiwan following the UN vote. Chiang Kai-shek was elected to a fifth term as president of the Republic of China in March 1972. Intellectuals, businessmen, and some KMT politicians were upset with his reelection, arguing Taiwan needed new blood and democracy needed to be established. The protests were low key, however, as students were organized by KMT cell units and took to the streets carrying signs that read, "President Chiang is the Nation's Savior."[31] Even more significant than the election of the president was the appointment of Chiang Ching-kuo as premier and vice-chairman of the party. This move solidified the younger Chiang's position to succeed his father as leader of the Republic. As in 1968 and 1969, other leaders took positions in the government who were not high-ranking cadres in the party organization. In some cases, they weren't even party members. Chiang Ching-kuo was no doubt instigator of the changes.[32]

In addition to government appointments much interest had focused on the upcoming elections promised the previous year. Opposition candidates objected to the campaign rules established by the KMT. Orders were sent down limiting where and when opposition candidates could give public speeches. In addition, candidates were again reminded they could not criticize the government in any way that would constitute a security concern. Despite the warnings, campaigning was furious and issues were debated freely, even though only five seats were allowed to be contested on the legislative yuan. As usual, the KMT won most of the seats on every body. In an important turn for the KMT, candidates ran more on the economic successes and less on stability, anti-communism, and other time-worn phrases of the KMT old guard. Indeed the economic successes were great. The diversity of agricultural exports increased 300% from 1952-1971. During this time, the economy had grown from being primarily agriculture based to include significant small and medium sized industries. Agricultural labor declined by 25%. Import substitution policies were successful in developing domestic consumption. By 1970, unemployment levels hovered around two percent.[33] All of these developments generated support for KMT candidates even though they also benifitted from unfair campaign advantages.

The government appointments and elections were in part considered a victory for pro-democracy advocates. Using diplomatic setbacks as a rallying call, intellectuals called on the government to make Taiwan a true democratic showcase for the rest of the world to admire. By packaging their concerns as patriotic duty, the intellectuals were able to gain the ear of party influentials. They argued that those with the greatest wisdom and vision had not always been permitted to speak. They called on the KMT to give the control yuan real power to stop corruption in the government. They advocated academic freedom so professors could write and discuss ideas in helping Taiwan become democratic.[34] After the UN vote, intellectuals increased their pressure to democratize representative bodies and party organs.

The party answered the movement with a campaign of its own. A book was published by the party recounting recent successes in Taiwan under KMT leadership. Party organs were required to distribute copies of the book and have their members study its pages. But eventually the KMT cracked-down on dissent, arresting leading professors, labeling them as communist sympathizers, and then released them but not before prohibiting them from returning to their jobs on campus. Despite this setback, the government did follow the crackdown with a series of reforms. It agreed to expand representation in elected organs, recruit younger leaders--especially Taiwanese, discipline bureaucrats and streamline government operations, seek closer contact with the people, and modernize agriculture and implement urban reforms.[35] Most observers believed the government's willingness to cooperate on reforms was a result of Chiang Ching-kuo's wanting to improve the government's image, and the image of the KMT through worthwhile reforms that would win high levels of popular support. It was also a tactic to distance himself from KMT leaders who were concerned at what they saw as the party's unhealthy liberalization and abandonment of revolutionary principles.[36]

Chiang Kai-shek fell ill in Autumn 1972. With his son premier and vice-chairman of the KMT, the transition was ready. The younger Chiang's efforts to open party and government posts to younger mainlanders and a few Taiwanese had created a core of support that went beyond his relationship to his father. His work in the public security sector gave him credentials needed to gain the support of those close to the Generalissimo. And his greater tolerance for dissent gave hope to those who favored more political liberalization. By the Spring of 1973, Chiang Kai-shek was too weak to run the day-to-day affairs of the party. Ching-kuo took over the primary functions of the party and government.

The Kuomintang on Taiwan: The First Two Decades

On numerous occassions, Chiang Kai-shek claimed to have introduced the first trappings of democracy in the Republic of China. There is no doubt that Chiang presided over a much better organization in Taiwan than he did on the mainland, and one that deserves high marks in many ways. Nevertheless, the party was still an authoritarian organization that shunned the democratic demands of the KMT's opponents.

1. Leadership

The party's reorganization and the bitter mainland defeat brought a new core of leaders capable of making long-term economic and political goals and seeing them to their completion. While Chiang Kai-shek remained the dominant force in the KMT, other leaders became well-known for their accomplishments. Chiang's willingness to rely on younger technocrats and political leaders laid the groundwork for others in Taiwan who would take their place in the party and the government as well. Party and government leaders were able to offer careful criticism of particular policies as long as they recognized the limits of acceptable dissent.

The Chiang family continued to hold the lion's share of power in the party and government, however. This proved to be a frustration to party and non-party individuals interested in democratic development. Despite the resentment felt toward Chiang Kai-shek at the time of his retreat to Taiwan, he was still able to build a popular base of support for his regime, even though political rights were granted only sparingly.

Stability is a good thing in laying the groundwork for liberal reforms. Chiang Kai-shek's desires to pursue vibrant economic policies and improve people's material well-being is a significant factor in the creation of a large middle class in Taiwan. It provided a stable base that would help ensure continuous, gradual change. It also prevented the emergence of extreme economic and social problems that surfaced in many Latin American regimes during this period and resulted in political chaos.

The Chiang family was not given to official graft in the way leaders of many other authoritarian states have been. Politics was seen as the path to economic success in the Philippines and in several Latin American states during this period.[37] While Chiang's fortune was no doubt significant, politics remained his primary interest. This factor helped keep critics at bay. As long as the people prospered and Chiang held to successful economic policies, there was little economic cause for the people to resent Chiang. In another sense Chiang was not a man of modern ideas. He held to old Chinese values. These included a general distrust of foreigners and a desire to lead a reflective non-materialist lifestyle.[38] These characteristics were most likely a reason for his resistance to modern democratic ideas.

2. Organization

The 1950 reorganization of the Kuomintang was probably Chiang Kai-shek's greatest accomplishment as leader of the Kuomintang. His recruitment of younger, better trained leaders, coupled with the forced retirement of many of the party leaders having served on the mainland, gave the KMT organizational strength it previously lacked.[39] Much of the corruption and poor work methods were eradicated with the reorganization. Standards were set, routines were established, and policies were evaluated. The Kuomintang was able to identify a clear purpose of its own that began to go beyond the personal whims of director-general Chiang. Chiang and key party leaders proved they had learned from their bitter mainland defeat and recognized that long-term success required a core of party leaders who had authority to operate on their own and make corrections when needed without fear of reprisal. The absence of war and overwhelming social problems also gave the KMT a boost in promoting and following through with development plans.

The Kuomintang became more inclusive on Taiwan than it had been on the mainland. As Chiang Ching-kuo's influence grew, the party's recruitment of Taiwanese became commonplace and some were given positions of importance. As the party became more inclusive, functions performed by the party became routinized, more conventional, and less revolutionary--but still not democratic. There was little inner-party democracy for the rank-and-file, and there were no plans to allow democracy to come about. The old phrases espousing tutelage were out of touch with the emerging reality that authoritarianism nurtured under the Chiang's could not last forever. Thus the contradiction between the party's advocacy of democracy and the realities of authoritarianism persisted.

There was also the problem of local factions. Though Chiang Kai-shek showed concern from time to time for the growth of factions and the presence of official corruption at the local level, he nevertheless knew local leaders did not seriously threaten the power-base of the KMT which was centered in the top Kuomintang organs in Taipei. So while the KMT continued to maintain their monopoly of power, many local factions continued to use local and provincial elected leaders and the few seats available on national elected bodies to increase their local power and influence. This factor would eventually thwart the party's ability to rally local support for the KMT's national agenda when the political system began to open up by the late 1980s. By this time, many factional leaders had long become reliant on party members within local party organizations to satisfy local business interests. This would make Taipei's calls for party discipline and support to fall upon deaf ears.

3. Ideology

At times the Kuomintang's official ideology clashed with reality. The first and foremost goal of party hardliners was to reclaim the mainland. The practical problem of projecting military power made this goal seem remote at best. For this reason, the KMT had to pay a great deal of attention to problems it neglected on the mainland. Land reform, the establishment of local elections, reforming education, establishing social-welfare standards and the like, became the day-to-day concerns of the KMT. The party came to realize that a party having no domestic plan to offer and no record to point to could never enjoy lasting success.

While progress was made in all of these areas, real democracy was slow in coming. Despite establishing local elections, the KMT did not allow opposition parties because the party maintained that special provisions over the constitution were still necessary. By the end of the 1960's Chiang Kai-shek was convinced that more had to be done to expand participation. But his dream of mainland recovery consumed him to such an extent that much was sacrificed in the name of suppressing the communist rebellion. Part of the problem rested with older KMT leaders who did not have a full enough understanding of Western democratic principles and why these principles were incompatible with strong-armed KMT rule. Too much time was spent trying to show similarities between KMT rule, Confucian principles, and modern democracy, without understanding the distinctive differences between Western liberalism's focus on individual rights and China's traditional concern with control by elites. On the other hand, while democracy needs a fertile ground to flourish, Taiwan lacked the institutions needed to support democracy. Calls for democracy were mainly made by intellectuals and other elites who opposed the KMT. As long as the Kuomintang could liberalize the system from above without direct involvement from the masses, reform would likely continue at a measured but certain pace. The Kuomintang state was still far too insecure and incapable of handling a broad-based democratic reform movement.

By claiming democracy as a goal for the party, Chiang avoided problems encountered by other authoritarian regimes. Oligarchic regimes in Southern Europe and Latin America were proclaimed to be the solution to the problems of weak parliaments and divided politics. This encouraged opposition groups to take extreme positions vis-a-vis the respective regimes.[40] Chiang's pledge to eventually democratize the system in conjunction with real improvements in Taiwan's standard of living, gave the KMT time to transform the system gradually.

4. Agenda Setting

For the first time since its fragile beginnings, the Kuomintang was able to make good on its promises. Claiming the San Min Chu I as its foundation, the KMT was able to define realistic economic goals and reach them successfully. While Chiang Kai-shek and party leaders were reluctant to give up their goal of launching a counterattack against the communists and reclaim the mainland, they realized by the mid 1960s they had built a showcase of economic development that could brighten their image even more by increasing political freedoms. The KMT's ability to foster broad-based economic development legitimized its rule and bought it time to consider political reforms that would not threaten the party's position of dominance. If democracy was to have a chance on Taiwan, it would have to take a back seat to KMT authoritarianism until elites within the party, most notably the party chairman, realized democratic change was the only viable option remaining for long-term political survival.

5. Quality of Governance

For all of its successes, the Kuomintang remained a brutal political party. Arrests, especially in the early 1950's, were commonplace. Trials were almost always conducted by military tribunals, and executions were frequent. Despite a pledge to promote academic freedom and freedom of the press, the KMT exercised overwhelming control over both of these institutions. Individuals or organizations advocating political opposition could be snuffed-out with little or no warning. Individual rights were respected as long as the party perceived no conflict with the KMT monopoly of power. So while the Kuomintang provided basic human needs on Taiwan, political rights and freedoms lagged far behind, cementing Chiang Kai-shek's legacy as a dictator in the process. Many authoritarian aspects of the KMT were giving way to greater openness. Openness was often followed by a temporary retreat to increased repression, though never so far as to halt the steady improvement in the political climate on Taiwan. Political opponents of the KMT suffered from a lack of organization. This was in part because of the effectiveness of the Kuomintang in stifling indigenous political movements. But it was also because Taiwan lacked a middle class political movement to make demands for greater political inclusion. Kuomintang economic policies would eventually improve Taiwan's standard of living and a middle class would emerge that would help build pressure for liberalization.

The Kuomintang's early efforts greatly improved the standard of living on Taiwan. Rulers in Iran, Nicaragua, and Cuba caused the growth of extreme opposition groups by excluding elites from political power and economic patronage.[41] In Taiwan real income levels grew, literacy rates skyrocketed, and housing conditions improved. People were optimistic about the future. Barring an unforeseen catastrophe, the KMT would temporarily be able to ride-out criticism of its dismal record on political rights.

6. Party-government Relations

Reorganization did help free the government from some party supervision. But for the most part, the government continued to be an extension of KMT power. Local elections were dominated by the Kuomintang organization, making it impossible to effectively separate the will of the government from the will of the party. As long as the KMT retained its Leninist organization, the government could have only limited independence. But the growth in the numbers of qualified government employees who were not party members had a significant effect on the KMT's attitude about government performance. For this reason, talented administrators were either co-opted into the party through membership drives or courted for their support of party policies. Better trained government employees would inevitably lead to competing loyalties--some favoring the party, others government autonomy.

Notes

1. "Manifesto of the Eighth National Congress of the Kuomintang," October 20, 1957, in Shieh *Kuomintang: Documents*, pp. 255-261.
2. "Political Platform Adopted by the Eighth National Congress of the Kuomintang," October 20, 1957, in Shieh, *Kuomintang: Documents*, pp. 263-266.
3. See chapter one in Alan P.L. Liu's, *Phoenix and the Lame Lion*.
4. *New York Times*, February 17, 1958.
5. Ibid., February 20, 1960.
6. Ibid., July 30, 1960.
7. Ibid., June 4, 1960.
8. Ibid., August 29, 1960.
9. Taiwan Home Service, 4 September 1960, FBIS *Daily Report*, Asia and Pacific, September 9, 1960, p. DDD.
10. *New York Times*, September 18, 1960.
11. For a translation of this document, see Chinese News Agency, 26 September 1960, FBIS *Daily Report*, Asia and Pacific, September 27, 1960, pp. DDD1-8.
12. Taipei, AFP, 23 September 1960, FBIS *Daily Report*, Asia and Pacific, September 23, 1960, p. DDD 2.
13. Taipei, AFP, 25 September 1960, FBIS *Daily Report*, September 27, 1960, p. DDD 13.
14. *New York Times*, April 24, 1961.
15. See Douglas Mendel, *The Politics of Formosan Nationalism* (Berkeley: University of California Press, 1970), p. 101.
16. Ibid., p. 103.
17. "Manifesto of the Ninth National Congress of the Kuomintang," November 23, 1963, in Shieh, *Kuomintang: Documents*, pp. 267-280.
18. "Platform of the of Party As Adopted by the Ninth National Congress of the Kuomintang," November 23, 1963, in Shieh, *Kuomintang: Documents*, pp. 281-5.

19. *New York Times*, December 21, 1964.
20. *New York Times*, April 7, 1965, and *Far Eastern Economic Review*, January 16, 1971, pp. 13-14.
21. "Principles For The Promotion of the Chinese Cultural Renaissance Movement," Document of the Fourth Plenary Session of the Ninth Central Committee of the Kuomintang, December 28, 1966. See Shieh, *Kuomintang: Documents*, pp. 309-312.
22. Such were the findings of Richard A. Wilson. See his "A Comparison of Political Attitudes of Taiwanese Children and Mainlander Children on Taiwan," in *Asian Survey* (December 1968), pp. 988-1000. Wilson found a high degree of political loyalty towards the KMT regime among both mainlander and Taiwanese children.
23. *New York Times*, April 24, 1968.
24. Interview with Tsiang Yen-si, Secretary-General to the President, Taipei, June 8, 1993.
25. See Mark Plummer, "Taiwan: The 'New Look' in Government," *Asian Survey* (January 1969), pp. 18-22.
26. *New York Times*, April 13, 1969.
27. "The Kuomintang Political Platform," Tenth Party Congress, April 5, 1969, in Shieh, *Kuomintang: Documents*, pp. 327-333.
28. Sheldon Appleton, "Taiwan: Portents of Change," *Asian Survey* (January 1971), pp. 68-73.
29. *New York Times*, January 10, 1971.
30. Ibid., December 24, 1971.
31. Ibid., March 22, 1972.
32. See J. Bruce Jacobs, "Taiwan 1972: Political System," *Asian Survey* (January 1973), pp. 102-112.
33. Shirley W.Y. Kuo, *The Taiwan Economy in Transition* (Boulder: Westview, 1983), pp. 57, 66-70.
34. See Mab Huang, *Intellectual Ferment for Political Reforms in Taiwan, 1971-1973* (Ann Arbor, Michigan: Michigan Papers in Chinese Studies, no. 28, 1976).
35. Ibid., p. 80.
36. Ibid., pp. 91, 110-101.
37. Jackson, "The Philippines," p. 237; Guillermo O'Donnell, "Introduction to the Latin American Cases," in *Transitions from Authoritarian Rule: Latin America*, p. 8.
38. I am grateful to Robert Scalapino for sharing his observations of Chiang Kai-shek with me.
39. Former KMT Secretary-General Ku Feng-Hsiang suggests Chiang's greatest leadership accomplishment on Taiwan was his selection of able leaders to head the party and government. Mr. Ku was interviewed by the author on August 17, 1988.
40. O'Donnell and Schmitter, *Tentative Conclusions*, p. 15.
41. Richard Snyder, "Explaining Transitions from Neopatrimonial Dictatorships," *Comparative Politics* (July 1992), p. 383.

4

Chiang Ching-kuo's Break from the Past

Leadership transitions in authoritarian regimes are often marked by instability and violence. This is especially true when the outgoing leader has held tight control over the ruling party. In a party organized along Leninist lines, factional disputes easily erupt after the exit of the party principal. In some cases, it is the former party leader who through his own political skill has been able to keep the factions together, by compromise, the mechanisms of party discipline, or by divide and rule tactics.

The transition of power from Chiang Kai-shek to Chiang Ching-kuo is unique among Leninist parties for several reasons. It was the first time that a Leninist leader passed the reigns of power to his son. Chiang Ching-Kuo's replacing his father was common knowledge and had been planned for years in advance. Most Leninist leaders may indicate who they prefer to succeed them, but this desire is not easily honored. The transition was one of political calm, both on the streets and within the top ranks of party power. Even before Chiang Kai-shek died, his son had effectively taken over the day-to-day affairs of the party. There is no doubt that Chiang Kai-shek's desire to have his son succeed him was supported by party leaders, even those who did not care for the younger Chiang. This loyalty for a deceased senior leader is not common in most Leninist organizations where top party leaders use transition periods to forward their own political fortunes.

This chapter looks at the pressures Chiang Ching-kuo faced in the initial phases of Taiwan's move towards democratization. It is not suggested that Chiang Ching-kuo was a democrat or that he favored the establishment of a democratic regime. At the time of his death, it was popular for party leaders to claim Chiang had presided over the process of democratic development.[1] But this is an exaggeration of Chiang's devotion to liberal democratic principles. As Samuel Huntington points out, the process of democratization is not one-sided. A successful democratic transformation requires courageous opponents to authoritarianism, and pragmatic authoritarians who realize they can no longer monopolize political power without risking a bloody political confrontation.²

For Chiang, democratic reform would become a necessity as social forces began to out pace the KMT's abilities to curb political activities outside the limits established by the party. The prestige the Kuomintang enjoyed in transforming Taiwan into an industrial and trading giant would be lost if political confrontation poured into the streets. Thus, Chiang Ching-kuo, the former head of the feared secret police, became Chiang the political reformer. The events that transpired during his thirteen years as chairman of the Kuomintang underscored the KMT's contradictory claims of the necessity for authoritarian control on the one hand, and democratic promise on the other.

Maintaining Political Calm

Even before Chiang Kai-shek's death, Chiang Ching-kuo was facing problems of a different magnitude than his father faced. The younger Chiang realized that the Republic of China's shrinking diplomatic world, and his relatively open style invited political dissent on a level not seen in Taiwan since 1947. In late 1973, a group calling themselves the United Independent Front gained a following by calling for rule by law rather than one-party rule. They advocated the popular election of mayors for Taipei, Kaohsiung, and the governor of Taiwan. They called for greater attention to constitutional principles and increased reliance on legislative processes rather than executive order. They also challenged the KMT to fully disclose its finances and stop government subsidies to the party.³ While the demands were not new ones, it was the first time that they had been advocated with such openness. KMT leaders warned the group about the accepted limits of political discussion, though serious retribution did not follow. Chiang Ching-kuo managed to keep the party and government in a holding pattern, and continued to move new leaders into positions of importance, though perhaps not with the speed he introduced change several years earlier. Those gaining positions of importance were both old and young mainlanders and Taiwanese. Li Huan was appointed general secretary and charged specifically with recruiting young supporters of reform. He used the party's youth league to promote capable young Taiwanese.⁴

Chiang Kai-shek died on April 5, 1975. A period of mourning was declared and security measures were increased. It proved to be a period of calm. Chiang's death left the people of Taiwan stunned. They realized it was the end of an era. Chiang Kai-shek died without realizing his goal of mainland recovery. Chiang Ching-kuo was given the title of chairman of the KMT in late April and maintained his government position as premier. By now Chiang Ching-kuo was a familiar face in politics, though nobody could be completely sure what kind of an agenda he would advocate.

One of Chiang's first acts was to release political prisoners. Chiang wanted to show that the Kuomintang could tolerate some dissent. The legislative yuan passed the clemency law in June and in July some 3,600 prisoners were released, many of them political prisoners.[5] Despite Chiang's willingness to show some tolerance for political dissent, the release of prisoners was similar to the previous releases in the years leading to 1975. In contrast to these signs of greater tolerance, the feared Taiwan Garrison Command continued to make arrests, some of them unexpected and arbitrary. Military courts continued to hear all cases of a political nature. Conservative KMT leaders who had been influential in supporting Chiang's father called for strict policies and the maintenance of order at all costs. The Kuomintang continued to have final say on reportage in all newspapers, radio, and television releases. Basic cell unit organizations continued to keep watch over neighborhoods, factories, military units, businesses, and government offices. In universities and colleges, professors' lectures were monitored by paid student informants or party officials to ensure that course content was not critical of Kuomintang policy.[6] Chiang's tolerance for dissent, therefore, was strictly defined within limits established under the rule of his father, and under guidelines he established as head of the security apparatus. Even though the government commuted the sentences of political prisoners and declared limited political discourse to be legal, Chiang warned that conditions still warranted extraconstitutional control--a stark warning to opposition leaders.

There were, however, certain changes within the party organization that indicated Chiang Ching-kuo would not be as heavy handed as his father. At the 11th National Congress of the Kuomintang held in 1976, the title of Tsung-ts'ai (supreme leader) was retired with the passing of Chiang Kai-shek. It was agreed that the new party leader and every leader henceforth should be referred to as Tsung-li (chairman). Chiang also oversaw the retirement of 69 party leaders into the central advisory committee, opening the way for younger leaders to express their ideas, including several Taiwanese leaders.[7] Significant gains were made on the central committee and central standing committee of the party (see table 4.1). Li Huan selected around 60 individuals, half of them Taiwanese, to attend the training course at the party school for top-level cadres. Included in their ranks were Chen Li-an (son of Ch'en Cheng and a future candidate for president), Lien Chan (a future premier and vice president), Wu Po-Hsiung (who would hold ministerial positions), Frederick Ch'ien (a specialist in foreign affairs), and James Soong (a future general secretary of the party, Taiwan governor, and presidential hopeful).[8]

The younger Chiang allowed concerns to be expressed that were shunned by his father. He knew some in and out of the party greatly feared that

Table 4.1 Taiwanese Composition in Party/Party Organs

Organ	Total	Taiwanese	% of Total
Kuomintang 1969	950,000	374,000	39
Kuomintang 1975	1,400,000	764,000	53
Central Committee:			
1952	32	1	3.1
1963	74	4	5.4
1969	99	6	6.1
1976	130	19	14.6
Standing Committee:			
1952	10	0	0
1963	16	2	12.5
1969	21	2	9.5
1976	22	5	22.7

Source: Adapted from Te-fu Huang, "Elections and the Evolution of the Kuomintang," in Tien, *Taiwan's Electoral Politics* (Armonk: M.E.Sharpe, 1996), pp. 114, 118-119. Reprinted by permission.

Chiang Ching-kuo's reign as party chairman could end any hope for making the KMT a more representative political party like the political parties of the West. Chiang promised to both extend government services to the people and to be more responsive to the people's concerns. He spoke of the party's modest efforts to liberalize the electoral system and portrayed them as serious political reforms that would continue. These gestures were not merely symbolic, however. He sensed that strong authoritarian rule that denied any hope of political liberalization would harm his chances of containing dissent and could lead to civil unrest.[9] And while many of the formalities of the party suggested little had changed with the younger Chiang taking over, substantial differences between the father and son emerged.

Chiang Ching-kuo's work style was predictable. His goals were easily identifiable, and his expectations known. He could take criticism from lower level leaders as long as they were considered constructive and helpful for the party and government. His trust for party and government leaders was known and this trust was reciprocated. The relaxation of tensions allowed the KMT to handle challenges to its power with a new-found confidence. Chiang was regularly seen on television meeting the people, touring the countryside, visiting factories and schools, and participating in festivals. To all but his most ardent opponents, Chiang was able to use the media spots to erase most lingering fears of his having headed the secret police establishment in Taiwan. He was a skilled authoritarian, speaking of reform without raising immediate expectations of democratization. And he was a populist, maintaining political control with measured reform, while convincing the people that there was no immediate need to open the system to competition.[10]

A proven record of economic growth helped Chiang considerably. By the early 1970s, Taiwan had entered a period of extensive investment in capital intensive industries such as chemicals and high tech electronics manufacturing. While private businesses and government agencies were often at odds with each other in Latin American states during this period, Taiwan businesses and their government counterparts enjoyed a favorable working relationship.[11] Leaders in the KMT-controlled state felt economic development would give them the political legitimacy they desired if they could incorporated local party factions and business interests into development schemes. This gave local businesses and factions an economic stake in supporting government projects and provided them with an avenue for limited political participation--first at the local level, and later at the national level.[12] Individuals and enterprises invested in each others' firms. Large textiles, electronics, plastics, and heavy manufacturing industries emerged.[13] The economy grew more complex and diversified. Per capita GNP reached 60,000 N.T. ($1,600) by 1980. Even during the oil shock of 1973-4, Taiwan managed real growth while other countries failed to recover from higher energy costs for the remainder of the 1970s.[14] Like Korea's Park Chung Hee, economic policies in Taiwan helped create the conditions for a viable middle class. This allowed both states to enjoy social stability alongside political repression.[15]

Economic success also took attention away from an inadequately developed political ideology. Like his father, the San Min Chu I was important to Chiang Ching-kuo primarily as a founding document rather than a viable political doctrine to live by. He was interested in political ideas, though few were of Western origin. One of the books he was especially fond of was a book on political reform dating to the T'ang Dynasty.[16] Chiang believed the book was helpful to leaders who were trying to establish reforms in an uncertain social climate. He felt the book helped him understand the hearts and minds of the people. But while the T'ang Dynasty is noted for its more benevolent rule compared to most periods of Chinese political history, this book is nevertheless a primer for maintaining authoritarianism.[17] Thus while Chiang was interested in reform, he continued to assert the superiority of the party in formulating and implementing reform.

Radical dissidents saw Chiang Ching-kuo's ascension to power as the establishment of a Chiang dynasty. Earlier political leaders had challenged the KMT on constitutional grounds and had even taken advantage of Chiang

Ching-kuo's greater degree of tolerance to challenge the KMT in court on charges of election fraud. But in 1977, legal attempts gave way to acts of terrorism. The threat of violence was widely feared. Vice President Hsieh Tung-min was severely injured opening a letter that had been booby-trapped with an explosive device. In spite of the violent actions, Chiang worried more about mainstream political activists. These members of the opposition were winning local elections (though they never came close to winning a majority of contested seats). They were young, educated, predominately Taiwanese who did not challenge the Kuomintang's right to exist, but objected to its monopoly of power. Chiang ordered lighter sentences for dissidents convicted of anti-government activities (with the exception of those associated with violent acts), and the press was given permission to scrutinize political policies and performance more carefully.[18]

A Quasi Opposition Party Emerges

Prior to the 1970s, no organized opposition group was powerful enough to stay in existence. Lei Chen's was the last significant attempt to form a new political party. But by the mid '70's, young businessmen, intellectuals, and others of Taiwan's sizable middle class gave form to an opposition movement. Most of the opposition leaders were Taiwanese. These included future opposition party leaders Huang Hsin-chieh, Shih Ming-teh, Yao Chia-wen, and opposition members who did or would hold significant county, city and national posts including Yu Ching, and Chen Shui-pien. Two prominent mainlanders were also a part of the growing opposition movement. Fei Hsi-ping and Lin Chin-chieh were especially important in forming an ideological base for the opposition movement to work from.

Collectively, opposition leaders and the media referred to their movement as the Tang-wai or outside party (TW). Its stated purpose was to help get non-KMT politicians elected to public office. The TW was closely connected to opposition magazines. Huang Hsin-shieh, Shih Ming-teh, and Yao Chia-wen were especially prominent in publishing political materials that dealt with everything from Taiwan independence to differences in the living standards of urban and rural areas. But the TW's interest in magazine publishing was primarily to inform the public of its political positions in a market where the KMT had dominated all media outlets.

By 1977 the KMT was to learn that with greater political openness, improvement must be made in political practice to avoid political turmoil. Members of the TW had exerted great effort in trying to show how frequently the Kuomintang had violated the rules of campaigning and thrown elections in its favor. Critics were somewhat willing to live with the fact that the KMT had advantages of media control and financial resources to give them an edge against opposition candidates. But when KMT officials were caught stuffing ballot boxes in Chungli, a town just south of Taipei, a riot ensued. During the course of the night, a police station and several police cars were burned. At first, local KMT leaders were disciplined in the incident for not taking better control of the election. But the KMT's final response was to assure the public that they would not tamper with election outcomes. This pronouncement was not reassuring for either TW candidates or KMT candidates not endorsed by the party apparatus. Rules for campaigning and election were changed to prevent future incidents from occurring. The KMT decided to hold party primaries to prevent local party factions from splitting the KMT vote in local elections. This clearly helped the party maintain unity in elections during the early '80s. The number of determined opposition candidates continued to grow. But the KMT did not halt elections, nor did they prevent opposition candidates from running. This helped routinize elections and kept the hope for meaningful political reform alive.[19]

Most people in Taiwan opposed the tactics taken by demonstrators in Chungli, but they did not excuse the party's attempts to throw the election. The KMT's willingness to give in to some of the demands of its opponents encouraged continued dissent. While KMT officials undoubtedly knew this was a likely consequence, they also knew that to simply dismiss their critics by repressive measures and fail to compromise in some way might risk even more dangerous challenges in the future.

Because of the power of national institutions, and most importantly the power of the Kuomintang, being a locally elected official at the county or provincial level was mostly a dignified position. Local politics was the place for young politicians to begin if they lacked real power within the Kuomintang and local businesses. But the events surrounding the Chungli riots were pivotal in the minds of opposition candidates and leaders. The TW was buoyed-up in its confidence that the time had come to take more pressing measures and challenge KMT power at the grassroots level throughout Taiwan. This was not as easy as winning seats in local elections, however.

Elected Kuomintang officials in the counties were responsible to county party chiefs. While village, branch, and district KMT cadres could rarely move up to higher positions of authority, county chiefs were anxious to tow the party line in hopes of being rewarded with appointments at the national level.[20] Most local leaders rose to their positions out of loyalty to the party rather than by leadership promise. Though many local leaders were college graduates, they worked for twenty years to secure a good pension and a second career outside of party service. Most of the work responsibilities at the local level were dignified, having no responsibilities of overarching importance. County party heads, on the other hand, came from the more prestigious colleges and attracted attention of KMT leaders (or party central) due to perceived leadership skills. County party chiefs were therefore quite ambitious and determined to succeed. Most county chiefs did not become leaders of national importance, however. Usually only those who truly distinguished themselves from the pack were able to move up. The problem for county chiefs was complicated even further by the fact that they were usually not locals and almost always appointed for only two years at a single post. This kept county leaders from forming factions that could challenge the party central, thus increasing party discipline.[21] KMT policies were therefore followed closely, especially those that could ensure success for the county leader. Innovative policies at the county level would only be tried if there was a high probability of success and if it would lend local support for the KMT. For the opposition to win a county post, the newly elected leader would run up against a hierarchically organized county government more accustomed to answering to the county party chief rather than the elected magistrate. This meant that opposition victories at the county and city levels were only first steps in breaking the KMT's hold on power in local Taiwan politics.

KMT critics renewed their criticism of rules governing national elections as well. Despite vociferous objections, the national assembly formally elected Chiang Ching-kuo president of the Republic of China in spring 1978, replacing the interim president Yen Chia-kan. Though the election was a formality, there were calls from academia and the opposition to end the special restrictions governing the election of the president and to hold popular elections. Most of these critics realized, however, that this could not be possible as long as the chairman of the Kuomintang continued to be the real power behind the government. For most non-KMT leaders, the ballot box was the only place they could legally challenge the Kuomintang. For this reason they focused their criticisms on the rubber-stamp national assembly which ratified all decisions sent-down by the Kuomintang's policy committee.

Diplomatic Setbacks and Liberalizing the System

The island-wide election scheduled for December 1978 was to be a turning point for the opposition. At stake in the elections were seats in the various national, provincial, county, and municipal representative bodies. A strong showing for non-Kuomintang candidates could prove to the ruling party and to the people of Taiwan that it was time to end KMT domination of the political system. But on the eve of the elections, the government cancelled the vote after President Jimmy Carter announced the United States would be switching its diplomatic representation from Taipei to Beijing.

The switch in diplomatic representation was not a surprise, though it occurred a little earlier than Taipei expected. The rise of Deng Xiao-ping on the mainland cemented Washington's efforts begun in 1971 to end the diplomatic isolation between the United States and mainland China. The derecognition of the KMT regime in Taipei created a new problem for the Kuomintang. How could the party maintain its pledge to liberate the mainland without outside recognition? With Taipei isolated on the diplomatic front, couldn't Taiwan independence forces be looked upon with legitimacy? Should the KMT open the political system to contestation now that the realities of restoring the mainland seemed remote? Had the Kuomintang miscalculated in claiming to represent all of China? Was it possible for the KMT to lose control of Taiwan?

The Kuomintang immediately held a plenary meeting to consider the crisis. Party leaders launched a major propaganda campaign emphasizing the nation's ability to thwart a communist attack and forge ahead with bold reforms. At the same time a highly successful program was introduced to build-up the strength of national defense. The citizens of Taiwan were encouraged to donate money to the government to purchase new equipment for the military and to increase the quality of the island's defense forces.[22] The party's efforts paid off both in financial terms, and more importantly in support for the government. Trade agreements with other countries remained solid, economic growth continued, and domestic support for the KMT was sured-up.

As in the past, changes on the international front prompted changes in the party. In order to further boost its image, the Kuomintang reshuffled its central committee, putting younger leaders in important policy posts, and in the youth and organization departments. Many of these positions went to young Taiwanese party members thereby boosting Chiang's image as a reformer, and opening the party to new ideas.[23] Accompanying these leadership changes were new policy guidelines. The Kuomintang decided to renovate the party by consolidating some of its duties, clarifying government-party responsibilities, improving the education and training of party members, and trying to increase honesty and efficiency in party work. In addition to the above points, the party also pledged to forge ahead to ensure trading partners for Taiwan's businesses. Most significantly, the party announced it would strive to become more domestic policy oriented, and strengthen the roles of the legislative yuan, the control yuan, and national assembly.[24]

Though seen as important, the changes the Kuomintang had committed itself to were more sweeping than perhaps party leaders had themselves realized. The U.S. derecognition of the Republic of China on Taiwan had forced the hand of the Kuomintang. Instead of being a revolutionary party first, Chiang Ching-kuo realized real progress had to be made in liberalizing the political system if the party was to have a legacy beyond that of facilitating economic growth. The KMT could do little of substance to realize its goal of ending communist rule of the mainland. Domestic politics had become more important in the eyes of Taiwan's people who realized there had been no political miracle to mirror the economic miracle so often referred to.

Continued political repression threatened the legitimacy of the party in spite of economic success. Political liberalization was therefore a necessity, but it would create a slippery slope for authoritarianism. The party's response would put in place the forces that would change the Kuomintang forever. The contradictions of authoritarian rule and espousal of democratic ideals was rapidly coming to a head.

Reform within the party continued well into the summer of 1979. Opposition leaders doubted the sincerity of the KMT arguing the changes were superficial and intended to extend the party's monopoly of power. The opposition's suspicions were not without basis. The KMT, after all, continued to reject any role for an opposition party, citing the dangers Taiwan faced in meeting the communist challenge without outside help.[25] Party leaders were trying to hold on to power as long as possible, and probably did not understand at the time how much they would have to give in the future to be the party of choice on Taiwan.

The late 1970s were significant for the number of TW and other opposition publications that appeared. Some periodicals like *Hsia-ch'ao* (*China Tide*), *The Eighties* and *Formosan* were closely linked to the Taiwan independence movement. The *Taiwan Political Review* was run by independent legislators and tended to focus more on legislative issues. One of the disadvantages publishers faced was the breadth of articles they were forced to publish. In order to secure enough financial backing to cover printing costs, magazines accepted articles representing extreme political viewpoints. This meant radical views received as much coverage as moderate views. This resulted in numerous confiscations of magazines and arrests, thus hampering the opposition's ability to get its positions out during campaigns. It also led to factional fights within the opposition, thus weakening its efforts vis-a-vis the KMT.

In a drive for unity, opposition candidates banded together in the campaigns of late 1979 in hopes of defeating KMT candidates. Although the details of the incident are unclear, a riot ensued in the southern city of Kaohsiung in December which tested the limits of the KMT's new policy of openness. Some argue the riot was started by KMT agents disguised as opposition supporters in order to make the opposition look bad. Others claim the KMT hired hooligans to start the riot. Recent reports verify the government's contention that members of the opposition, most with connections to the controversial opposition *Formosan* magazine were the instigators of the riot.[26] Scores of policemen were injured (who, according to some, were told not to use force to put down the demonstration), and eight principals were arrested for their alleged involvement in the riot, including TW leaders Shih Ming-te and Huang Hsin-chieh. Even though people in Taiwan were unaccustomed to violent political activity and had reservations about the opposition's role in the Kaohsiung affair, they did not support the Kuomintang's position in the incident. In the investigation that followed, tactics the garrison command used in interrogating prisoners came under fire, thus calling into question the Kuomintang's role in the riot's aftermath. These revelations lent support to the opposition's contention that the KMT needed to answer for its behavior during the riot and in the trial that followed.

The eight defendants were held in seclusion, and according to the government, each confessed to the crime of sedition. But attorneys and family members were unable to gain access to the defendants to verify these claims. The garrison command also announced that a pretrial hearing had been set when in reality the pretrial hearing had already occurred in secret. At the same time, defense attorneys could not gain access to the documents the state planned to use against the defendants despite claims otherwise.[27] Once the actual trial began, more details emerged on how the government prepared its case against the defendants. All eight of the defendants reported they had been subjected to long periods of questioning where police had coerced them to confess the crimes against their will. All defendants but one absolved the police of physical beatings,[28] though all reported they had been subjected to "fatigue bombings," or long periods of interrogation where the detainee is forced to stand under threat of physical punishment. One defendant said she was shown a photograph of a bullet-ripped body and was forced to repeatedly read her own obituary until she agreed to sign her confession.[29]

A central contention of the government was that the defendants were advocates of Taiwan independence. International observers contend the government was never able to clearly demonstrate this point. Furthermore, it was clear nearly all of the defendants merely advocated self-determination, not independence. Despite these circumstances, the court accepted the confessions and determined the case to be legal. In the decision handed-down, the court declared:

> The defendants have received higher education and have had adequate social experience. Some have been lawyers for years. They should have realized the consequences of the confession. Should they have committed no crime, they would not falsely accuse themselves of sedition.[30]

The Kaohsiung incident reiterated the Kuomintang's position that Taiwan independence was not an issue open for debate and furthermore, that the party would take strong measures to keep it that way. The issue to most if not all of the defendants was Taiwan independence and democracy. The use of terms like self determination presupposes a growing grassroots movement towards independent statehood for Taiwan. But while the people of Taiwan were nervous about how Beijing would view discussions of Taiwan independence, they nevertheless voted against the Kuomintang in the 1980 elections in those seats where jailed opposition leaders had intended to run. Family members of the jailed leaders ran in their stead and were elected by a huge margin. The KMT's efforts at damage control over the Kaohsiung incident had backfired. The opposition was buoyed-up by its successes at the polls, but nevertheless focused their attention, at least temporarily, on issues other than independence.

At the same time the Kaohsiung incident was capturing headlines, the Kuomintang continued to make sweeping changes within. In December, nine Taiwanese party members were put in the central standing committee, among them owners of the widely read *China Times* and *United Daily News*.[31] Table 4.2 indicates the changes brought more diversity to top levels of the party at a time when political challenges throughout the island demanded new insights.

For the next several years, the reshuffle continued. Chiang first replaced leaders that had been close to his father but had proven unable to keep up with party reforms for reasons of health or political disagreement. He then began to turn those out of office he originally selected to help with his transition to power. Some were considered to be compromise leaders that were acceptable to both Chiang Ching-kuo and the party hardliners, while others were seen as progressives that cleared the way for future leaders. As Chiang's critics began to lose their places of importance, newer leaders were needed to replace the first wave of reformers in order to meet the demands of increased political activity on Taiwan.[32] The Kuomintang had a record it could run on in elections, and it needed to build on that record to be successful in the future.

The 12th National Party Congress of the KMT was different from previous congresses in one key respect. The 12th was not as anticipated as other party congresses had been. Each national party congress provided party members

Table 4.2 Taiwanese Composition on CC, CSC, 1981

Organ	Total	Taiwanese	% of Total
CC	150	29	19.3
CSC	27	9	33

Source: Te-fu Huang, "Elections and Evolution of the Kuomintang," in Tien, *Taiwan's Electoral Politics* (Armonk: M.E. Sharpe, 1996), pp. 118-120. Reprinted by permission.

and outsiders an idea of new policies and personnel changes. But the rise of Chiang Ching-kuo changed the importance of the party congresses. Chiang no longer waited for party congresses to assess goals or suggest policy changes. Every meeting of the central committee became much more important as policy changes were introduced with scarce warning in advance, sometimes without even convening a plenary session. The decline in importance of the party congress pointed to a major change within the Kuomintang. Not only had younger progressive leaders embraced the call for change initiated by Chiang, but the party had entered an important transition period by abandoning the overarching importance of the party congress, a Leninist institution, for more pragmatic changes as they needed to be made. It was also a larger indicator of the relative absence of factional strife in the party. Party congresses tend to be more important when disagreements are strong.[33] As time passed, the KMT was becoming a more inclusive party.

In July 1981, an American professor from Carnegie Mellon University was killed in Taipei. Chen Wen-cheng was visiting Taiwan to do scholarly research. A noted critic of the Kuomintang, Chen was a permanent resident of the United States. He had been picked up by the police and questioned and later released. The next day he was found dead in his office. Speculation focused on members of the garrison command. Later the focus was directed at individual interrogators. Though the case was never solved, most experts believe Chen was probably killed by a police officer acting on his own. The government closed the case too soon, raising questions about its investigation. Some believed the government was afraid the investigation would uncover too much about the security apparatus or individuals involved in the case.[34] The United States government raised objections to the way the case was handled, though little could be done to urge the government to reopen the case.

In 1982, repercussions of the Kaohsiung Incident and other challenges to KMT authority resulted in several significant changes.[35] The garrison command shut down over a dozen magazines that crossed the line of acceptable political limits, though no punishments were given to individuals running the magazines. But after a taxi driver was killed during questioning under police custody, the legislative yuan passed a law requiring legal representation to defendants during interrogation, though it allowed police to continue to make arrests without warrants and issue summons without court authorization.[36] The actions of the legislative yuan seriously curtailed the abilities of the police and the garrison command to carry out interrogations as they had done in the past. It also forced police agencies to work more closely with the courts in respecting rights of the accused.

As newer leaders found their way into important posts, Chiang continued to release political prisoners. Most notably, those accused of involvement of the famed 2-28 incident of 1947 were released in early 1983. By August of the following year, four of the Kaohsiung defendants were paroled, partially as a result of U.S. pressure.[37]

In September 1982, the TW formed the Tang-wai Campaign Assistance Association to perform all of the functions of an opposition party, but without the official designation as a political party. Fei Hsi-ping presented two important points in founding the organization. The first was to allow the people of Taiwan to determine whether Taiwan was to be a part of China, or an independent state. The second was a call to abolish martial law, establish constitutional rule, and remove all prohibitions against the media and potential political parties.[38] The organization further evolved a year later into the Tang-wai Public Policy Study Association. The change in name and function of the TW organization reflected a growing rift from within over whether the TW should pursue a campaign of mass protest, or an electoral strategy. It was just one of several debates that would divide TW members, even after its formal organization as a political party.

At the Brink of Change

Since Chiang Ching-kuo had ascended to power, much had changed. If looked at on a year-by-year basis, there seemed to be little difference. But if one looks at the period 1975 to 1983, it is easy to see that Taiwan was on the brink of a major political change. A genuine middle class had emerged, an opposition group functioned in many ways like an opposition party, and pressures were being felt within the party to change as well. Chiang Ching-kuo's first eight years as chairman of the Kuomintang saw a steady transition process taking shape. At times the KMT tried to clamp down on the opposition. But repression threatened the party's legitimacy even more than tolerating dissent. Chiang had presided over sweeping political changes. His remaining six years would be even more dramatic as the liberalization process would lead to the first trappings of democracy.

Notes

1. From interviews with Feng Hu-Hsiang of the Chinese Democratic Reformers Alliance, Taipei July 22, 1993, and Tsiang Yen-si, secretary general to the president, Taipei, June 8, 1993.

2. Huntington, *The Third Wave*, Chapter Two.

3. *New York Times*, November 25, 1973.

4. Tien, *The Great Transition*, p. 69.

5. See the *New York Times*, June 1, 1975, and Peter P. Cheng, "Taiwan 1975: A Year of Transition," *Asian Survey* (January 1976), pp. 61-5.

6. Interview with Alexander Ya-li Lu, National Taiwan University, Taipei, May 19, 1993.
7. Ministry of Information, *China Yearbook, 1977* (Taipei: China Publishing, 1977).
8. Tien, *The Great Transition*, pp. 69-70.
9. A point also eventually realized by General Pinochet in Chile. Arturo Valenzuela, "Chile: Origins, Consolidation, and Breakdown of a Democratic Regime," in Volume Four of Diamond, Linz, and Lipset, eds., *Democracy in Developing Countries: Latin America*, pp. 187-192. See Nathan and Ho, "Chiang Ching-kuo's Decision for Political Reform," pp. 37-38, and Herman Halbeisen, "In Search of a New Political Order? Political Reform in Taiwan," in Steve Tsang's *In the Shadow of China: Political Developments in Taiwan Since 1949* (Honolulu: University of Hawaii Press, 1993), p. 81.
10. Interview, Ya-li Lu, May 19, 1993.
11. Robert R. Kaufman, "Liberalization and Democratization in South America: Perspectives from the 1970s, in O'Donnell, Schmitter, and Whitehead, *Transitions From Authoritarian Rule: Comparative Perspectives*, p. 101.
12. Chyuan-Jeng Shiau, "Elections and the Changing State-Business Relationship," in Hung-mao Tien, ed., *Taiwan's Electoral Politics and Democratic Transition*, pp. 216-218.
13. Gold, *State and Society in the Taiwan Miracle*, pp. 88-9.
14. Kuo, *The Taiwan Economy*, pp. 97, 201; Jackson, "The Philippines," p. 245.
15. Han, "South Korea," p. 277.
16. According to Feng Hu-hsiang, Chiang frequently studied and quoted from *Cheng-kuan Cheng-yao* (Political Governance and Political Expediency), considered a classic in Chinese political theory. Interview with Feng, July 22, 1993.
17. See Volume II, Chapter 10, of Feng Yu-lan's *A History of Chinese Philosophy*, Edited by Derk Bodde (Princeton: Princeton University Press, 1953).
18. See Gerald McBeath, "Taiwan in 1977: Holding the Reins," *Asian Survey* (January 1978).
19. Ming-tong Chen, "Local Factions and Elections in Taiwan's Democratization," in Tien, *Taiwan's Electoral Politics*, pp. 180-1.
20. Much of the information on local party chiefs in this sections was gathered from interviews with Tao Yuan and I-lan county party cadres and Taipei City party cadres during May and June, 1993.
21. Interview, Yang T'ai-shuenn, May 24, 1993. While elected officials are now allowed much independence from county party chiefs, the importance of county party chiefs remains important to the party central for policy implementation as well as national recruitment. Local KMT officials still have only limited responsibilities.
22. Taipei Domestic Service, 18 December 1978, FBIS *Daily Report*, Asia and the Pacific, December 18, 1978, pp. B12-15.
23. CNA, 7 February 1979, FBIS *Daily Report*, Asia and the Pacific, February 8, 1979, pp. B2-3.
24. CNA 10 February 1979, FBIS *Daily Report*, Asia and the Pacific, February 14, 1979, pp. B2-3.
25. *Chung-yang Jih-pao*, 3 October 1979, FBIS *Daily Report*, Asia and the Pacific, October 18, 1979, p. B1.

26. Interview, Ya-li Lu, May 19, 1993. For a full report of the riot and its aftermath see John Kaplan's *The Court-Martial of the Kaohsiung Defendants* (Berkeley: Institute of East Asian Studies, University of California Press, 1981).

27. Ibid., pp. 19-24. It should also be noted that the government claimed they had to assign defense attorneys due to the defendants refusal to secure themselves defense early enough.

28. Defendant Lin Yi-hsiung had been beaten severely. Lin was released temporarily to attend the funeral of family members who had been murdered and witnesses clearly saw that he had been subjected to physical mistreatment.

29. Ibid., pp. 29-31.

30. Ibid., p. 47.

31. Hong Kong AFP, 14 December 1979, FBIS *Daily Report*, Asia and the Pacific, December 14, 1979, p. B6.

32. Interview with Tsiang Yen-si, June 8, 1993.

33. Interview with Ya-li Lu, May 19, 1993.

34. John Copper, "Taiwan in 1981: In a Holding Pattern," *Asian Survey*, January 1982.

35. Andrew J. Nathan and Helena V.S. Ho, "Chiang Ching-kuo's Decision for Political Reform," p. 45.

36. Parris Chang, "Taiwan in 1982: Diplomatic Setback Abroad and Demands for Reforms at Home," *Asian Survey* (January 1983), pp. 38-47.

37. *China Post*, 17 August 1984, FBIS *Daily Report*, China, August 22, 1984.

38. Lu, "Political Opposition in Taiwan: The Development of the Democratic Progressive Party," in Cheng and Haggard, *Political Change in Taiwan*, p. 126.

5

Liberalizing the Political System

Increased openness within the party encouraged some to express their opinions without fear of party discipline. KMT secretary-general Y.S. Tsiang called on the party to respect outside criticism and public opinion more readily. Local KMT leaders had already made such calls and had even tried to appeal to the voters by distinguishing differences between themselves and the party or other party candidates. Indeed, by 1983, elections in Taiwan had become a focus of political debate. The KMT realized that allowing local elections to carry-on with little interference was a good way of deflecting criticism of the party at the national level.

After the 1978 elections were cancelled, most observers noticed the rescheduled elections of 1980 were open beyond any that had occurred in the past. Due to the declaration of martial law, elections since 1969 were only permitted by presidential decree. But a new "Act of Election and Recall of Public Officers During the Period of Communist Rebellion" passed in 1980, gave official sanction to elections (an reaffirmed martial law).[1] But press control, limitations on public campaign rallies, organization strengths, and vote buying all favored the KMT. Opposition candidates accused the KMT of being undemocratic and called for a reformation of the three main parliamentary bodies to make them truly democratic. TW candidates wrote a common platform in attempt to show party-like unity, which contained calls for greater democratization at all levels of government. They also called for freedom of speech and assembly, and called for the KMT to lift the special restrictions that suspended important articles of the constitution. In addition, Tang-wai candidates called on the KMT to become a regular political party and abandon its special relationship to the government.[2]

Many were surprised at the KMT's relatively low-keyed response to the Tang-wai's demands. Others suggested the KMT realized its popularity was secure and could therefore run on its accomplishments and still handily defeat the Tang-wai in elections. The success of the 1980 election carried over into the elections of 1981 and 1982. TW candidates were buoyed-up in their

Table 5.1 Electoral Support for the KMT and TW in Selected Elections

Year	Election For:	KMT% of vote	TW% of vote
1977	Magistrate (County Head)	70	29.6
1981	Magistrate	59	23
1985	Magistrate	61	13.5
1981	Nat. Assembly	71	24
1980	Legislature	72	13
1983	Legislature	71	19
1986	Legislature	66.7	24.5

Source: Adapted from Cheng and Hsu, "Issue, Structure, Factionalism, and Party Realignment," in Tien, *Taiwan's Electoral Politics*, p. 138.

growing electoral success. Both TW and KMT candidates began to look at each other as legitimate contenders for political office and less as enemies that threatened the well-being of Taiwan.[3] Of more importance than actually winning the elections, the institutionalization of the campaign and election process gave the Kuomintang confidence to expand reforms and allow dissent from other sectors of society.

The Growing Pressure to Liberalize

The steps towards recognizing the legitimacy of elections also had negative effects on the KMT's ability to maintain party discipline and curb corruption. During the 1950's and 60's there was a low level of financial corruption because Taiwan was relatively poor. As growth rates soared, the people of Taiwan quickly found it to their advantage to support policies that would help develop their localities. Like all local KMT officials, those taking party jobs in the 70's were acquainted with local businesses and their owners. As electoral participation increased, so did the competition to attract votes. Small businesses sought out local officials to arrange favorable treatment and contracts in exchange for votes and financial support. Though not all local KMT officials were involved in graft, the problem exploded as the system began to open up. In some cases, government and party officials went looking for local opportunities to make deals. It became common practice to sell products or services to the government at artificially high prices and split the difference of the windfall with officials arranging the deals. A lucrative deal of this sort often resulted in long-term financial rewards for both parties as officials would guarantee additional contracts, trips overseas, and other deals involving money for continued agreements.[4] The Chinese tradition of doing favors through personal contacts (kuansyi), justified the practice in the minds of some business owners, though others reported they avoided the temptation to engage in illegal deals entirely or participated once or twice and then avoided further involvement.[5]

Seats previously belonging to mainlanders were filled by Taiwanese representatives on the legislative yuan, and deals became commonplace between the newly elected officials and local enterprises. As real decision making power still rested with KMT party central, local KMT legislators provided what largess they could. Aware that their political careers were limited to their localities which offered little hope for gaining national prominence, many KMT officials made deals with bus companies, real estate companies, and newly established savings and loans firms. Once these connections were made, officials would grant these businesses favorable treatment by influencing local policies and overlooking regulations. In return, businesses gave money to these officials, or offered positions in their firms after they retired from party and government service.[6]

National political leaders stayed relatively clear of these corruptive influences. Because most national leaders of significance were mainlanders they lacked connections to Taiwan's businesses which are mostly small family-run firms. This allowed the KMT to maintain a relatively clean image at top party circles even though the problem of corruption continued to grow at the local level.

In spite of these negative influences, the feeling of political liberalization was beginning to take hold. Chiang Ching-kuo was seen as a determined reformer and sometimes democrat, especially compared to his father.[7] The younger Chiang was able to not only match the economic success achieved during his father's rule, but began moving the island's economy in much more complex and diversified ways. This type of economic transition required political change to sustain the move. Political development lagged behind economic growth, but there was no doubt the Kuomintang was moving in the direction of political reform. In terms of party composition alone, the KMT had become a party of young technocrats, many of whom were Taiwanese.

One study found that by 1985, 40% of the party's policy-level officials were of Taiwanese origin. At the provincial level 75% of the policy-level officials were Taiwanese, and 100% of those at the city and county level were Taiwanese.[8] Changes in party composition led to changes in the nation's three parliamentary bodies. In the national assembly, 91 out of 955 members were elected on Taiwan, 78 out of 251 in the legislative yuan, and 24 out of 38 in the control yuan. With the exception of the control yuan, the other two bodies continued to be dominated by older KMT officials who were rarely part of the day-to-day political routine of the Kuomintang. These members represented an earlier era of party rule and for many in and out of the Kuomintang, their presence was considered a nuisance. For this reason, the number of Taiwanese placed in important party posts was more significant than the gains made by Taiwanese on the elected bodies, because the political climate of Taiwan was still largely determined by internal KMT policy.

The opposition and the Kuomintang realized, however, that this would change as further democratic reforms placed new importance on elected bodies. This would in turn alter the way policy proposals would be debated and enacted into law. For the time being, however, the large number of Taiwanese party members holding significant positions of power weakened the opposition's contention that the KMT had been unresponsive to the needs of native Taiwanese.

Younger party leaders were making inroads to high organs of power. The Central Standing Committee of the Central Committee had been a bastion of mainlander political dominance under Chiang Kai-shek. Because of the CSC's large membership, the introduction of younger leaders into the body, and Chiang Ching-kuo's increasing reliance on technocracy, the CSC had decreased in importance in the decade since Chiang had taken over formal leadership of the party. An informal group consisting of the party secretary general, premier, general secretary to the president, minister of defense, and a few others, became the defacto CSC by 1979. The group's existence kept relevant voices in the CSC from making their views heard. It also limited some technocrats from having the impact on policy they desired in pushing for reforms in the party and government.[9] In 1983 Chiang Ching-kuo disbanded the group. But instead of strengthening the CSC significantly, the body only marginally increased in power. Decision making power became dispersed to other entities, including government bodies thus allowing for some real separation of party-government functions.

Party appointments, delegation of responsibility, and electoral success had given the KMT a new look, though aspects of the old regime continued to haunt the Kuomintang. Chiang worried about military leaders and the possibility of their attempting to influence political events. General Wang Sheng had been critical of Chiang Ching-kuo in private circles. In 1983, Chiang made Wang an ambassador to Paraguay after rumors surfaced of

Wang's efforts to challenge Chiang's political power. Wang's "banishment" from the Taiwan political scene sent a message to other military leaders including Chiang's half-brother Chiang Wei-kuo, that the party controlled the political system--and the military.

Institutionalized violence and extra-legal methods of handling political opposition continued despite the fact that most KMT leaders opposed such tactics. In 1985, a California newspaper man, and advocate of Taiwan independence, was found murdered in his suburban San Francisco home. Henry Liu had long been the target of Kuomintang criticism for his efforts to end the KMT's domination of political power. He also fought for the establishment of an independent Taiwan republic. At first, the Kuomintang denied any connection to the Liu murder. But officials in the United States, and a simultaneous investigation in Taiwan uncovered evidence that the murder was ordered by Admiral Wong Hsi-ling, chief of the ROC Defense Ministry's Intelligence Bureau. Through subordinates in the bureau, Wong hired underworld figures to kill Liu. The killing refocused attention on the KMT security apparatus. It is likely the order to kill Liu came from Admiral Wong himself, not any other high level KMT leader. But the killing was a reminder of the vast security network organized by the KMT to squelch political opposition. It also rekindled the fears of U.S. officials that the Taiwan authorities were again involved in brutal acts to intimidate their opposition. Responding to such fears, the party eventually offered limited cooperation in the case, taking every opportunity to distance the actions of Admiral Wong from any official policy of the party or government.[10]

While it is not likely that any KMT officials higher than Wong ordered the assassination, critics argue the incident was a reflection of how the security network operated in Taiwan. In earlier times security people were charged with knowing which voices needed to be silenced without top KMT officials having to issue direct orders. Thus the desire of a superior was carried out without the leader having to make his wish known. One of Admiral Wong's mistakes was not realizing how quickly the political times had changed, thus exposing the KMT to criticism at home and abroad.[11]

There were other serious problems for the KMT in 1985. Opposition leaders had been calling for a full disclosure of KMT finances since the Lei Chen case in 1960.[12] The KMT had been attempting to separate party enterprises from government enterprises since the 1970s. While success was realized in this area, the closed nature of the KMT's financial dealings made it tempting for some to commit illegal acts believing the veil of secrecy would hide their deeds. Such was the thinking behind some officials involved in the bankruptcy of the Tenth Credit Corporation, a financial institution with direct Kuomintang ties. The scandal resulted in the indictment of several prominent officials and a promise that the KMT would review its business connections to make sure that no improprieties would continue.[13]

The positive side to both the Henry Liu case and the failure of the Tenth Credit Cooperative was that the KMT had to commit itself to reform its most obvious errant ways. This kind of reform was primarily internal and required the KMT to establish new rules of conduct.[14] The Taiwan electorate gave the KMT over 66% of the vote in the 1986 elections for the legislative yuan in spite of the scandals. But TW candidates had gained over 24% of the vote. They had seen their share of the vote nearly double since the 1980 legislative elections. They were showing confidence in their growing popularity, and the KMT was worried about its continued decline in popularity. As quickly as the KMT bounced back from its mistakes, new challenges faced its leaders.

In 1986 a Taiwan-based 747 airliner was hijacked to mainland China. The incident caused the government to abandon a long-held policy not to negotiate with the mainland authorities on political matters. In order to get the airplane back, Taipei was forced to hold talks with government officials from Beijing. Taipei tried to downplay the significance of the talks, publicly declaring the efforts to be a law enforcement matter that China Airlines and some government officials were trying to resolve. Despite its disclaimers, the government had in fact engaged in official negotiations with the mainland authorities. In doing so, the KMT had broken a political barrier that would clear the way for them to negotiate scholarly and tourist visits in the years to come. All in all, officials privately acknowledged these were fortunate aspects of the incident.

The Emergence of an Opposition Party and an End to Martial Law

Unfurling the banner of democratization, Tang-wai leaders attempted to focus attention on the KMT's continued monopoly of power. Demonstrations became commonplace, speeches included subject matter that was considered illegal such as Taiwan independence. By May 1986, the KMT was sitting down with influential TW leaders in negotiations to consider measures that would be mutually agreeable in moving Taiwan towards democratization. Little progress was made throughout the spring and summer amid growing criticism that the KMT was resisting real change that would undermine its power base. The Tang-wai demands centered on breaking the prohibition on opposition parties, ending martial law, allowing for the popular election of major leaders such as the president and vice president of the country, governor of Taiwan, and mayors of Taipei and Kaohsiung, and a separation of Kuomintang-government functions.

The demands were not unreasonable, though the tactics used by opposition leaders were not always helpful to their cause. Disruptions of legislative yuan sessions by Tang-wai leaders, and other acts of rebellion were viewed unsympathetically by many. People who had historically held a grudge against the Kuomintang had grown to hate the Tang-wai as much or more because of its tactics. A common complaint was that the Tang-wai showed little competence to take the reins of leadership and would probably not perform as well as the Kuomintang were it to receive a majority of seats in a fully representative legislature.[15] Some felt political change was occurring too quickly and expressed worry about continued economic growth and social stability.

These concerns are common in developing regimes. Luciano Martins notes potential critics of the military regime in Brazil became passive supporters because of stable and successful economic policies. When economic benefits were realized by key groups, the demands for political freedoms were not as prominent.[16] The people of Taiwan were also willing to temporarily forego political freedoms in exchange for continued economic growth and stability. It was nevertheless clear to most KMT leaders that political reform had been carried to the point where there could be no turning back. To oppose further reform would invite the same kind of violent activity that rocked South Korea in the early 1980s.[17] They feared putting off liberalization would risk a complete loss of political power. It was therefore apparent that to be successful, the KMT had to become a competitive party in a multi-party system.

Indeed authoritarianism had reached its usable limit.[18] A sense of democratic inevitability had overtaken the Taiwan political scene and the Kuomintang had reached a critical juncture in its political evolution. Its experience in handling earlier crises built confidence to face up to the need for sweeping political change.[19] With each passing day, more and more conservative leaders came to realize that continued resistance to democracy would surely lead to undesirable results.[20]

It is not clear at what point Chiang Ching-kuo accepted this conclusion. Aides close to Chiang report he was determined to forge ahead with democratization.[21] Ma Ying-jeou, a secretary to Chiang Ching-kuo during the 1980s reported that by 1984 Chiang was embarrassed about Taiwan's image abroad, given that the island was still under martial law.[22] But when questioned about the particulars of Chiang's comments in regards to democracy, the evidence is not as certain. Supposedly in private conversations, Chiang spoke of democracy in connection with the *San Min Chu I* and the need for better education as a way of improving people's lives and making the country healthier economically. While economic stability has direct connections to democratic development, the evidence of Chiang supporting democracy is not overwhelming. Chiang offered no new interpretations of how the *San Min Chu I* related to democracy, nor did he propose any other formulations of what he felt democracy meant in the context of Taiwan politics. It is apparent, however, that Chiang attempted to keep up with the ever-increasing calls for democratic reform. He was adept at finding short-term political paths to take, though events were transpiring so quickly that he struggled to develop a long-term political strategy to facilitate change.[23] His repeated claims of democratic support legitimized rule by law and weakened authoritarianism. And like his authoritarian counterparts in Brazil, Uruguay, and Argentina, Chiang was forced to open the system to justify decades of democratic rhetoric.[24] His decision was no doubt aided by the realization that the opposition was not likely to oppose the KMT's right to exist in a competitive system, and the opposition was not likely to take risks that threatened the economic and political stability of Taiwan.[25]

In September 1986, Chiang Ching-kuo formally announced martial law would soon be lifted and a new national security law would be established in its place.[26] At the same time, the Tang-wai took advantage of the government's promise to allow opposition parties, and announced the formal organization of the Min-chu Chin-pu Tang (Democratic Progressive Party or DPP).

The DPP suffered from many of the same problems that plagued the TW. At first it constituted more of a party movement than a tightly organized political party. Its initial efforts were to get the KMT to open the political system. It was predominantly Taiwanese, though a few mainlanders were counted among its ranks. This caused problems for some who did not want the DPP to become a Taiwanese-only party. Mainland-born DPP members Fei Hsi-ping and Lin Chin-chieh would eventually quit the party after feeling excluded by the DPP rank-and-file.

The party was as much an agent of political agitation as it was a body seeking elective office. Most of its members tended to be in favor of Taiwan independence and policies directed more to what they saw as the economic disadvantaged, though they were still middle class in orientation. Typical DPP supporters were younger than KMT supporters, and included many young intellectuals and professionals.[27]

The DPP's announcement, though not totally unexpected, created a problem for the KMT. The Kuomintang had almost always been able to keep ahead of major political developments. The creation of the DPP tested the ruling party's patience. While martial law was to be ended soon, and new guidelines were in the works allowing for the creation of opposition parties, the DPP had jumped the gun. If the Kuomintang decided not to act against the DPP it could give the new party and any other potential party organizers the impression that its word had decreased in importance. If it acted to ban the DPP, the Kuomintang would become the target of attacks both at home and abroad for using repressive measures to thwart the forces of democracy. The *United Daily News* urged the government to be careful in its handling of the DPP. Others also took the higher ground arguing that swift actions against the DPP would not only reflect poorly on the KMT, but could severely damage the march towards democratization that Taiwan had experienced in recent years.[28]

The Kuomintang's response was a measured one. Although it did not instruct the government take formal action against the DPP, it did declare the party to be illegal. The inevitability of an organized political opposition made it impossible for the Kuomintang to take a stronger stand. At the same time the government made it clear that the organization of opposition parties would only be permitted if the new parties were anti-communist and did not advocate Taiwan independence.[29] The Kuomintang's insistence on the above two points was important because of Taiwan's precarious international position. Leaders in Beijing had taken notice of Taiwan's move towards democracy and worried about the island making overtures for independence. The government warned that Taiwan was the legitimate temporary seat of government for all of China and any move to the contrary would be met with resistance from both the government of the Republic of China and the Communist authorities in Beijing.

Despite these warnings, a wing of the DPP that favored independence for Taiwan made plans for the return of exiled opposition leaders associated with the overseas Taiwan Independence Movement (TIM). The most prominent figure was Hsu Hsin-liang who was refused admittance on grounds that his return threatened national security. The refusal to admit Hsu resulted in demonstrations at Chiang Kai-shek airport and in Kaohsiung and Taipei. The Taipei demonstration was the most serious since the Kaohsiung riot of 1979. One dissident died when he entered a building and refused to come out. Police fired tear gas on the building, engulfing it in flames, and by some reports, prevented the man from exiting the burning structure.[30] But the actions of this more vocal wing of the DPP angered other factions of the party who either thought the drive for Taiwan independence was premature, or believed the idea of independence to be a political mistake because of public opposition to the idea.

Inter-factional strife weakened the DPP's effectiveness as a broad based party, and solidified the already well-entrenched support for the Kuomintang. Despite some initial electoral success in local elections, the DPP had become so fragmented in 1987 that various party leaders openly attacked each other in the press, each claiming to lead the faction with the most grassroots' support. By late 1986 only 60% of the population had heard of the DPP and just over 8% approved of its tactics. In addition, about half of people surveyed were evenly divided on whether or not the party should be banned from participating in Taiwan politics, while the other half had no strong feelings one way or another.[31]

As long as the DPP remained seriously divided, the KMT had time to carefully think through policies regarding opposition parties and the removal of martial law. In July the government officially lifted martial law, ending the temporary provisions that granted extra-constitutional authority to the KMT-controlled government since 1947. While the new National Security Law did not go as far as some had hoped in terms of granting full constitutional government, significant changes were initiated. Most importantly, military law was lifted with new emphasis given to constitutional rights and civil law. While the government continued to arrest political opponents, prisoners were quickly released and all forms of physical torture ended.[32] Security agents overseas, primarily in the United States operating under the guise of the Taiwan Trading Company in New York City, stopped monitoring Taiwan students at American universities, and also ended surveillance of pro-Taiwan independence groups operating in American cities.[33] Censorship of magazines and other media materials was gradually brought to a stop. The result was an explosion of political magazines and increased news coverage in newspapers.[34]

Provisions regarding contact with families on the mainland were established, as were liberalized rules regarding overseas travel. There was a huge increase in the number of private institutions, political and non-political that emerged. Long considered essential in the life of democratic societies, these associations became advocates for democratic change.[35] Existing institutions that had been co-opted by the Kuomintang became vocal in their support for greater liberalization.[36] Some of the special privileges given to the executive office were lifted. The issue of electing the President and Vice President remained unsettled, though the government promised to take up this problem with the next round of reforms. It remained the most sensitive issue remaining from martial law. The 1947 constitution intended for the office of president to be weak. The president was to be the head of state, while the government would be headed by the premier. The extraconstitutional practices institutionalized by Chiang Kai-shek and Chiang Ching-kuo, however, made it difficult to turn back to the intent of the constitution. It immediately became the focus of contention and a major obstacle to the emergence of democracy.[37]

The main tenets of the new National Security Law made it a crime to advocate communism or to allow political groups to organize if they tolerated communism in any fashion. It also forbade any attempt at Taiwan independence or support for any group advocating an independent Taiwan republic.[38] While there was little desire on Taiwan to assimilate communism, there was a small though powerful drive to move Taiwan towards independence. Most residents of Taiwan feared military conflict with the mainland, and at the same time, felt some attachment to the people of mainland China even though few had actually been to the mainland. At the same time, most Taiwanese held a distaste for the kind of political activism that was advocated by many in the opposition. Indeed, political interest in Taiwan was not nearly as heightened as it had been in some other developing countries. For most people, the reforms were gradual but sure, thus suiting their immediate interests. These factors gave the government the legitimacy it needed to enforce the anti-Taiwan independence clause of the new National Security Law. In September, the first arrests were made of those advocating Taiwan independence. While some opposition leaders accused the KMT of returning to its paranoid ways, others considered the move a positive one for the DPP as it would allow the struggling party to regroup.

Opening the Party and Representative Institutions

By late 1987, the KMT embarked on one last significant reform before Chiang Ching-kuo's death. Many older KMT leaders opposed the rapid pace by which martial law had ended and the government's subsequent willingness to allow opposition parties to organize. They realized that with the abolishment of the extraconstitutional laws that had given the KMT its unique status, the KMT's monopoly on power would be gone forever.

Younger KMT leaders like Kuan Chung and Jaw Shao-kang saw this as a positive step and believed the next area of reform needed to be the nation's representative organizations. Their power base had been established not as much in the party as in the representative institutions. They were outspoken advocates of electoral reform. The KMT itself had become significantly more liberalized. Young talented leaders who favored the KMT agenda could join the KMT, do their best to improve their political position, and expect to move-up in the party's ranks for a job well done. Liberalization gave way to more broad-based decision making at the county and city party organization level. Electoral reforms increased the power of elected officials vis-a-vis party chiefs. This meant local party organizations had to work more with elected leaders, whereas they had previously made all significant local decisions without direct input from mayors and county magistrates.

Party leaders began to question the legitimacy of party central in sending down policies that they felt were out of touch with local conditions.[39] At the same time, party chiefs began to be challenged by lower level party officials who wanted to be consulted before accepting policies sent from Taipei or from the local party leader's office.[40] These developments made it more difficult to maintain party discipline in the way the Kuomintang was accustomed to.

More attention was needed to consider the three national representative bodies if the Republic of China was to begin a more sweeping transition towards democracy. In December, the KMT announced it was working on a plan to retire senior KMT officials from these parliamentary bodies. This would clear the way for the first fully contested national elections.[41] At the same time, it would create new problems in trying to decide what to do with the Taiwan Provincial Assembly. This body would be even more redundant with the legislative yuan becoming more democratic.

The Kuomintang cited a number of reasons for its willingness to address the problems of the three bodies. Among them was the admission that the opposition and academics had encouraged the KMT to move in this direction. The KMT's tolerance of ideas previously considered treasonous had resulted in the party being more responsive to important public discourse which in turn helped make the KMT an effective engine of liberalization. At the same time Kuomintang leaders realized liberalization was a two-edged sword. While the party had so far been able to survive reforms and maintain a high degree of public support, even tougher challenges were emerging. Liberalization freed voices to criticize the quality and extent of reforms. These voices were readily found both in and out of the party. Young KMT members had become involved in factional disputes at the local and national levels. Conservative leaders became increasingly concerned about what would happen to the party after the departure of Chiang Ching-kuo. As a result, opposition to Lee Teng-hui as a successor was expressed openly by some senior leaders, despite Lee's being hand-picked by Chiang as the latter's successor.

The political system in Taiwan had been stable for so many years because the party had been able to control so many aspects of life in Taiwan. Unlike developing countries in Latin America and elsewhere, the KMT had built extensive ties to business, education, and social groups. But these connections had begun to erode as had the Kuomintang's monopoly on political power and its capacity to control the pace of reform. The contradictions of party authoritarianism and calls for democratic reform had peaked and the Kuomintang would be changed forever.

Chiang Ching-kuo and the Politics of Reform

The party seemed poised to face other reforms when Chiang Ching-kuo died in January 1988. He was a more complex man than his father was. On the one hand, he was the Soviet-trained hardliner who became the enforcer of his father's policies with the KMT's escape to Taiwan in 1949. He showed little tolerance for opposing viewpoints, even from influential party leaders. At the same time, Chiang Ching-kuo had foresight that Chiang Kai-shek lacked. The elder Chiang was consumed with recovering the mainland to the point of forgetting about the long-term political needs of Taiwan. The younger Chiang saw the continuance of his father's harsh authoritarian ways to be dangerous to KMT survival and harmful to both his and his father's personal legacy. Chiang Ching-kuo came to understand that long-term success needed to be planned for in the present, not put off until events forced the Kuomintang to accommodate meaningful political change.

Some scholars believed Chiang was able to stay ahead of the game at least until the mid 1980's.[42] But by the end of the decade, liberalization was expedient if the KMT was going to have a future role in Taiwan politics. Chiang had to stop controlling elections to give the KMT renewed legitimacy. It meant phasing-out the security system and making the party more inclusive by bringing in younger and better skilled Taiwanese party members to take significant posts. In the final years of his life, it meant breaking down the barriers to broad-based political competition by ending martial law, formally announcing that opposition parties would be allowed to organize, and rethinking the way national representative bodies were supposed to work.

The policies of Chiang Ching-kuo's later life contradicted those of his earlier life, demonstrating that political leaders often mature in their thinking when challenged by those claiming their political rights. His not claiming authoritarianism to be an acceptable long-term alternative to democracy gave him credibility not enjoyed by authoritarians in Europe.[43] At the same time, Chiang's policies and the opposition's challenge to the KMT brought attention to the party's contradictory claims as an authoritarian party that advocated democracy.

1. Leadership

Mistakes by KMT leaders and challenges from the opposition helped move the Kuomintang from hard to soft authoritarianism.[44] By the late 1980s, the party's reliance on authoritarianism had become permanently shaken. Chiang Ching-kuo found it necessary to face challenges to the party's authority in a manner that would accommodate liberalization rather than oppose it. Democratization seemed inevitable and the KMT needed to be a partner in this process if it was to have a role int he political future of Taiwan.

The loss of U.S. recognition, human rights abuses, and the financial scandal of the Tenth Credit Cooperative forced KMT leaders to be respond to the public and to KMT members who demanded the party behave responsibly. Talented political leaders were in no short supply in the economic sector. Chiang had been able to keep up with challenges from the political opposition, though it meant making good on the promise of democracy. The party leadership became increasingly concerned with pragmatic approaches to problem solving and what the long term effects of these approaches would be in implementing particular policies. Soft liners like Jaw Shao-kang, James Soong, and Kuan Chung were able to convince hard liners of the necessity of reform. This was as important in the democratic transition process as the role of the opposition because it forced to party to take moderate approaches to political challenges.[45] Public opinion mattered to younger KMT members who were finding their places as newly elected leaders, administrators, and members of top party organs. They believed their political fortunes were based on the public's perception of party competence and therefore developed a more public spirited method of operation. But top leaders in the CSC were becoming increasingly divided over which path the KMT should take. Some older party leaders and a few younger party members preferred the authoritarian Kuomintang to the liberalized Kuomintang because the former was more sensitive to mainland recovery. They felt the liberalized Kuomintang was too willing to sacrifice this principle. Thus the Taiwanese-mainlander division within the party began to grow. Chiang's death heightened the concerns as the mantle was to fall upon Taiwan-born Lee Teng-hui.

Chiang Ching-kuo's role in the Taiwan regime's transformation was crucial. His efforts to gain a popular mandate for the party increased its acceptance during difficult political times. It also eased the political system into gradual liberalization, thus increasing the chances for democracy to take hold. If he had resisted this transition, liberalization would have had to wait for a leader who was not nearly as well situated as Chiang was to make reforms, or risk violent attempts by the opposition to open the party.[46] Chiang's efforts kept liberalization on a centrist path, thereby avoiding political extremism from more radical elements. It also helped keep potential differences between mainlander KMT leaders and Taiwanese leaders in and out of the party from coming to a head. A quasi-ethnic struggle of this kind had the potential of bringing the same undesirable situation that plagued some Latin American countries, often resulting in serious bloodshed.[47]

2. *Organization*

Though the transition was by no means complete, Chiang Ching-kuo managed to bring the Kuomintang closer to a typical Western political party than it had ever been. During the 1980's, the KMT gave up many of its privileges of monopolizing political power and became a more competitive party in Taiwan elections with island-wide support. The party began to lose its identity as a party dominated by a single party leader. There is no doubt Chiang Ching-kuo held the most significant position of power in the party, and that major decisions required his approval. But others within the party like Li Huan and Lee Teng-hui were freer and in fact expected to make suggestions without fearing harsh reprisals from Chiang or the party's old guard.

Local party organs attempted to attract public support by sponsoring community activities. The party lost control over much of the day-to-day business of local organizations. This strengthened local factions. Strife was beginning to build between local factional leaders and party central. In spite of this the KMT was the party of choice, even after the DPP organized itself with the belief it could rally the people after years of exclusive KMT rule. But the Kuomintang could only go so far with its existing organization. It remained too Leninist to fully embrace democracy. The role of the party chairman had to be challenged. Until this happened, the party would be seriously limited in its abilities to support democracy.

3. Ideology

The Kuomintang dropped almost all references to it being a revolutionary party during the chairmanship of Chiang Ching-kuo. The *San Min Chu I*, was only important to the KMT as a concept rather than a specific blueprint for political development. The strength of constitutional principles and pragmatic steps towards democratization offered more to the party as a political plan than the vagueness of the *San Min Chu I*. The party's positions on issues increasingly sounded like those supported by Western political parties in terms of offering peace and prosperity rather than the somewhat anachronistic sounding phrases of restoring the mainland and developing the Three Principles of the People. This became even more apparent as the KMT's role in government began to be tested. More importantly, though democratization was beginning to take a firm hold, there is no evidence to suggest that Chiang Ching-kuo or any other major KMT figures understood what that entailed philosophically. To them it meant an end of an era. But there is no evidence to suggest senior Kuomintang leaders spent very much time thinking about how to implement democracy. For this reason, further reform and consolidation of democratic gains would require increased ideological justification by KMT leaders. It would also necessitate the development of democratic mores such as toleration, moderation, compromise, and a dedication to recognize the sacred nature of political rights.

It is often said that the acceptance of democratic mores is not easy in East Asia. Thomas Metzger suggests the Chinese do not realize the depth of their devotion to Confucian principles. A major proof of this is the superficial acceptance of liberal democracy.[48] Lucian Pye argues Asians emphasize leaders as morally superior persons, and in the process minimize the importance of individual citizens. This results in a limited appeal to Western forms of democracy.[49] The structure of family life in East Asia is cited by both scholars as a support for authoritarian rule. But Alexis De Tocqueville argued families are profoundly changed in democratic societies. Democratic principles change the family culture, altering the role of father from lord and master over his children to one of provider and caretaker.[50] Tocqueville's contention is that democracy brings an expectation of equality to all human relationships, even those traditionally considered non-political. Similarly, Francis Fukuyama suggests Confucianism plays a larger role in family life, though the influence of Confucian teaching diminishes in democratic settings.[51] The Taiwan case verifies the arguments of Tocqueville and Fukuyama, suggesting that leaders in Taiwan need to emphasize Western democratic mores to improve and stabilize democracy on the island.

4. Agenda Setting

The KMT had developed a proven record of economic success to base its support, but realized that political progress was a key aspect that had been neglected. Promises of greater political liberalization were kept by the party, thus improving its chances to effect political change over time and win the support of Taiwan's population. The linkage of an improved living standard and ongoing liberal reforms helped develop a sense of democratic promise in Taiwan. This in turn influenced the formation of policies Chiang introduced in his later years.[52] While Chiang Ching-kuo played a large role in setting this agenda, there is no doubt other leaders were instrumental in formulating the details and enforcing the changes amidst opposition from party conservatives who felt the Kuomintang's goals were being abandoned too quickly. In some respects the KMT had lost control of the agenda with the emergence of political openness. Disagreements grew within the party as the KMT was forced to give-in to the realities of a new political climate. But the measured pace of reform kept the transition process from getting out of hand and upsetting political calm. It also stabilized leadership replacement within the KMT. In turn, replacement set the party on a more direct path of reform, giving Chiang's successor the support he needed to keep up the gradual pace of liberalization.

5. Quality of Governance

Because of its dependence on public support and its composition of native Taiwanese, the KMT was successful in persuading the people of Taiwan that it could provide economic security for the population. It continued to demonstrate this during Chiang Ching-kuo's tenure as party chairman, and seemed able to proceed with the same confidence in the future. The party learned to rely less on secret police and intelligence services and more on

Liberalizing the Political System 89

confronting the issues and taking responsibility for scandal and policy failures. In ending martial law, the party strengthened the role of civil courts and removed much of its influence from the day-to-day operation of the judiciary. At the same time, the party saw government excess as a negative reflection on them. For this reason, the party also made strides in encouraging its members to be more responsive to the needs of the people and in being more professional.

While Taiwanization and greater reliance on technocracy is not the same as democracy, these policies were influential in introducing a new cast of characters ready to move in when the political moment was right.[53] With each reform introduced by the KMT, skilled personnel were ready to do their part in the liberalization process.

During the later part of Chiang's rule, the people of Taiwan showed increased interest in quality of life issues such as environmental protection, social security, health, and civil rights. The media began to function as it does in democratic societies. Political openness began to be accepted as commonplace--thus bringing legitimacy and stability to the reforms.[54] Opposition leaders, particularly key TW and DPP figures played an invaluable role in opening the system. Despite being torn by factional rifts of its own, the opposition showed courage and unquestioned resolve to stake a claim in the political system and fight for the expansion of political rights. It was the catalyst that brought about decisive change in the system. Without them, liberalization would have been stalled, and the promise of democratization would have remained unrealized.

The development of civil society in this way has proven to be a major difference between the stronger performances of newly developed countries in Europe than those in Latin America.[55] It is also a major difference between the relative success Taiwan has enjoyed in the democratization process and the troubles the Philippines has faced.[56] But the limits of civil society would still be tested in Taiwan as Chiang's successor would learn.

6. Party-Government Relations

The party continued to dominate the government at the national level. Top government officials were still significant party leaders. The negative effects of this were financial scandal, duplication of duties, unfair meddling in government affairs, and anger from the opposition. This was also a concern for the people of Taiwan who viewed Taiwan's democratization to be incomplete until the marriage between the KMT and government organs was completely broken. The key to breaking this relationship in part depended on the three nationally elected bodies becoming truly representative. As chairman of the KMT, Chiang Kai-shek and Chiang Ching-kuo institutionalized an imbalance of power that favored the chairman in his role as president of the republic. This allowed the Chiangs to control much of the day-to-day activities of the government. Renewed attention to constitutional principles was needed to bring balance to the various branches of government and end illegitimate party rule. As party influence began to decline, the strength of government agencies and representative bodies grew in importance. This provided new political opportunities for aspiring politicians and added to the legitimacy of the government as a focus of political authority.

The Kuomintang made tremendous progress during the years of Chiang Ching-kuo's chairmanship in unloading aspects of authoritarian control. But the battle was not over. The transition to democratic rule is dangerous and can be thwarted in many ways. Many worried about the prospects for democracy in Taiwan when Chiang Ching-kuo took over. Now that he was gone, many worried if the drive for democratic reform would continue.

Notes

1. Fei-lung Lui, "The Electoral System and Voting Behavior in Taiwan," in Cheng and Haggard's *Political Change in Taiwan*, p. 156.
2. Tien, *The Great Transition*, pp. 177-181.
3. Ibid., pp. 193-4.
4. Information gathered from businessmen interviewed in May 1993.
5. Corruption continues to plague Taiwan politics. The Taiwan electorate considers it to be one of the most serious problems of the political system.
6. Interview with Yang T'ai-shuenn, May 24, 1993.
7. Yangsun Chou and Andrew J. Nathan, "Democratizing Transition in Taiwan," *Asian Survey*, March 1987, pp. 282-3.
8. See Alexander Ya-li Lu, "Future Domestic Developments in the Republic of China," *Asian Survey* (November 1985).
9. Hung-Mao Tien, *The Great Transformation*, p. 81.
10. CNA 16 March 1985, FBIS *Daily Report*, China, March 18, 1985.
11. Interview, Chiang Ch'un-nan, May 19, 1993.
12. Former KMT leader K.C. Wu and others had called for an end to government subsidy of the KMT and a full audit of KMT books as early as the 1950s.
13. See *Washington Post*, October 7, 1985.
14. A point readily admitted by most prominent KMT officials including Tsiang Yen-si in an interview with the author, June 8, 1993.
15. This was a concern frequently expressed to me during the early summer of 1986 in Taipei. Many young entrepreneurs had grown uncomfortable with the Tang-wai and had an allegiance to the Kuomintang despite grievances they held against the KMT.
16. Luciano Martins, "The Liberalization of Authoritarian Rule in Brazil," in O'Donnell, Schmitter, and Whitehead, *Transitions from Authoritarian Rule: Latin America*, pp. 79-81.

17. Han, "South Korea," p. 283.
18. Linz and Stepan, *The Breakdown of Democratic Regimes*, pp. 53-4.
19. Sidney Verba, "Sequences and Development," in Leonard Binder, James S. Coleman, Joseph LaPalombara, Lucian Pye, and Myron Weiner, eds., *Crises and Sequences in Political Development* (Princeton: Princeton University Press, 1971), pp. 302-3.
20. Rustow, "Transitions to Democracy," p. 357.
21. Interviews with Tsiang Yen-si and Feng Hu-hsiang.
22. Ho and Nathan, "Chiang Ching-kuo's Decision," p. 36.
23. Ya-li Lu, May 9, 1993.
24. Alain Rouquie, "Demilitarization and the Institutionalization of Military-dominated Polities in Latin America," in O'Donnell, Schmitter, and Whitehead, *Transitions from Authoritarian Rule: Comparative Perspectives*, pp. 110-112.
25. Dahl, *Polyarchy*, p. 15.
26. *China Post*, 10 September 1986, FBIS *Daily Report*, China, September 17, 1986.
27. Ya-li Lu, "Political Opposition in Taiwan: The Development of the Democratic Progressive Party," in Cheng and Haggard, *Political Change In Taiwan*, pp. 132-3.
28. Hong Kong, AFP, 30 September 1986, FBIS *Daily Report*, China, October 3, 1986.
29. *China Post*, 15 November 1986, FBIS *Daily Report*, China November 21, 1986.
30. The government states the man was able to leave the building but refused out of protest.
31. John Copper, "Taiwan in 1986: Back on Top Again," *Asian Survey* (January 1987), p. 84.
32. Interview with Ya-li Lu, May 19, 1993.
33. Interview with Chang Ch'un-nan, May 19, 1993.
34. Censorship did not end for Television and radio stations, however. While they benefitted also from the lifting of martial law, the lifting of restrictions over T.V. and radio did not begin in earnest until 1994.
35. Alexis De Tocqueville, *Democracy in America*, Henry Reeve Text, Volume I (New York: Alfred A. Knopf, 1980), p. 195.
36. Tien, *The Great Transition*, p. 57.
37. Hu Fo, Interview, May 28, 1993.
38. CNA, 1 July 1987, FBIS *Daily Report*, China, July 2, 1987.
39. Hansen Chien (Chien Han-sheng), Taipei City KMT Chairman, interview, June 14, 1993.
40. Johnny Jen-nan Sand (Sheng Chien-nan), Cultural Affairs Office of the KMT, interview, May 28, 1993.
41. The Kuomintang has asserted that the 1947 elections were fully democratic. This is not entirely true do to rules established by the nationalists on the mainland that prohibited individuals and independent parties from putting their names on the slate.
42. See for example Edwin A. Winckler's "Institutionalization and Participation on Taiwan: From Hard to Soft Authoritarianism," *China Quarterly* (September 1984).
43. O'Donnell and Schmitter, *Tentative Conclusions*, p. 15.
44. Ibid.
45. O'Donnell and Schmitter, *Tentative Conclusions*, p. 19.

46. Andrew J. Nathan, *China's Crisis: Dilemmas of Reform and Prospects for Democracy* (New York: Columbia University Press, 1990), p. 136.

47. Diamond and Linz, "Politics, Society, and Democracy in Latin America," in *Democracy in Developing Countries*, Volume Four, pp. 3-5.

48. Thomas A. Metzger, *Escape from Predicament: Neo-Confucianism and China's Evolving Political Culture* (New York: Columbia University Press, 1977) pp. 194-5.

49. Lucian W. Pye, *Asian Power and Politics: The Cultural Dimensions of Authority* (Cambridge, Mass: Belknap Press of Harvard University Press, 1985), PP. 339-341.

50. Tocqueville, *Democracy in America*, Book II, pp. 193-4.

51. Francis Fukuyama, "Democracy's Future: The Primacy of Culture," *Journal of Democracy* (January 1995), p. 13.

52. Diamond and Linz, "Politics, Society, and Democracy in Latin America," p. 11.

53. Constance Squires Meaney, "Liberalization, Democratization, and the Role of the KMT," in Cheng and Haggard, *Political Change in Taiwan*, p. 114.

54. Li Cheng and Lynn White, "Elite Transformation and Modern Change in Mainland China and Taiwan: Empirical Data and the Theory of Technocracy," *China Quarterly* (March 1990), pp. 3-9.

55. Philippe C. Schmitter, "An Introduction to Southern Europe Transitions: Italy, Greece, Portugal, Spain, Turkey," in *Transitions from Authoritarian Rule: Southern Europe*, pp. 5-7.

56. Jackson, "The Philippines," p. 263.

6

Inner-Party Conflict and the Emergence of Democracy

Lee Teng-hui's ascent to the top Kuomintang post was not as well orchestrated or as sure as Chiang Ching-kuo's. Lee received formal educational training in Japan and the United States. His PhD from Cornell helped him land a position as section chief and advisor to the Joint Commission on Rural Reconstruction, the government agency charged with overseeing land reform and agricultural development. The success of the program was one of the main components of Taiwan's phenomenal economic development plan. Lee's competence in rural reform helped launch his political career. He served as minister without portfolio in the national government, where he was further able to demonstrate his abilities as an administrator. In 1978 he was named mayor of Taipei, and because of excellent service there, was appointed governor of Taiwan in 1981. In 1984, Lee became Vice President of the republic.

Despite his capable record in government service, Lee's experience in the KMT has been limited compared to others who used the party as their primary conduit to power. This was especially concerning to party conservatives who viewed the party as the only road to power in the Republic of China. Lee's disposition towards technocracy mirrored Chiang Ching-kuo's concern with practical ability in politics, but did not allay the concerns of those consumed with party orthodoxy. These worries grew with Lee's appointment as KMT vice-chairman and with the deterioration of Chiang Ching-kuo's health.

Securing the Party Chairmanship

Chiang Ching-kuo's death set off a flurry of activity within the top ranks of the Kuomintang. Even though Lee Teng-hui was both party vice-chairman and vice president of the republic, party hardliners, especially conservatives Yu

Kuo-hwa, Li Huan, and those close to Madame Chiang Kai-shek opposed Lee's taking command of the party and the government. They realized nothing could be done to prevent him from becoming president. There was an established constitutional precedent that had been followed in 1975 when vice president Yen Chia-kan took over the formal position of president at Chiang Kai-shek's death. But Chiang's son took charge of the party, and therefore defacto power after his father's death. Hardliners favored a similar arrangement in the case of Lee Teng-hui. Lee's support for party reform and occasional advocacy for political liberalization, and the fact that he was a native Taiwanese, brought opposition from KMT hardliners.

Chiang Ching-kuo's departure came at a critical time for the party and the people of Taiwan. Chiang's willingness to consider ways to reform the national assembly, legislative yuan, and control yuan, and growing discussion surrounding the procedure for electing the president and vice president of the republic, the governor of Taiwan, and mayors of Taipei and Kaohsiung, worried some older party stalwarts. They believed too much reform, particularly the reforms mentioned above, would not only fundamentally change the party, but could also result in the demise of the KMT. Lee Teng-hui fought hard to dispel such worries by trying to convince party members that reforms must continue if the KMT was to be a vital force in the future. Madame Chiang Kai-shek returned to Taiwan from the United States in an attempt to block Lee's appointment as party chief. Premier Yu Kuo-hwa backed Madame Chiang's efforts to thwart Lee's bid for the top party post. The debates, mostly fought behind closed doors, caused an impasse, eventually resulting in the party's having to cancel a meeting of the central committee that was supposed to take place in mid January 1988.[1] Many speculated Lee would not be able to claim the chairmanship of the party. By late January, however, Lee succeeded in rallying enough influential party leaders to support his bid as party chief. In the end, many party hardliners, including Madame Chiang, embarrassed themselves in their effort to block Lee's appointment by not only causing internal problems for the party, but in giving the opposition and many within the KMT ammunition in their contention that the KMT hierarchy was an anti-Taiwanese, pro-mainlander club.

There was little time for Lee and his supporters to savor their victory. Debates surrounding the procedures for electing the governor of Taiwan and mayors of Taipei and Kaohsiung demanded immediate attention. If the governor of Taiwan was to be chosen by general election, Lee and others knew that this person would be the highest executive in government popularly elected by the people. This would directly challenge the legitimacy of the president of the republic, who in reality was formally appointed by the Kuomintang hierarchy and ratified by the rubber-stamp national assembly. Similarly, general elections for the mayors of Taiwan's two largest cities could mean loosing the municipalities to the opposition. A temporary decision was made to have the premier nominate the governor of Taiwan and have the nominee ratified by the provincial assembly rather than by presidential appointment. This allowed the KMT to keep control over the selection of nominees, thus ensuring that the provincial assembly did not gain too much power vis-a-vis the legislative yuan. This decision also invited more public scrutiny in the process by having members of the provincial assembly, popularly elected themselves, ratify or reject the nominee. But many key KMT leaders feared too much was happening too fast, prompting a postponement of discussions concerning the election of the mayors of Taipei and Kaohsiung.[2]

Attention turned to preparations for the 13th National Congress of the Kuomintang. The congress was originally scheduled for early 1988, but was postponed to July due to the factional squabbling following Chiang Ching-kuo's death. Lee's agenda for the party congress was far more ambitious than those of previous party congresses. In one respect this was predictable in that Lee had to establish his own base of support in the party that distinguished him on his own terms and not merely as the hand-picked successor to Chiang Ching-kuo. On the other hand, Lee's proposals were hardly easy pills for party conservatives to swallow. The platform for the congress emphasized more policy-oriented goals traditionally associated with the platforms of democratic parties of the West. Environmental protection, democratic development, improved labor relations, economic growth, consideration of the structure of parliamentary bodies, and freedom and human rights issues, were clearly emphasized while the traditional focus of recapturing the mainland was mentioned in only passing terms.[3] The attention to reforms couched in democratic rhetoric marked yet another turning point for the Kuomintang, as Lee attempted to push reforms even more quickly than his predecessor. He hoped the reform agenda would weaken his rivals in the party.

Despite getting the central standing committee's nod to serve as party chairman, Lee's appointment could be overturned at the party congress if party conservatives were able to convince the central committee to vote against him. When the congress finally convened, one of the first matters of business was the election of Lee Teng-hui as party chairman and selection of new central standing committee members and central committee members. Yu Kuo-hwa and other party conservatives, and other party members, called for a secret ballot to nominate and elect the party chairman. Kuomintang practice had always been to use an open ballot because it helped party elders maintain party discipline. Party members who publicly voted against measures supported by the party hierarchy could be identified by party elders. It was argued that since pluralism was gaining ground throughout society, the party ought to set a standard by convening more democratic elections themselves. Lee and his supporters, though having advocated increased liberalization, saw the secret ballot proposal as an attempt to keep Lee from being formally elected. Using their influence, Lee's supporters saw to it that the elections remained an open-ballot affair, thus ensuring Lee a large margin of victory in the election. Though the election was clearly non-democratic, Lee saw it as a victory against those who had opposed or wanted to restrict ongoing reforms that would have benefitted him. The denial of secret balloting was a clear pronouncement that as leader of the Kuomintang, Lee intended to use some of the same disciplinary tactics routinely employed by his predecessors.

All in all, the elections went well for Lee and his supporters. Over 65% of the central committee were new members, and the average age of the body dropped from 70 to 59. Taiwanese representation on the body increased from 20 to 45%. More importantly, a majority of the 31 central standing committee members were Taiwanese nominated by Lee, thus increasing the chasm between Taiwanese and mainlander party leaders. Former president Yen Chia-kan and Chiang Ching-kuo's half-brother General Chiang Wei-kuo, were "nominated" to the presidium of the central advisory council, thus limiting their influence in the party hierarchy.[4] A good number of other conservative and elder party members were also retired at the congress, giving newcomers a freer hand to propose changes.[5] Li Huan retained his post as party general secretary, as did premier Yu Kuo-hwa. Lee gave clear indications he intended to move Hau Pei-tsun, a critic of the new party chairman and a party conservative with extensive military experience, into high political office, possibly premier. Reformers were stunned by Lee's willingness to promote Hau, though nearly everyone saw it as an attempt to buy the military's loyalty.[6]

Trying to keep pace with the times, the party decided to change the standing policy on contacts with the mainland. The policy was worded in far more scholarly and less inflammatory language than previous KMT statements. For the first time, official cultural and economic contacts were approved by the party, assuring their passage by the government. In some respects the party's allowance of semi-official contact with the mainland was pro-forma. Taipei chose not to do much to those engaged in illegal trade with the mainland in the year or so prior to the congress.[7] The new policy gave allowance for contacts between academics on both sides of the Taiwan Straits, thus lifting some party control over higher education. The official new approach was not as clear as officials hoped it would be. Lee had difficulty clearly articulating his mainland policy. He restated the KMT's long standing policy of not having official contact with the communist authorities. At the same time, he stressed that low level contacts were essential for humanitarian reasons and for providing a model of openness for Beijing.[8]

The party congress cemented many of the goals Lee set-out to accomplish. He established his power base on a firm footing. The 13th congress was more open than any previous party congress. Journalists had more freedom to report internal debates. The reportage helped mount popular support for reforms. While party congresses under Chiang Ching-kuo decreased in importance because of his ability to control factional debates, Lee needed to build a critical mass of support during the 13th congress. He gained the backing of younger Taiwan-born KMT leaders and the public. Many younger mainlander KMT members were skeptical of the new chairman. Conservative leaders disliked what was happening to the party under Lee, primarily because they worried the goal of mainland recovery was being sacrificed for Lee's "Taiwan-first" policy.

Extending Reforms and Lee's Fight for the Presidency

The party congress did not deal with the question of legalizing opposition parties. Though still technically illegal, the DPP continued to operate openly. Other groups opposed to both the DPP and the KMT felt free enough to organize political demonstrations. Most notably, farmers, workers, students, and even some soldiers, demonstrated for a more representative government that paid attention to their concerns. The KMT tried to show sensitivity to these demands at the congress, though these groups were not satisfied that enough had been done. At the same time, in spite of increasing openness, Lee Teng-hui and other party officials continued to censor news reports. Much of this was done through informal threat rather than through official agencies.

By early 1989, the Civic Organization Law was passed, finally legalizing the creation of opposition parties. The passing of the law failed to give the DPP the broad-based strength it desired. Instead, some 34 parties registered with the government, thus weakening the opposition's voice in the elected bodies.[9] This was one of the contributing factors behind the wild debates that rocked the legislative yuan during the year. Shouting matches and fist fights were too often the course taken to settle differences. At the root of the problem were arguments surrounding special procedures claimed and practiced by the ruling party, and divisions among opposition legislators over how to deal with these privileges. In particular, the opposition challenged the KMT's right to control the agenda and specify what kinds of bills were to be considered in the legislative yuan. It objected to the heavy-handed tactics the KMT used to force party members to vote along party lines. Despite disagreements within the party, the KMT could still depend on its members of the legislature to deliver the vote on most issues important to the party hierarchy.

Party reforms and the call for liberalization resulted in greater openness in government affairs. In January the executive yuan announced that it had cut defense from 50% of the budget to 40%. The decrease in military expenditures was a victory for reformers who wanted to focus more on domestic problems and less on mainland issues and what they saw as outdated worries over internal and external security.[10]

Leadership worries continued to concern reformers in and out of the party. While Yu Kuo-hwa's days as premier seemed numbered by the end of 1988, liberal reformers worried about a possible successor. When Yu was finally pushed out of office in 1989 and KMT general secretary Li Huan was announced as his successor, reformers worried that the slightly-more moderate Li Huan may not be much of an alternative to the conservative Yu. The appointment of reformer James Soong to replace Li Huan as general secretary of the party reassured some in the liberal faction, but Li's outspoken characterizations of the political opposition as lawless hooligans and other inflammatory remarks threatened to stall reforms in an increasingly charged political climate. Some in Taiwan believed the time had come for KMT politicians to stop characterizing political opponents as enemies of the people.[11] Li Huan tried to assuage these concerns by tempering his rhetoric and by making efforts to meet with DPP leaders. The meetings were encouraged by many in Lee Teng-hui's faction who wanted Li to take a softer approach.[12]

Government reform did proceed. Following the pledge at the 13th party congress, the party moved towards greater social responsibility in government. The ministries of Social Welfare, Agriculture, Labor, and Culture were organized to address quality of life issues that had been neglected for so long in Taiwan.[13] The creation of the ministries was also a victory for the opposition. Despite the fact that the public showed strong support for the KMT as the party of choice, the creation of the new ministries came at a time when party and government functions were under serious scrutiny. The increase in government power meant a devolution of KMT power and a chance for the opposition to point to inefficiencies in the system. Many government employees saw increased government responsibilities as a way to rid the government of excessive KMT oversight and meddling.

The December 1989 elections for the legislative yuan were significant for a number of reasons. As in previous elections, only a limited number of seats were contested. In spite of this the DPP did better than expected. This worried the KMT even though it kept a huge majority in the body. Most of the KMT's problems were of its own making. KMT candidates ran against other KMT candidates who were not endorsed by the party. There was squabbling between candidates which had a negative effect on the electorate. Predictably, KMT candidates split the votes in some races, thus handing victories to DPP candidates. Some conservative party leaders argued the campaign problems underscored the drawbacks of party reform. They worried about short and long-term KMT influence in a competitive party system. But in the 1989 race such worries were unjustified. As one U.S. observer complained, even if the DPP had won every contested seat on the legislative yuan, it still would have been a minority party in the legislature.[14] The 1989 race was a harbinger of democratic progress. Although there were strict limitations on the number of seats contested, elections had become institutionalized on Taiwan.[15] Party leaders knew subsequent elections had to be fully representative or risk instability.

The unsolved problem of how to elect the president of the republic resurfaced in early 1990 as the national assembly prepared to meet in Taipei. Most people in Taiwan favored popular elections. Despite Lee Teng-hui's popularity, many in the KMT feared a nation-wide ballot for the presidency because it would put Lee head-to-head with an opposition challenger. The political stakes for the presidency were great because of the special privileges associated with the presidency but not granted by the constitution. Party conservatives realized if a non-KMT candidate was elected, that president would also have the sweeping powers enjoyed by previous presidents. On the other hand, reformers feared a conservative president could resist reform or worse still, fight to roll-back reforms. KMT members generally feared an opposition party president might push for Taiwan independence and would certainly work for the complete separation of government and KMT responsibility, thereby weakening the KMT's role in politics forever. Thus the special privileges given the president and KMT chairman proved to be a major problem for democratic reform. Yet without addressing the issue, reform could not be complete, as it constituted a major obstacle to political liberalization.

In a February party meeting, Li Huan, Lin Yang-kang, Hau Pei-tsun, and Yu Kuo-hwa fought for a secret ballot in nominating the party's candidate for president. While the conservative group justified its proposal on democratic grounds, there was no doubt the group wanted to take power from Lee Teng-hui and felt a secret ballot gave them their greatest chance. KMT general secretary Soong, despite being a public advocate of democracy, spoke in favor of a voice vote in order to keep the KMT unified behind Chairman Lee. He knew conservative party members would feel obligated to support Lee in a public ballot.[16] Despite loosing their bid for a secret ballot, Lin Yang-kang and Chiang Wei-kuo decided to formally challenge Lee's power by announcing their candidacy for the presidency and vice-presidency respectively. Their efforts were short lived, as younger leaders accused conservative party members of trying to force their will on the party.

Though Lee's election to the presidency seemed a sure thing, this did not mean the Kuomintang formula of presidential selection could last forever. In March, 1990, 10,000 students took to the streets to protest the lack of democracy in Taiwan. Specifically, they demanded an end to the temporary provisions established on the mainland that gave the president sweeping powers. They called for popular elections to choose the chief executive. They also demanded more representation in elected government bodies. Both

Chiang Ching-kuo and Lee Teng-hui promised to consider the question of elections to parliamentary bodies, and Lee admitted the extraconstitutional privileges of the presidency needed to be rethought. In an attempt to satisfy some of the students' demands, Lee Teng-hui promised a conference to study these and other constitutional issues. At the same time, the demonstrations moved the KMT to consider other measures of political liberalization. Li Huan announced the KMT would retire older leaders, remove the ban on mainland visitation, and allow direct trade with the mainland. He also pledged to empower the Taiwan Provincial Assembly and make it more representative. He acknowledged the government was rethinking the communist rebellion clause that granted the presidency special powers, and committed to popular elections of the Kaohsiung and Taipei mayors.[17]

Li's proposals committed the party to specific democratic reforms. At the same time, all of Li's comments (with the exception of the retirement of older KMT leaders) either directly or indirectly dealt with presidential privileges. If adopted, these changes would strictly limit the power of Lee Teng-hui. Li Huan had a growing base of support within the KMT from older party leaders, and some younger members as well. Several groups within the KMT openly threw their support behind Li and his campaign for government reform. Li's efforts formally created two factions, one headed by Li Huan and another by Lee Teng-hui. A showdown was eminent.

Lee Teng-hui was officially elected president in April. He managed to secure both the top Kuomintang and top government position, though the KMT suffered during the spring meetings of the national assembly. Open debates between party members exposed an ugly side of the Kuomintang--the side the party fought to keep hidden from public view. Both Chiang Kai-shek and his son were able to keep most party debates confined to select gatherings. The climate of increased openness fueled debates, which in turn widened the rift between leaders. Lee wanted to rid his cabinet of the most vocal opponents to his power.

One of the first to go was Li Huan. Long considered to be a close friend of the Chiang family, Lee replaced him with Hau Pei-tsun. Hau's appointment as premier initially sent shock waves through the country due to his military background and his association with the conservative arm of the party. Lee's selection of Hau reflected Lee's need to appoint a man capable of winning some conservative support, and at the same time, someone who could retain the loyalty of party members who previously supported Li Huan. While it was clear President Lee and Premier Hau were not the best of friends, Hau was not Li Huan, which gave Lee some breathing room. Lee knew, however, the things Li Huan advocated in the months preceding his dismissal could not be neglected.

The Rise of Constitutional Questions

In July, government and party leaders sat down with the opposition and academics to discuss prominent constitutional questions. Both the KMT and the opposition felt the conference was significant in that substantive issues were discussed. There was disappointment, however, that the decisions of the conference had no binding power. But the conferees reached general agreement on five areas of reform:

1. Lifetime members of the legislative yuan and national assembly were to be retired. Fully competitive elections for those bodies were to be held.

2. The governor of Taiwan, and the mayors of Kaohsiung and Taipei were to be popularly elected. This would end the presidential privilege of appointing these officials.

3. The President of the Republic of China would be popularly elected.

4. The extraconstitutional provisions proclaimed because of the communist rebellion, were to be done away with, as well as the prohibitions against amending the constitution.

5. Taiwan's population was to be considered the first priority of the government. Mainland Chinese issues was an important secondary concern.[18]

Though some were distressed that no time table had been set for implementing the reforms, President Lee committed himself and the party to address and enact the five points into law. Despite this commitment, President Lee found it difficult to consider the five points because of disharmony within the party. He began a campaign to build support within the party for further reforms. He believed the party had to respond to the reform agenda if it was to maintain a popular image.[19] At the same time, pressures exerted by the opposition, in particular the DPP, weakened the party's and government's abilities to deal directly with the reform measures. More and more opposition leaders were openly calling for Taiwan independence despite the fact that the KMT, the government, and people of Taiwan opposed moving towards independence. President Lee faced increased pressure from some in the party to use government authority to punish the DPP for its advocacy of independence.[20] Lee refused legal action, instead calling on the government to reason with independence advocates. He believed such efforts would mount popular resentment against those advocating Taiwan independence.

In spring 1991, President Lee pushed ahead with his agenda. At a meeting of the national assembly, approval was given for renewing the three parliamentary bodies. By the end of the year, the national assembly was to retire all permanent members and elect a new body of 325 members, 225 elected by districts throughout Taiwan, 80 elected as national representatives, and 20 as overseas representatives. By the end of 1992, the legislative yuan would be renewed. Of its 161 members, 135 would be elected by district, 20 in nationwide elections, and 6 would represent the overseas population. Originally, the control yuan was to be renewed in 1993, with 25 of its 52 members elected by the provincial assembly, ten each elected by the Taipei and Kaohsiung city councils, 5 elected at the national level, and 2 elected by the national assembly. (It was later decided to appoint the 29 members of the control yuan and have the nominations ratified by the national assembly. The change was made to streamline the selection process and to emphasize the importance of elections for the legislature and national assembly.)

Despite the agreement to renew the parliamentary bodies, several important problems remained. Most of these related to the problem of overlapping responsibilities. It is one thing to renew existing bodies, but what if the bodies have redundant responsibilities? Renewal did not address the problem of the provincial assembly and how it differed from the legislative yuan. There were similar questions surrounding the duties of the national assembly. The duties of the control yuan also overlapped with those of the other elected bodies, as well as those of the judicial yuan, executive yuan, and examination yuan. The problem of overseas Chinese is also important. Hu Shih first questioned the legitimacy of overseas Chinese participating in elective bodies given the fact that they resided in foreign lands and in some cases, were citizens of other countries. The presence of overseas Chinese on the elective bodies buoyed-up the Kuomintang's contention that the government represented all of China. Party members increasingly questioned the practice. Some argued overseas representation was anti-democratic because representatives did not reside on Chinese soil.

These problems aside, the agreement to rejuvenate representative bodies was a significant step. It was followed by President Lee declaring the special provisions enacted in response to the communist rebellion were null and void. Another chapter of the Chiang Kai-shek legacy had come to a close. The ending of the special provisions resulted in greater freedom of the press and protection of speech generally. In July, the KMT sponsored legislation proposing the party's Chinese News Agency be turned over to the Government Information Office. But members of the opposition argued the Government Information Office should be privatized because it too was dominated by the KMT.[21] In spite of their objections, the legislation passed. It would take several years to complete the transition.

With the question surrounding representative institutions and press agencies temporarily solved, attention turned to the election of the president. At first the KMT announced it was willing to allow the president to be elected directly by the people. A party committee was struck to study this question and to consider the redundancy problems of the government yuans.[22] But after a few months of deliberations, the committee announced it was inclined to allow the existing system of presidential appointment stand given the full democratization of the national assembly, or have assembly members vote on the basis of his or her district's desire--a type of electoral college.[23] Both suggestions generated a huge controversy among KMT and non-KMT officials alike. In addition, numerous disagreements surfaced on the problem of administrative redundancy. The assembly meetings broke-up with no resolution on either problem.

Liberalization, Elections, and Lingering Constitutional Issues

While Lee Teng-hui continued to push his agenda, he still had to confront dissent in and out of the party. A faction of the KMT received permission to form a separate political organization. Though founded as a study group, the organization closely resembled an independent party. The political interests of the KMT's membership had grown more complex in the freer political climate.[24] The party was no longer seen as the only path to power. The DPP renewed its campaign to create an independent Taiwan. It included a proposal to submit a formal application to the United Nations to recognize Taiwan as an independent republic. In a surprise statement, President Lee declared there was no need to establish an independent Taiwan republic since it had been de facto independent since 1949.[25] Such an admission would have been considered treasonous during the rule of Chiang Kai-shek. But in the new political climate of Taiwan, the KMT would have to abandon old philosophies to be successful. Lee's statement gave the government some room to spar with the DPP over Taiwan's status. At the same time it was benign enough to ward off interference from the Beijing authorities. Party conservatives were nevertheless stunned at Lee's statement. They believed the Taiwanese president was mortgaging KMT principles to sure up his political success on Taiwan. But Lee's pronouncement helped calm people's uneasiness over the independence issue. For the time being, the people of Taiwan continued to oppose Taiwan independence. Some vocal DPP members resisted demands to reconsider their position.

In December, the first island-wide elections for the national assembly were held. It was a tremendous victory for the Kuomintang, capturing 71% of the vote. The DPP received 23% of the vote. Party leaders noted the major reason for the party's success at the polls was due to the work of local KMT factions. The growth of factional influence worried some mainlander KMT officials who feared the party was becoming too much of a Taiwan-based political party.[26] They viewed Lee Teng-hui as a supporter of local factions, and local factions as anti-mainlander and supporters of Lee.

The limited number of seats captured by the DPP was as much a reflection of the KMT's success in campaigning as it was the unpopularity of an opposition that had come to be seen as radically out of step with the desires of Taiwan's people and lacking policy development. The KMT not only survived the full democratization of the first representative body, it had done so with a mandate from the people.

The newly elected national assembly's first task was the consideration of controversial tenets of the constitution. If democracy was to be fully established, lingering constitutional questions had to be settled. The greatest concerns continued to surround be the method for electing the president and how to divide government responsibilities to ensure administrative efficiency. Lee Teng-hui made early overtures that he would not seek reelection in order to establish the succession process in the office of the presidency.[27] He also suggested he would take himself out of the running to prevent the appearance of him trying to move the discussion of how to choose the president in one direction or another. On this issue there was considerable debate. The people wanted to popularly elect the president. Some KMT leaders wanted to continue to have the president nominated by the majority party and ratified by the national assembly. There was also the issue of selecting the membership of the control yuan. Since the body was supposed to be a watchdog organization, the DPP argued its members should be elected by the people. Most influential KMT leaders felt the president should be able to appoint its members and have them ratified by the national assembly.

While the national assembly met in the spring to consider these issues, it was apparent the Kuomintang majority was trying to follow the will of party leaders. This was not an easy task, however. On one side was the mainstream faction led by Lee Teng-hui who believed the president should be directly elected by the people. The party mainstream had been buoyed-up by elections for the national assembly and believed it could deliver the votes needed to popularly elect a president suitable to their faction. On the other side was the non-mainstream party members, mostly mainlanders, who wanted the national assembly to continue appointing the president. They believed there was great risk in any KMT candidate running for office against a popular DPP candidate. In addition, a popular KMT candidate would probably not be much to the liking of mainlander KMT members who had a growing distrust towards the Taiwanese-majority membership. KMT assembly members fought openly over the issue, and in the process, marginalized DPP input in the debates. Angered over the KMT's refusal to consider their voice, DPP members walked out of assembly sessions in an attempt to delegitimize the KMT's heavy-handed efforts to reform the constitution.

While the assembly's KMT delegates managed to approve the amendment for direct election of the president and vice president, other issues were left unchanged or only marginally touched upon. It was decided that rather than electing control yuan members, the responsibility would be given to the president to appoint its membership and have them approved by the national assembly. The compromise was an attempt to secure a strong role for the president at a time when others were suggesting the premier should be the chief executive. Other questions about presidential authority lingered. Under Chiang Kai-shek, presidential powers had been expanded beyond original constitutional intent. These powers had become institutionalized under Chiang Ching-kuo and Lee Teng-hui. The national assembly failed to specifically curtail these powers, leaving this debate and the role of the president vis-a-vis the premier unresolved. The assembly also failed to clarify overlapping responsibilities of the five yuans.

One of the major reasons so little had been accomplished in terms of constitutional reform was disagreement within the KMT over the extent and nature of proposed reforms. KMT rank and file members complained that the views of the party's majority were being disregarded by influential conservatives like Li Huan and Hau Pei-tsun. Outside observers also blamed the lack of progress of reforms on party elders who felt their influence within the party slipping away.[28] The reform agenda formulated by the KMT majority, in particular those elected to seats in the national assembly, was closely scrutinized by those who worried about the efforts of the Taiwanese majority. This made it difficult for Lee Teng-hui to keep the party unified. As chairman of the KMT, Lee knew infighting could harm the KMT's chances in the upcoming legislative elections. For this reason, Lee allowed backsliding on reform proposals in order to keep unity.

In May 1992, the sedition law was formally suspended. The law contained many provisions that gave the government a free hand to detain and arrest people for many actions routinely protected in democracies. A new law was established in its place designed to punish only violent attempts to overthrow the government. This was followed by the dissolution of the feared Taiwan Garrison Command in August. Most of the activities of this political police force were abolished with one notable exception. Party conservatives wanted the garrison command to watch coastal areas to check illegal contact to and from the mainland. These duties were shifted to other government agencies who were charged with coastal protection and law enforcement. In spite of the garrison command's disbandment, critics charged the government had not gone far enough in ensuring an end to censorship and spying on Taiwan's citizens. These fears proved to be largely unwarranted, however, as even some of the most ardent critics of the KMT found they were able to write and speak as the pleased.[29]

The major events of the first half of 1992 (constitutional reform, repeal of the sedition law, and dissolution of the Taiwan Garrison Command) complicated matters for the KMT in fielding candidates and focusing on issues for the year-end legislative Yuan elections. Under secretary-general James Soong, KMT headquarters intended to control the slate of KMT candidates by endorsing only those acceptable to the party leadership. This would help the KMT hold the line on controversial issues such as mainland reunification and Taiwan independence. It was also an attempt to keep the party united by appointing enough candidates to satisfy party hardliners and local KMT factions alike.

Soong's attempts were met with strong resistance, however. Local factions, buoyed-up by their success in winning seats for their party in the 1991 national assembly elections, ignored Taipei's endorsements and nominated their own candidates. Many local officials believed Lee Teng-hui supported their attempts to run for office without party endorsement because it would build Lee's support within the party to have more Taiwanese in positions of authority. Local KMT officials complained that party central had never done anything for them other than expect obedience to party directives. They believed it was time for the party to accept the fact that party locals knew their constituencies better than Taipei. In addition, some candidates disregarded the party platform and openly campaigned for Taiwan independence and spoke of the KMT as a Taiwanese party. Once again many districts had two KMT candidates running for the same legislative seat--one the candidate of the local party faction, the other candidate carrying Taipei's endorsement.

This inner-party competition benefitted DPP candidates. After having done poorly in the national assembly elections, the DPP's hopes soared with increased squabbling between local KMT leaders and party central. It also set-up a level of campaign competition previously unknown in Taiwan. Despite the existence of election laws that set spending limits at N.T. 8 million (U.S. $300,000), candidates were routinely spending $4 million U.S. The money was used not just for getting their message out, but for buying votes and paying consultants to help them develop their image. One candidate in Chang Hua spent more than $20 million U.S. dollars on his campaign.[30]

The election did not go well for the KMT. Angered by blatant attempts to buy votes, the public chose candidates it believed to be the most honest and paid little attention to official endorsements. Candidates who campaigned against corruption did extremely well. This was especially true of a Kuomintang faction known as the New KMT Alliance. The New Alliance platform singled out honesty in government service as its primary concern. Its electoral success in securing 11 of the 12 legislative yuan seats it ran in worried Lee's cohorts. In all, the party won only 53% of the seats, the DPP 31%. For the first time since coming to Taiwan, the KMT realized the risk of loosing political control was real in the new era of political competition. Issues relating to Taiwan's international political status and its relation to mainland China proved to be of only marginal importance to voters. Islanders' contempt for vote buying and preoccupation with economic well-being mirrored the concerns of voters in other democratic states. Old guard party leaders and Lee's party mainstream both sought a popular mandate in waging their political battles with each other. Both had proven unable to win that endorsement.

In the post-election fallout, Lee Teng-hui and party secretary Soong admitted the party had made mistakes during the campaign. They pointed to pre-election infighting and corruption in the campaign process as a major reason for the KMT's poor showing at the polls. They also believed the issue of Taiwan independence had sent a mixed message to the public. Lee set-up a task force to look at the process of nominating candidates so a better strategy would be in place for future campaigns.[31] But the admission of mistakes failed to halt infighting. The rift between mainlander and Taiwanese party members intensified. Despite admitting mistakes, Lee also argued the party had to establish stronger local organizations to enable local leaders to work better with their constituents. Party conservatives saw this as a direct attempt to empower the party mainstream. Differences previously papered-over now became sharper with each passing day. Pressure to fire secretary Soong was great within Lee's party mainstream, from the KMT old guard, and second generation mainlanders. Soong left his position as general secretary and accepted an appointment as provincial governor. Hau Pei-tsun also stepped down from the premiership because of his growing contempt for Lee Teng-hui who he held largely responsible for party infighting. Lee nominated moderate Hsu Shui-te as party secretary, and Lien Chan as the new premier. Both nominees were Taiwanese. Lee hoped the nominations of Hsu and Lien would be a first step in regaining the KMT's popularity. A Gallup Poll showed a dismal 36.5% approval rating for the KMT, the lowest since the party had been on Taiwan.[32]

Hsu Shui-te was not as well-positioned as Soong had been. Soong was more of an activist secretary than Hsu would be. But Hsu's less aggressive style was in part made up by his willingness to work with factions in the party in trying to build a consensus. For this reason, Hsu was seen as a weaker, though more conciliatory secretary than Soong. Lee hoped his appointment would build support for the chairman's agenda leading to the 14th party congress scheduled for late summer.

Lien Chan had earned the respect of many within the party, though he was seen by many mainlander party members as too supportive of the party mainstream. Under new constitutional provisions, the national assembly held confirmation hearings on the Lien appointment. The hearings were significant for two reasons. First, it was clear the unresolved debate over the duties of the premier in relation to the president caused some confusion over what assembly members should actually be asking Lien in the confirmation process. Previous confirmation hearings did not provide an adequate standard to judge the premier-designate, since no one was clear on what duties premiers would have to perform in the future. The second significant development was the inflammatory questions posed to Lien from mainlanders opposed to his nomination. A reasonable observer would have expected the sharpest criticisms to come from DPP members of the national assembly. This proved not to be the case, however. Working closely with members of the New Alliance, some mainlander KMT assembly members claimed to have secret information on Lien's private business dealings that cast doubt on his worthiness to serve as premier. Evidence was never produced, however, though New Alliance members of the legislative yuan claimed they planned to use the evidence in future battles with Lien and President Lee.[33]

The fallout of the December 1992 elections proved to be detrimental to the health of the Kuomintang. Factions within the party used the KMT's poor performance as a base to launch their attacks against the party mainstream. The mainstream needed to strengthen the role of local KMT leaders to be successful at the polls. At the same time, Lee Teng-hui resisted this trend, realizing his position as party chairman would be weakened from demands made by powerful local leaders. By the Spring of 1993, the battle lines of inner-party strife became especially clear, with the creation of the Chinese Democratic Reformers Alliance (Hsin T'ung Meng Hui, to be explained below). Factional splits within the party now threatened the future of the KMT's electoral success. More importantly, non-mainstream factions came to view a KMT loss in upcoming year-end county elections to be in their favor because the mainstream would have to call on the mainlander factions for help. It is necessary to consider these factions separately.

The Development of Party Factions

Scholars who study Western systems are accustomed to identifying conservative and liberal factions within political parties. Identifying conservative or liberal factions within the KMT is not as easy, however. The party is divided more among mainlanders and Taiwanese, older party members and younger party members, urban and rural interests. For this reason, while one faction may be conservative on some issues, it may be considerably liberal on others. Mainlanders tend to be more conservative on issues regarding Taiwan independence. Older mainlanders are also more willing to keep the party hierarchically run, provided it is run by them.

Mainstream party members (mostly Taiwanese) are more pragmatic in their approach to politics, tending to pay more attention to local business interests. At the local level, factions tend to be built around personalities rather than particular ideological issues. This means the major national factions (New Alliance, Chinese Democratic Reformers Alliance, and Wisdom Club), tend to have little significance in local politics.

The Party Mainstream

Popular press accounts often refer to the party mainstream as the mainstream faction, though in reality it is the majority, not a faction. The mainstream is predominantly Taiwanese. Recent elections attest that its power is now greater than that of KMT mainlanders. The party mainstream is not a closely knit group, however. It is beholden to local interests and support Lee Teng-hui primarily because he is Taiwanese. For this reason, the mainstream lacks an ideological center. It does have final say on some nominations and party decisions because of its ability to tip the balance in its favor on issues where the party is sharply divided.

Powerless under Chiang Kai-shek and Chiang Ching-kuo, mainstream members spent a good deal of time in the margins of power, though they built significant contacts with local businessmen. When the system began to open-up, they suddenly realized the benefits of rewarding those who supported them. One of the unfortunate but predictable results has been a high degree of corruption. Many in the mainstream, through local factional interests, receive money from businesses in exchange for political favors. The kinds of favors vary according to the immediate interests of the businesses. Sometimes government contracts are awarded. At other times government regulations relating to environmental protection and worker safety are overlooked. Small real estate firms, credit unions, transportation companies, and construction companies are involved in a number of corrupt schemes involving mainstream members (large businesses tend not to be as interested in influencing local officials). Some KMT members are courted by village or town leaders who represent local financial interests. They ensure strong voter turnout for a candidate running for the legislative yuan by providing transportation and other conveniences to residents on election day.[34] The draw of money has encouraged many in the party mainstream to build personal fortunes rather than construct a political agenda. It is a major reason why candidates for the legislative yuan spend millions of dollars in getting elected.

The stench of corruption has harmed the party mainstream, however. The relatively poor showing by the party mainstream in comparison to New Alliance candidates in the 1992 legislative yuan elections demonstrated the public's distaste for the pernicious influence of money in politics. Party leaders believed the public's dislike for corruption would help curb the influence of graft in the years to come.[35] But others see the party mainstream as a disloyal group who hold no real political opinions and only use the KMT for personal gain. Critics believe mainstream members can be easily convinced to abandon the KMT and join an array of political parties or factions, depending on what disaffection could offer them in terms of political and financial success.[36]

Because there is no real bond for the party mainstream besides being Taiwanese, the mainstream is in many respects, a collection of local factions. On a practical level factions exist because they have a greater awareness of the local needs of constituents and how to get candidates elected to office. Local KMT organs must have good contacts with organizations like the rotary and lions clubs, and others in the community who can offer advice. This helps party strategists determine not simply who is best qualified for office, but who is likely to get elected. At times this puts local factional interests at odds with KMT headquarters. This has been the source of some discontent and has made it difficult to keep the party unified not just in large metropolitan areas like Taipei, but even in remote places like Peng Hu Island.[37] But these are the kinds of problems every political party faces in free electoral contests. What is more troublesome for the mainstream is that conflict put factions in direct opposition to one another or in opposition to national party leaders. In most cases the source of these conflicts is not ideologically based, but differences of opinion over political strategies. This has threatened the tenuous unity of the party mainstream and caused senior party leaders to worry about a total disintegration of the party.

Much of the growth of local factions came about naturally. Even though the KMT was not a democratic party when it came to Taiwan, it was still necessary to develop close contact with businesses, educators, and other interests in the local communities.[38] Over the years, local party members in the KMT's seven working committees (organization, society, youth, mainland affairs, overseas Chinese, women, and training) developed close relationships with various constituencies. These contacts made them intimately aware of the needs and desires of people in their locales. As the political system opened-up not only for the opposition, but for the KMT rank-and-file as well, factions began to exert greater pressure on KMT headquarters to go along with local demands. In part this meant traditional KMT power holders had to share power with local factions when it came to formulating the party's agenda, and the national political agenda as well. This was one of the strongest messages of the 13th party congress, when Lee Teng-hui sought rank-and-file support for his formal election to the chairmanship of the party. It was also apparent in the national assembly elections of 1991, when party headquarters admitted the KMT's electoral successes were in no small measure dependent on local factions getting the vote out. Thus mainstream members believe recent KMT success is attributable to the people wanting a Taiwanese chief executive and Taiwanese representatives in elected bodies, and less on the substance of the party platform.

Central party headquarters has tried to lessen the influence of local factions through improved training and communication. The main ideological organ of the party is the journal *Chung Yang*, but it does not interest local members because its primary focus on national issues. It also tends to be more theoretical than most rank-and-file members care for. Most local KMT cadres are woefully unaware of the party's history either on the mainland or on Taiwan. They are content to minimize problems of the past and tend to focus on the primacy of current issues to give them legitimacy. In recent years, little has been done by the party to educate party members on the history and purpose of the party.[39] Local training sessions are held at the county, district, and branch levels, but they are practical in content. Much of the training literature is printed locally and is primarily public relations oriented. While party central communicates regularly with Taiwan's county headquarters, there is no formal reporting process between county headquarters and the district and branch levels. Though occasional meetings do occur between county cadres and district and branch leaders, most communication is handled by word of mouth and very little feedback is expected.[40]

This relatively relaxed method of conducting local party business has given factions relative freedom to conduct their own affairs independent of supervision by party superiors. Campaigning is largely left to the individual. The importance of personal connections between the candidate and influential members of his or her constituency rank high in importance. The party offers little or no financial assistance to the candidate seeking office. This has led to a sharp increase in businesses buying a candidate running for office, and the candidate in turn buying votes from the people of his district. But in addition to the graft associated with campaigns, there is also considerable money exchanging hands between business interests and party cadres as well. KMT employees are courted by business interests just as candidates and elected officials are. In many cases, party cadres can be counted on to act as go-betweens for business concerns and elected officials. This is especially true for retired KMT cadres. Many cadres have been able to count on lucrative second careers once they leave the party's employment by acting as consultants between business leaders and other party cadres or elected officials. While a retired cadre could be employed in a legitimate consulting capacity, many local cadres do not distinguish between legitimate and illegitimate contacts.

While it would be inaccurate to claim that all local factions are driven by the corrupting influences of money, the public views it as the defining characteristic of the party mainstream. It is this very issue that the New Alliance used to gain influence with the Taiwan electorate.

The Wisdom Club

Liberalization gave party members the freedom to express their own policy ideas. The Wisdom Club (Chi-shi Hui), was formed by Taiwanese KMT members of the legislative yuan. In contrast to other factions, the Wisdom Club has always been associated with the party mainstream. Since its establishment in 1989, the Wisdom Club embraced a "Taiwan First" agenda, meaning the KMT needed to focus on Taiwan's needs, and less time dwelling on mainland China. Most members of the Wisdom Club believed Taiwan should be an independent nation-state, and therefore quietly opposed the Kuomintang's claim to rule all of China. Officially, however, the Wisdom Club advocated an "independent Taiwan," rather than Taiwan independence. Its intent was to show that Taiwan is defacto independent, though it did not rule out the possibility of a unified China in the future. This is referred to as the one country, two systems formula.[41]

The influence of the Wisdom Club has been modest. While it is true that Lee Teng-hui has acknowledged publicly that Taiwan is presently independent of China, he tried not to be a vocal advocate of the formula suggested by the Wisdom Club. The Wisdom Club has actually had no other notable policy statement other than attempting to focus the political agenda on Taiwan. It has been an extremely pragmatic group warning party elders that without a more direct approach in addressing the needs of Taiwan's electorate, the KMT could be easily replaced as the ruling party in Taiwan.

Wisdom Club candidates did poorly in the 1992 legislative yuan elections. Although they won 20 of 30 seats contested, several influential incumbents went down to defeat because of allegations of campaign corruption.[42] The rejection of Wisdom Club incumbents surprised other members of the faction who believed that its "Taiwan First" agenda would attract voters interested in a solution, albeit a temporary one, to the debate surrounding Taiwan's unique political status. As a result, the Wisdom Club fell into disarray by early 1993. In June, an attempt was made to rejuvenate the organization into a nonpartisan organization called the Public Interest Alliance. The organizers hoped the new group would help in the peaceful transition to democracy in Taiwan.[43] But the new organization's goals were broader than those of the Wisdom Club, thus further weakening the parent organization. By summer 1993, the Wisdom Club had all but disappeared.

The New KMT Alliance

The New KMT Alliance (Hsin Kuomintang Lien-hsien) was one of several factions belonging to the group sometimes referred to as the non-mainstream faction. Several KMT candidates running in the December 1989 legislative yuan elections ran on an anti-corruption platform and won sizable majorities in their districts. This led to the formal organization of the New Alliance the following May.

Most members of the New Alliance were young or second generation mainlanders and members of the legislature. They included well known lawmakers like Wang Chien-shien, Jaw Shao-kang, Yok Mu-ming and Lee Ching-hua. They developed a two-fold agenda, focusing on reform within the party, and electoral success. On the former point, they sought to make votes within KMT bodies more reflective of practical political needs and less reliant on the party line.[44] This was more than just a call for democracy, however. It was also an attempt to weaken Lee Teng-hui's support within the party and begin to rebuild the party in a way that would benefit the pro-mainland views of the New Alliance. Electoral success was intended to increase its influence in the legislature and to use the high profile status elected office gave them to shape party policy. The tactic of pointing to corruption within the government made the alliance popular with the electorate, and despised within the party. Its most vocal attacks were launched against party mainstream candidates tainted by corruption. New Alliance members criticized national leaders like Lien Chan and Lee Teng-hui for being too aggressive in redistributing power in Taiwan. They openly admitted that a DPP victory in the 1993 year-end county elections would directly benefit the New Alliance's image by having challenged the KMT on corruption. They believed a KMT defeat would increase their influence in reforming the party.[45] They further believed a significant increase in DPP representation would cause the KMT mainstream to have to broker a deal with the New Alliance in order to secure a KMT majority.[46] But scholars and KMT party members alike viewed the New Alliance as a group of mainlanders trying to take the party away from a Taiwanese majority that had abandoned the Kuomintang of earlier days.[47]

The DPP viewed the New Alliance with skepticism as well. On the one hand it was encouraged with the factional fighting that plagued the KMT. The DPP believed they would be the beneficiaries of KMT strife. On the other hand, it also believed the New Alliance to be a group of opportunist mainlanders who wanted a restoration of the privileges mainlanders used to enjoy on Taiwan before liberalization.[48] It also pointed to what it believed was a double standard. Despite claiming to be against the corrupting influences that plagued the party mainstream, the DPP argued the New Alliance was also tainted by graft.[49] Critics also doubted the New Alliance's claims for democracy by pointing to individual alliance members' positions taken before marital law ended. New Alliance leader Jaw Shao-kang is singled out as a KMT leader who opposed the lifting of martial law restrictions. He was an outspoken advocate of wiretapping political opponents phones prior to liberalization.[50]

Members of the New Alliance shared some similarities in their philosophical approach with others who opposed the party mainstream, but were anxious to distinguish their uniqueness. Like the Wisdom Club, it tried to generate support from the Taiwan electorate to avoid being seen as too entrenched in mainland interests. The New Alliance believed the Chinese Democratic Reformers Alliance (see below) had alienated Taiwanese voters because of its mainland Chinese zeal. It tried to convince people they were not out for political power, but for political reform. At the same time, the New Alliance took note of the success of the Japan New Party and held out the possibility of creating a new party if the KMT failed to listen to its demands (New Alliance members split from the KMT and created the New China Party in August 1993). It advocated strong business ties with the mainland in order to build institutions that could facilitate reunification, and shunned talk of an independent Taiwan republic. But its popularity was largely based on the appeal for honesty in politics, not because of their stand for a unified Chinese Republic.

The Chinese Democratic Reformers Alliance

In May 1992, a group of disgruntled party members founded a journal to criticize the direction the party had taken under the leadership of Lee Teng-hui. Many of the journal's sponsors were senior party leaders and numerous overseas Chinese who expressed the belief that Lee Teng-hui had to be replaced if the party was to survive. They hoped the *China Forum* (*Kuo-shih P'ing-lun*) would help get their message out and attract a majority of party members who were not part of the party mainstream. They raised a considerable sum of money enabling them to purchase several floors of an expensive building overlooking the Chiang Kai-shek Memorial in Taipei. On March 12, 1993, they founded the Chinese Democratic Reformers Alliance (Hsin T'ung-meng Hui).

The Chinese Democratic Reformers Alliance (CDRA) employs a multi-faceted approach in its efforts to gain followers. The CDRA is composed of scholars, senior party leaders, military leaders, overseas Chinese, and legislators all united in a common effort to restore the KMT's focus on the *San Min Chu I* and mainland recovery. Prominent leaders of the CDRA include Hau Pei-tsun, Li Huan, Lin Yang-kang, Chiang Wei-kuo, and Wu Po-hsiung. Critics have referred to the leaders of the CDRA who meet every

Monday evening as the "underground central committee" of the KMT.[51] In these meetings CDRA leaders tried to formulate a strategy for the 14th Party Congress. They also tried to build close contacts with members of the New Alliance, notably Jaw Shao-kang, though the New Alliance resisted inclusion. Organizers chose the Chinese name of their organization (Hsin T'ung Meng Hui, or New T'ung Meng Hui) because they see the most important features of the KMT legacy to be products of the T'ung Meng Hui era--the development of the *San Min Chu I*, the founding of the Republic of China, and the concept of people's revolution.[52]

When joining the CDRA, candidates sign a membership application form indicating that they want to return to the original principles and purposes of Kuomintang. For most younger applicants, the CDRA conducts a series of education seminars on the top floor of its Taipei complex where Sun Yat-sen's political tenets are taught. They are also taught how the CDRA believes these principles have been abandoned by the KMT under Lee Teng-hui's chairmanship. Once a candidate has proven loyal to the CDRA cause, they are issued a membership card containing the tenets of the *San Min Chu I*, along with a pledge to avoid the corrupting influences of money and power in politics, and to reject any efforts at establishing an independent Taiwan state.[53]

CDRA leaders claim Lee Teng-hui has been corrupted by the temptations of power and money. They also believe he abandoned the party's responsibility to restore the mainland and tacitly fought for Taiwan independence.[54] In a book that establishes the theoretical base of the CDRA, two primary mistakes are identified as having harmed the KMT: early collaboration with Yuan Shih-kai and the KMT-CCP union. Lee Teng-hui's chairmanship is considered to be third in importance to those events. The CDRA likens him to Wang Chingwei, the KMT leader who collaborated with the Japanese during the 1930s.[55] The CDRA complains that like Wang, Lee maintains a flashy appearance, but lacks leadership skills, intelligence, courage, familiarity with the party's history, and confidence in military leadership. They accuse him of shouting empty slogans about democracy while ruling with an iron will.[56] But the CDRA's calls for democracy in the party and a restoration to the founding principles of the KMT lacks legitimacy in the minds of most people in Taiwan, and within the Kuomintang as well.

The T'ung Meng Hui was a secret society. Despite the assurances of founders that the main difference between the CDRA and the T'ung Meng Hui is the former is devoted to democratic principles, the evidence seems to suggest otherwise. The CDRA is beholden to overseas Chinese who have donated huge sums of money to found the organization. CDRA founders argue the support of overseas Chinese is important because the KMT is supposed to be an all-China party, not a Taiwan-based party. Support of the overseas Chinese is also important because even before Chiang Ching-kuo's death, they were sharply critical of Lee Teng-hui being heir apparent to the presidency of the republic and chairman of the party. Critics in and out of the Kuomintang have always questioned the legitimacy of overseas Chinese involvement in government and party matters, especially in the case of Taiwan. They suggest Taiwan is a place where many overseas Chinese have little or no familiarity with the island's particular needs. But the heavy influence of Chinese who cannot vote in Taiwan's elections is just one aspect of the CDRA's unconvincing advocacy of liberal democratic principles.

Many in the CDRA hierarchy have never been known to be outspoken advocates of democracy until political liberalization on Taiwan began to swing the pendulum in favor of the Kuomintang's Taiwanese majority. By then their calls for secret ballots and greater party democracy were really efforts to oust Lee Teng-hui. CDRA leaders knew greater party liberalization would invite criticism of the party chairman and hopefully increase their chances to gain positions of power. Their cavalier criticisms of Lee Teng-hui have sounded more like sour grapes than carefully articulated principles needed to win over an electorate interested in continued peace and prosperity. Furthermore, the group's ideological tenets resemble the rhetoric used by the mainlander-dominated KMT of the '60s and '70s than a party interested in winning over a people who have rejected authoritarianism. Most scholars doubt the CDRA's commitment to democracy and believe the organization would be willing to forego many aspects of political liberalization in order to reestablish the KMT as the kind of party it was a few decades ago.[57] The justification for this is based on the CDRA's belief that the KMT must represent all of China and that democratization on Taiwan cannot change the necessity of restoring the mainland.

Facing an Uncertain Future

The increase in party factions encouraged party central to increase its efforts in recruitment. The party stepped-up public service programs in areas of public interest such as computer literacy, foreign language study, and forums on history and culture.[58] It also tried to distance itself from its earlier image as watchdog and increased its efforts to present the party in a more popular light to attract talented recruits. The rise of national and local factions thwarted its efforts, however, and recruitment became more difficult. Several issues continued to fuel the fires of factionalization, most notably the party's efforts to gain recognition for Taiwan in the United Nations, preparations for the 14th Kuomintang Congress, and the 1993 year-end city/county elections. These events and subsequent elections in 1994 kept the KMT from losing ground vis-a-vis the other factions. They also sealed Lee

Teng-hui's position as the leading candidate for the 1996 presidential race. We now turn to a discussion of these issues in chapter seven.

Notes

1. *Hong Kong Standard*, January 19, 1988, FBIS *Daily Report*, China, January 20, 1988.
2. CNA, February 11, 1988, FBIS *Daily Report*, China, February 11, 1988.
3. CNA, July 11, 1988, FBIS *Daily Report*, China, July 11, 1988.
4. CNA, July 14, 1988, FBIS *Daily Report*, China, July 14, 1988.
5. CNA July 13, 1988, FBIS *Daily Report*, July 13, 1988.
6. James D. Seymour, "Taiwan in 1988: No More Bandits," *Asian Survey* (January 1989).
7. CNA, July 13, 1988, FBIS *Daily Report*, China, July 13, 1988.
8. *Chung-yang Jih-pao*, 13 July 1988, FBIS *Daily Report*, China, July 22, 1988. High-ranking KMT and government officials were still prohibited from visiting the mainland. This policy was tested by Hu Chiu-yuen, a KMT member and legislator. His trip to the mainland resulted in his expulsion from the party in late 1988.
9. CNA February 2, 1989, FBIS *Daily Report*, China, February 3, 1989.
10. Tokyo, Kyodo, January 30, 1989, FBIS *Daily Report*, China, February 1, 1989. Kyodo also reports government officials acknowledged that defense expenditure in the 1960's accounted for 70% of the total government budget.
11. Ts'ai Ling and Ramon H. Myers, "Surviving the Rough-and-Tumble of Presidential Politics in an Emerging Democracy: The 1990 Elections in the Republic of China on Taiwan," *China Quarterly* (March 1992), p. 125.
12. *China Post*, December 16, 1989, FBIS *Daily Report*, China, December 27, 1989.
13. CNA, October 14, 1989, FBIS *Daily Report*, October 16, 1989.
14. Comments by Representative Stephen Solarz on page 1 of *Taiwan: The National Affairs Council and Implications for Democracy*; Hearing Before the Subcommittee on Asian and Pacific Affairs of the Committee on Foreign Relations of the House of Representatives, October 11, 1990.
15. Fei-Lung Lui, "The Electoral System and Voting Behavior in Taiwan," in Cheng and Haggard, *Political Change in Taiwan*, p. 149.
16. *Hong Kong Standard*, February 23, 1990, FBIS *Daily Report*, China, February 26, 1990.
17. Taipei Domestic Service, March 24, 1990, FBIS *Daily Report*, China, March 28, 1990.
18. Points summarized by Maysing Yang, *National Affairs Council*, Hearing Before Subcommittee on Asian and Pacific Affairs, pp. 30-31.
19. CNA November 9, 1990, FBIS *Daily Report*, China, November 13, 1990.
20. *China Post*, November 22, 1990, FBIS *Daily Report*, November 26, 1990.
21. Taipei Voice of Free China, July 1, 1991, FBIS, *Daily Report*, China, July 3, 1991.
22. CNA August 16, 1991, FBIS *Daily Report*, China, August 20, 1991.
23. CNA November 14, 1991, FBIS *Daily Report*, China, November 15, 1991.

24. CBC October 3, 1991, FBIS *Daily Report*, China, October 8, 1991.

25. See Jurgen Domes, "Taiwan in 1991: Searching for Political Consensus," *Asian Survey* (January 1992).

26. *FEER*, January 9, 1992.

27. CNA, March 6, 1993; FBIS, *Daily Report*, China, March 6, 1993, p. 66.

28. *FEER*, June 18, 1992.

29. Chang Ch'un-nan, interview, May 19, 1993.

30. *FEER*, December 17, 1992.

31. CNA December 23, 24, 1992; FBIS *Daily Report*, China, December 23, 24, 1992.

32. Gallup poll results reported in *FEER*, March 18, 1993.

33. CNA April 13, 1993; FBIS *Daily Report*, China, April 13, 1993.

34. Chu Yun-han, interview, May 20, 1993.

35. Tsiang Yien-si, interview, June 8, 1993.

36. Ye Chu-lan, DPP legislator, interview, Taipei, July 1, 1993; and Feng Hu-hsiang, interview, July 22, 1993.

37. Hansen Chien, interview, June 14, 1993.

38. Ts'ao Chun-han, "Su-tsao Chung-kuo Kuomintang Wei Kung-kung Cheng-ts'e Cheng-tang Tse-yi," pp. 58-9.

39. These are impressions the author has gathered in interviews with members of the Taipei City, Tao Yuan County, and I-Lan County party committees.

40. Interview with members of the I-lan county KMT committee, June 15, 1993.

41. Lin Chia-lung, interview, July 22, 1993, National Taiwan University. At the time, Lin was a PhD candidate at Yale University.

42. *FEER*, January 7, 1993.

43. *The China News*, June 25, 1993.

44. *Tse-li Pao*, July 19, 1993.

45. Chung Jih-hong, interview, New Alliance Headquarters, Taipei, July 20, 1993.

46. Chu Yun-han, interview, May 20, 1993.

47. Yang Tai-shuenn, interview, May 24, 1993.

48. Ye Chu-lan, interview, July 1, 1993.

49. DPP partisans and KMT supporters alike claim Jaw Shao-kang, Yok Mu-ming and others have used their offices for financial gain.

50. Chang Ch'un-nan, interview, May 19, 1993.

51. *Ts'ai Hsun* (Wealth Magazine), July 1, 1993, p. 88.

52. "Hsin T'ung Meng Hui Ch'eng-li Shuo-ming," (Explanation of the Founding of the Chinese Democratic Reformers Alliance), *Kuo-shih P'ing-lun*, (China Forum), March 15, 1993, p. 7.

53. Membership form and card given to the author on July 22, 1993.

54. Feng Hu-hsiang, interview, Taipei, CDRA Headquarters, July 22, 1993.

55. Chiang Yung-ching, *Pai-nyan Lau Tien: Kuomintang Ts'an-sang Shih* (One-Hundred Year-Old Store: The Kuomintang's Turbulent History (Taipei: Ch'uan Chi Wen Hsueh Ch'u-pan She, 1993.)

56. Ibid., pp. 310-314.

57. Lu Ya-li, interview, Taipei, May 19, 1993.

58. Information supplied by the Chung Shan District Party Office, Taipei, June 15, 1993.

7

Testing Democratic Reforms in Taiwan

Lee Teng-hui and other KMT leaders have long understood the implications of Taiwan's unique political identity. The debate has been the source of the greatest share of political hostility between the DPP and KMT. It is also the reason for continuous infighting within the KMT before, during, and after the 14th and 15th party congresses, and continues to be the overarching political problem facing politicians in Taiwan today. The question was a focal point in the 1996 campaign for president, punctuated by military threats from the mainland and a show of American naval power to check Beijing's attempts to influence the elections. Lee Teng-hui knows that his popularity is in large part dependent on his handling discussions surrounding Taiwan's political status and the related issue of subethnic rivalry. The issue concerns all politicians, but attention is especially focused on the president to articulate his vision of Taiwan's political future. Lee chose to present his views of Taiwan's political identity in what he thought was a comparatively benign corner of politics--foreign policy. It proved to be a hornets nest of controversy, eliciting strong reactions at home and from Beijing.

Lee Teng-hui's Diplomatic Agenda

The KMT's non mainstream faction and members of the CNP contend Lee Teng-hui has abandoned the KMT goal of mainland recovery. High ranking Lee supporters have rejected these accusations by arguing mainland recovery is the very reason Lee has supported business investment in the mainland--to uphold the livelihood principle of the *San Min Chu I* in order to help the mainland make the transition to democracy and join with Taiwan. If the mainland is not ready to make this transition to democracy by having reached some degree of economic maturity, mainland recovery will not be accepted by the people of Taiwan.[1] But by acknowledging that the people of Taiwan may have a say in mainland recovery rather than sticking to the

KMT's long-standing promise to seek recovery at all costs creates a major point of contention between the party mainstream and the party's factions. Scholars argue Lee Teng-hui has not always been consistent in his convictions on recovering the mainland. While his official rhetoric suggests the importance of mainland recovery, political appointments and compromises have given critics room to question his actual thinking on the matter.[2]

Lee Teng-hui's drive for membership in the United Nations can be seen as either a commitment to the concept of a united China, or an independent Taiwan. Membership would give Taiwan the prestige it deserves as a major trading power and newly democratized state. It would likely clear the way for many nation-states to establish or reestablish relations with Taiwan. If the desire for an independent Taiwan state grows, and conditions between Taiwan and China suggest the creation of a Taiwan republic is possible, UN membership would legitimize the creation of an independent state. The KMT would benefit from UN membership if the mainland attempts to use force to retake Taiwan, or in the event that a solution is reached between Beijing and Taipei on the one China issue. In 1993, most people believed UN membership would enhance the island's security vis-a-vis the mainland. Presidential elections in 1996 caused voters to reconsider as Beijing used military threats to counter such efforts.

Taiwan's success in joining Asian Pacific Economic Cooperation (APEC) and progress towards gaining membership on the General Agreement on Tariffs and Treaties (GATT) has buoyed-up the party's hopes of success in gaining a UN seat. Lien Chan has made the case that denying Taiwan UN status is unfair given that both East and West Germany held separate UN seats, and North and South Korea currently enjoy the same arrangement. Lien has also declared that the Beijing authorities do not represent the people of Taiwan (nor by implication does Taipei represent the population on the mainland).[3]

The KMT's efforts to win UN membership have not been nor are they expected to be honored in the near future. The attempt for membership is understandable because the effort robs the DPP of political ammunition in its contests with the KMT on Taiwan's unusual international status. DPP leaders have realized the KMT's efforts to gain UN membership have given the Kuomintang an advantage in enhancing the image of Taiwan. The DPP cannot oppose the KMT's efforts and still advocate Taiwan independence. At the same time, as an opposition party, it has no role in the UN effort. Whether Lee Teng-hui is ultimately successful or not, the KMT stands to benefit in the attempt. The DPP's disadvantage is similarly problematic for the major factions that oppose Lee Teng-hui. They cannot reject the KMT's efforts for UN membership without being seen as traitors to the people of Taiwan, especially since many of the factional leaders lamented the Republic of China's expulsion from the UN in 1971.

Testing Democratic Reforms 121

The issue surrounding Taiwan's status as a province of China or an independent republic, and the subethnic conflict, are the principle problems for politicians on the island. The KMT party mainstream realizes the creation of an independent Taiwan will either destroy the Kuomintang or enable them to create a party largely free of mainland loyalties. At the same time, the major factions realize an independent Taiwan will most likely end their dream of reunification with the mainland. Furthermore, their influence in the political system is likely to disappear altogether. The DPP needs to have the issue of Taiwan independence in order to survive. In the event Taiwan and the mainland are reunified, the DPP is not likely to have national influence. But the creation of an independent Taiwan is likely to enhance the DPP's prestige, having been the first political party to have advocated the creation of a formal Taiwanese state.

Discussions surrounding the political status of Taiwan has generated much interest in recent years. During the spring and summer of 1993 people watched the debate intently, though they recognized that much depended on the political situation in Beijing, particularly the succession to Deng Xiaoping, as well as Taiwan's success in winning greater international recognition on other important organizations. By July 1993, however, political interest had turned sharply towards the Kuomintang's 14th party congress.

The Fourteenth Party Congress and a Splinter Party

The most important party congress for Lee Teng-hui had been the 13th party congress. At that time, Lee was able to consolidate power and formally win endorsement as party chairman from the party's rank-and-file. The 14th party congress was fascinating because it marked the death of the old KMT and birth of a new KMT into the uncertain world of democratic politics. This party congress differed from all previous party congresses in three major ways:

1-Liberalization had cut deeply into the power of the party chairman. Chiang Ching-kuo and Lee Teng-hui helped facilitate the shift from authoritarianism to democracy. In so doing, liberalism had been legitimized and authoritarianism had become increasingly rejected. Thus the power of the KMT chairman's office had been changed forever. The recognized office of power in Taiwan was to be the elected president, not the KMT party chairman, or any other chairman of a contending party. Similarly, the central committee and central standing committee of the Kuomintang was weakened by the growth in importance of the legislative yuan. The KMT's power base had to be established in the legislature in order for the KMT to be a viable party in the future. For this reason, party leaders had to do the things legislators do in democratic states--compromise, bargain, debate openly, and persuade the people--things the csc never had to do, and could not do given their detachment from the new circles of political power.

2-As the KMT's Leninist power structure came under increasing scrutiny, so did the party's ability to maintain unity. The party was too broadly defined for the world of democratic politics. It had no ideological center. Factionalization was a natural outcome, and threatened the strength and long-term health of the organization generally.

3-Taiwanese members in the party, particularly those who had been elected to representative bodies, had new ideas and goals they wanted the party to address. The party's mainstream believed the KMT's policy to recover the mainland was important, though not as important as Taiwan's needs. In fact most KMT members were finding the whole issue over mainland recovery to be a nuisance. They stressed economic wealth for Taiwan's people over settlement of the long-term political stalemate with mainland China. But the issue of Taiwan's relationship with the mainland could not be escaped without some sort of policy to deal with the issue. Thus, the national identity question became an open political wound not just for the KMT vis-a-vis other parties, but within the KMT itself.

One of the most important questions prior to the 14th congress was how democratic would the meetings be? Would Lee Teng-hui and his followers object to secret ballots in the elections for party chairman? In late May the party tentatively decided to go with a secret ballot. Lee's opponents saw an opportunity to nominate a challenger to Lee, but doubted any contender's chances for defeating him, given the strength of his support from the party mainstream. This placed new emphasis on the election of people who could challenge the power of the party chairman through the auspices of other official party positions, either as party vice-chairmen, or members of the central committee and central standing committee.

Party central issued a declaration stating the party congress would stress unity of purpose. It reiterated its policy of placing the interests of Taiwan's people above all other goals. It pledged to continue the fight for greater international recognition for Taiwan.[4] But while party headquarters was attempting to set an agenda that would lend strength to the party generally, New Alliance members and the CDRA had a different strategy. New Alliance legislators were bolder in their attempts to go against the party on a number of important bills, among them, a high speed railway, a nuclear power plant, and a watered-down version of the Sunshine Law (a bill requiring public officials to disclose their financial records). President Lee had been a staunch supporter of both the high speed rail project and the nuclear power plant. Justice minister Ma ying-jeou fought hard for passage of the Sunshine Law. New Alliance members argued the first two projects were a waste of money, dangerous to the environment, and tainted by bribes taken by legislators and other government officials having a personal financial stake in the projects. They also spoke out against mainstream legislators who weakened tenets of the Sunshine Law. Alliance members said the stronger law would have seriously implicated corrupt KMT officials in illegal financial schemes. KMT party central viewed open opposition to the party as a direct attempt to subvert the agenda of the party congress. To counter these efforts, party officials declared they would hold a disciplinary meeting for members of the New Alliance and other KMT members who voted against the party's sponsorship of legislative bills. In return New Alliance members announced their intent to break away from the KMT and create a new political party.[5] By early August, party leaders believed the New Alliance defection might lessen conflict between factions during the congress.

Factional pressure was great at the outset of the congress. Lee Teng-hui appealed for unity in his opening address to the congress. In an attempt to minimize factional strife, delegates voted to amend the party's constitution so the party could convene a congress every two years instead of every five. It was hoped more frequent meetings would improve communication and understanding among factions. While these measures were welcomed by the delegates, all knew the real fireworks of the congress were the controversial issues surrounding the elections of party vice chairmen and members to the central committee.

The non-mainstream members of the party believed their most important task to be the election of vice chairmen who shared their concern that the party had been damaged under the leadership of Lee Teng-hui. Because Lee Teng-hui would be reelected chairman, they favored strong organizational men with experience and a following to challenge Lee's dominance. In particular, they believed Hau Pei-tsun, Li Huan, and Lin Yang-kang would be most effective in fulfilling this task. Supporters of Lee Teng-hui feared a powerful senior party leader like Hau Pei-tsun could limit Lee's ability to run the party. For this reason, the central standing committee agreed before the congress convened to add vice chairmen, enabling the party mainstream to bolster Lee's power.[6] This meant Lee would be able to nominate several candidates for the position, some who opposed him, but others acceptable to him.[7] Lee would likely be able to maintain his power as before.

When the congress actually began, the issue of vice chairmen immediately became a point of contention between mainstream and non-mainstream members. Although most party members were willing to go along with the CSC's proposal to elect several vice chairmen, there were not enough votes to ensure the required two-thirds margin of victory. The heated exchange between non-mainstream members who overwhelmingly approved of the measure, and mainstream members who viewed the multiple vice-chair proposition as an effort to appease mainlander interests, led to fist fights.[8] Fearing the issue could split the party, Lee Teng-hui spoke on behalf of the measure, thus ensuring its success in the second vote. With the issue finally agreed upon, attention turned to the actual elections.

In the first secret ballot for party chairman ever held, Lee Teng-hui came away with 82% of the vote, thereby sealing his next term as party chairman. In order to build unity in the party, Lee nominated two non-mainstream party members and ardent critics of Lee's leadership style. The selection of Hau Pei-tsun and Lin Yang-kang was a partial victory for non-mainstream party members especially the CDRA. But the abilities of Hau and Lin to bring some power back to non-mainstream members were tempered by Lee's other two appointments. The selection of premier Lien Chan and vice president Li Yuan-zu, both closely aligned with Lee, strengthened Lee's power within the party. Still, many Taiwanese party members worried that the strength of Lin Yang-kang's and Hau-Pei-tsun's faction would cause problems because of serious policy differences within the party. They feared Lee would have to give in to many mainlander demands. Despite these misgivings, Lee's nominations were accepted by party delegates.[9] Attention then turned to central committee elections.

The elections for membership to the 210 member central committee was important mainly because party delegates would be selecting the group that would in turn elect half of the important CSC. In another respect, the CC had become increasingly independent as the political system liberalized, causing the party leadership to compromise with the CC on various issues. Election issues included delegates' concerns that the party's image had become tainted because of increased corruption. They also worried about the party's remaining authoritarian practices that were out of sync with democratic reforms. The party elected 59 party members to the CC who were members of the legislative yuan or national assembly, satisfying a need to be more sensitive to public opinion. At the same time, a number of party delegates dubbed "gold bulls" because of their reputation as people who use their money to buy political influence, were denied seats on the CC.[10] As indicated in Table 7.1, membership in the KMT, CC, and CSC more closely mirrored the island's demographics and public opinion. With the growth in importance of the legislative yuan, CC members who were also legislators could be depended on to bring pressure on the party to reform in ways that could transform the Kuomintang into a party more akin to Western political parties. But this was also contingent on the composition of the CSC because it was the body responsible for the day-to-day policy issues of the party.

At the close of the party congress, the CC met in its first plenary session to select its 31 member central standing committee. Lee Teng-hui appointed the first 15 members as party-designates. As indicated by Table 7.2, all were pro-mainstream members of the party with the exception of Li Huan. The 16 elected members to the CSC included a number of officials who were elected lawmakers, thus continuing the trend begun in the elections to the CC. John

Table 7.1 Membership in the KMT, CC, and CSC

Year	Body	Total Membership	% Taiwanese
1980	KMT	1,940,000	60
1987	KMT	2,400,000	66
1992	KMT	2,600,000	70
1981	CC	150	20
1988	CC	180	35
1993	CC	210	53
1952	CSC	10	0
1957	CSC	10	10
1976	CSC	22	22
1981	CSC	26	35
1988	CSC	31	52
1993	CSC	31	57

Source: Te-fu Huang, "Elections and Evolution of the Kuomintang," in Tien, *Taiwan's Electoral Politics*, (M.E. Sharpe, 1996) pp. 113-121. Reprinted by permission.

Kuan was the only non-mainstream party member elected to the CSC, thus limiting the immediate influence of that group on the CSC. Taiwanese members gained a 18-13 majority on the CSC, though the strong showing for mainlanders surprised many within the party. The five oldest members of the CSC were mainlanders in their seventies, though younger mainlanders did fairly well in securing seats as well.[11] The new CSC was slightly younger and enjoyed more popular support than the previous CSC, though the threat of factional strife endangered the prospects of unity. The problem was not that Lee had many opponents on the CSC. By selecting members more representative of the party's and people's interests, the CSC was less likely to honor every desire of the party chairman. This meant there would be broader discussion of the issues and a greater chance for reform within the party, especially with party congresses convening every two years. As more decision making power shifted to the party's deliberative bodies, the relative importance of the positions of chairman and vice chairmen of the party were likely to decline.

While the KMT was embroiled in its party debates, the New Alliance attempted to use the party's problems to gain support in forming a new political organization. New Alliance members originally asked the interior ministry for permission to register their organization under the name New

Table 7.2 Factional Composition of KMT Party Elite, 1993

P = Party Official Only
C = Cabinet Member or Government Service
L = Lawmaker

Body	Total	%Taiwanese	Ave.Age	Occupation
CSC	31	58	60	C=11, P=4, L=16
Vice Chairmen	4	50		C=4
CSC Mainstream	29	66	59	C=10, P=3, L=16
Non-mainstream	2	0	64	C=1, P=1, L=0
Vice Chairmen/ Mainstream	2	50		C=2
Vice Chairmen/ Non-mainstream	2	50		C=2

Source: KMT Central Committee, *China Post*, and *Shih-jie Ryh-pao*, August 24, 1993.

Kuomintang Alliance. But the ministry rejected the request arguing the Kuomintang name was held by the Kuomintang party and could not be shared. The ministry did give permission to the group's second request to name the party the Chinese New Party (Hsin Tang).[12] The Chinese New Party (CNP) leadership believed the name reflected the same kind of success and optimism the Japan New Party generated in Japan. They hoped to enjoy the same kind of electoral success against the KMT that the Japan New Party enjoyed running against Japan's ruling Liberal Democracy Party in parliamentary elections.

But despite the fact that over 10,000 enthusiasts attended a rally celebrating the founding of the CNP, the party's base of support was limited. The party attracted a good deal of support from mainlanders disenchanted with the Kuomintang party mainstream. While it was able to address the public's dissatisfaction over political corruption, policy development was weak, making it difficult to distinguish the CNP from the Kuomintang. Critics of the CNP argued the party was really a mainlander-only party, not a party that represented the needs of Taiwan's citizens. CNP officials tried to counter these accusations by arguing the party was for all of China but represented primarily the needs of people living in Taiwan.[13] CNP leaders realized it would be difficult for the party to distance itself from the stigma of being dominated by mainlander interests. They also realized how much the

Kuomintang had become a Taiwan-based party. Because of these worries, KMT officials predicted trouble for the CNP in elections. At the same time the animosity of the Kuomintang towards CNP organizers emerged. KMT party officials accused CNP leaders of rejecting the mission of the KMT. Predictably, CNP leaders used the same argument against the Kuomintang.[14]

The CNP held its first congress at the same time the KMT was holding its 14th congress in an attempt to steal the media spotlight. The Chinese New Party made an initial splash, but failed to upstage the Kuomintang. The press paid the most attention to the KMT congress because it was the ruling and largest political party on Taiwan. The KMT controlled not only the legislature, but the national assembly, the presidency of the country, and most of the provincial, county, and city posts. For this reason the CNP was viewed as a novelty, and failed to generate the wide interest organizers hoped for.

The City/County Campaign and Election

With the party congress behind them, the KMT leadership turned their attention to the year end elections for city and county chiefs. In earlier years, the KMT could depend on the party machine to control local government offices. But in democratic Taiwan, the KMT was increasingly forced to play by democratic rules. The Kuomintang was now much more of a competitive political party than the Leninist KMT of the past. The election for city and county chiefs was a major test, as every subsequent election would be, of the Kuomintang's ability to compete as a legitimate party in a democratic system. The election was also important because most observers believed it to be a confidence measure for President Lee Teng-hui. Opposition parties hoped a strong showing against the KMT would improve chances for their candidates in the presidential election. Given the relative strength of the president on Taiwan, every party viewed local elections as a key to each party's ability to win the coveted spot and set a new political agenda. Lee Teng-hui showed signs of reneging on his pledge to not seek a second term as president, thereby adding to the excitement of the elections.

In early September, the press failed to recognize the CNP's weak political base and speculated it would do well in the upcoming elections. The media's assessment was based on the high profile issue of political corruption that CNP members had used so convincingly in earlier elections as New Alliance candidates running for office.[15] It was also based on renewed fighting within the KMT on issues ranging from foreign policy to Lee Teng-hui's leadership abilities. Hau Pei-tsun publicly proclaimed that the only reason Lee Teng-hui was selected to succeed Chiang Ching-kuo was that Sun Yuen, the designated successor to Chiang, was ill at the time and would have been unable to perform his duties.[16] Hau's intention was to suggest Lee should have only been a temporary fill-in as president and party chairman. But few beyond Hau's immediate circle paid much attention to his complaints.

As the campaign went on, it became apparent there was little difference between political parties on the issues, other than on some matters of foreign policy and defence, and on inner-party policies.[17] This realization was damaging to the DPP and CNP who experienced difficulties convincing the Taiwan electorate of the pressing need for change when the people of Taiwan wanted neither drastic change nor a party that failed to distinguish itself from the ruling party in any significant way. Polls indicated party identification had very little effect on the people's views of the issues. Like most democratic societies, the people of Taiwan prided themselves on making their election decisions based on whether a candidate was free of corruption and how he or she stood on the issues.[18]

The lack of policy differentiation and public preference meant each party would have to run on its experiences from previous elections rather than on promising new ideas. For the KMT this meant making better use of its basic organizations in enlisting the support of women and young people.[19] The CNP, unable to keep momentum going, tried to convince well-known KMT figures to defect and join their party.[20] But this strategy could not create the groundswell it needed to make a major difference in race results. The KMT's organizational strengths proved to be too much for the CNP to contend with. Lee Teng-hui used his popularity as president to rally enthusiasm for candidates as he toured cities and counties. The Kuomintang portrayed the CNP as a opportunist party that reflected primarily mainlander interests and lacked policy development. Kuomintang party central worked better with the local organs in binding the party's wounds and smoothing-over public quarrels that plagued the party at the national level following the party congress.

Opponents tried to present an image of the KMT as a greedy political organization possessing phenomenal financial wealth. The Kuomintang released financial reports estimating the party's assets to be around 900 billion New Taiwan dollars (about $36 billion U.S.). But the figure was not as impressive as some had hoped. The KMT was running industries that failed to make profits, owed considerable sums of money to banks, and was only partial owner of many firms where profits were shared with non-KMT entities.[21] Most voters did not seemed impressed enough by the financial disclosures to rethink their support for the KMT.

On the eve of the election, CNP leader Jaw Shao-kang was already apologizing for the CNP's expected poor turnout at the polls. There was a last-minute KMT defection by a senior legislator who joined the CNP. Some thought the defection would boost the new party's chances in the elections. But CNP leaders knew otherwise. Jaw proclaimed the CNP to be the party of the future because it had not had time to adequately prepare for elections given the lateness of the party's founding and KMT smear tactics.[22] The

KMT's confidence had grown. The despair party central felt the previous spring seemed to lift as it became apparent the KMT would still maintain a clear majority of seats in the city and county races. In fact, race results showed the KMT was able to hold on to the same number of seats at the county and city level, with the exception of one loss to an independent candidate. The KMT won 15 seats, the DPP 6, and the CNP failed to win a single seat. But all was not rosy for the Kuomintang. With 71% of eligible voters participating, the DPP's overall vote percentage climbed to 41% from 36% in the 1989 elections, while the KMT's declined from 54% to 47%. KMT general secretary Hsu Shui-te seemed relieved the KMT had escaped a beating, but he did not proclaim the election a victory. Acting on a pre-election pledge, the DPP party hierarchy decided to resign their posts because of the election loss, while the CNP continued to blame KMT smear tactics as the primary reason the party did not win a seat.[23]

Scholars identified poor policy development as reasons for the DPP's and CNP's inability to challenge the KMT more effectively. At the same time, DPP party members blamed internal factions in their own party for weakening the DPP's unity at election time.[24]

The elections pointed to several problems for the CNP. Despite their differences with the KMT, CNP leaders realized the KMT's economic policies were successful and popular. At the same time there was little hope it could build an organization capable of challenging the Kuomintang on an island-wide basis. The CNP's popularity was primarily limited to the Taipei metropolitan area.

Lee Teng-hui managed to keep the party unified enough to capitalize on the weaknesses of the opposition. In doing so, he slowed the erosion of support for the party and increased his chances of performing well in the first fully democratic race for president. But for now attention turned to the 1994 mid-winter elections for city and county councils and mayors and town chiefs, and the year-end elections for mayors of Taipei and Kaohsiung and governor of Taiwan.

A Year of Endless Campaigning

For many in Taiwan, the 1994 campaigns brought out the worst in Taiwan politics. In late January elections were held to elect city and county councils, and mayors and chiefs of small cities, townships, and villages. The KMT won an impressive 578 council seats (67%) and 254 mayoral and chief seats (82%). By comparison, the DPP managed to win 92 council seats (11%) and only 23 mayoral and chief positions (7%). The CNP won 8 seats on councils, and independents won 180 seats.[25] The local elections were only marginally important to KMT national strength because most of the issues in the campaigns were of local importance. But the KMT's strong showing was indicative of the collective strength of the mainstream's numerous local factions.

The elections were marked by unprecedented violence and gross examples of political corruption. The Ministry of Justice investigated five incidents of gunfire at campaign headquarters or candidates homes. There were hundreds of reports of vote buying. The buying of votes did not end with the general election, however. On March 1, councils were to select speakers and deputy speakers of each respective council. The KMT euphoria of having done so well in the local elections quickly disappeared as council members openly sought bribes or tried to bribe others for support. By mid April, 215 individuals had been formally charged with corruption. These included 10 elected speakers, 7 deputy speakers, 145 councilors, a provincial assemblyman, and 52 associates.[26] Four individuals were given the equivalent of $132,000 to vote for a particular candidate, and 46 others were paid $18,000 for their votes.

Though the KMT was not exclusively involved in the scandal, the vast majority of cases involved KMT officials or supporters. President Lee vowed the KMT would shoulder responsibility for the violations and begin to clean its own house. Corruption became the leading issue of the campaigns leading up to the December elections for mayors of Taipei and Kaohsiung, and race for governor. Throughout the spring, newspapers carried stories of shameless acts of political graft, government incompetency, waste of public money, and politicians' indifference to the public's desires. But as the elections drew nearer, the issue of Taiwan independence and subethnic matters once again captured center stage.

Lee Teng-hui saw the promise of continued prosperity as the best way to handle concerns over Taiwan's political status and continued Taiwanese-mainlander rivalry. Since trade is the key to a prosperous future for Taiwan, Lee intensified his efforts abroad.

As the national assembly began meeting to discuss constitutional revisions, President Lee made numerous visits to other countries. In May the government announced a plan to make Taiwan an economic hub for the Asia-Pacific area, focusing not only on the North and South America, but on Asia as well. This was augmented by a reshuffle of the KMT's central standing committee in September that brought trade specialists and their supporters into more influential positions of power. These individuals were sympathetic to mainland investment, but were also interested in Taiwan reaching out to countries in Southeast Asia. Taiwan's prospects for increased mainland investment were complicated by the Taiwan independence issue and the murder of 24 tourists from Taiwan on a lake in mainland China. Beijing's handling of the incident was disastrous, putting ROC officials in the difficult position of having to explain why investment in the mainland was important to Taiwan's future. Public opinion polls indicated support for unification with the mainland sagged to 21% while uncertainty over Taiwan's international status grew from 31% to 43%.[27] The public's enthusiasm for mainland investment also lagged.

Lee continued his campaign for Taiwan representation on the U.N., GATT membership, and for full membership on international and Asian sports committees. All of these efforts generated greater public interest in Taiwan than they had in the past, though there was no breakthrough in any of these areas. But Lee's efforts were important because it allowed him to play the role of statesman--an important image to establish for a man with his sights set on the upcoming presidential election. As opposition parties, the DPP and the CNP could not get the same kind of press coverage or international respect that Lee commanded, even though he was handicapped by Taiwan's lack of official relations with most countries.

The national assembly's approval of constitutional amendments regarding presidential elections helped focus attention on the issue. All ROC citizens, including overseas Chinese, would be allowed to vote in the election. DPP revisions to the constitution were rejected, as was a proposal to lengthen legislative yuan terms from three years to four. Though the Assembly's approval of the presidential election amendment was expected, its passage increased the importance of the upcoming mayors' and governor's races, and legislative yuan elections as tests of KMT popularity and the abilities of Lee Teng-hui as a campaigner.

Some speculated James Soong, the KMT incumbent governor, might have a difficult time defeating his DPP challenger. But Soong proved to be too strong for the opposition. His victory established him as a future candidate for president in a post-Lee Teng-hui era. Soong was popular as an appointed governor. On the campaign trail he attempted to deliver some of his speeches in Taiwanese to bridge the gap between his mainland roots and the Taiwanese majority. His strategy of pointing to the KMT's accomplishments in economic growth and stability for the island's people proved to be better than the DPP's platform which could easily be portrayed as a program of risky change. He also benefitted from Lee Teng-hui's willingness to campaign on his behalf. This brought support from local factions and further strengthened Taiwanese support for the mainlander governor. In the end, Soong beat his DPP rival by a near 20% margin. The CNP candidate trailed far behind. The KMT also maintained a two-to-one margin over the DPP in the provincial assembly.

The KMT mayor of Kaohsiung also handily held on to his seat. But the most interesting races turned out to be in Taipei. DPP candidate Chen Shui-pien benefitted from KMT mayor Huang Ta-chou's lack of charisma and a poor record of supervision over public works and resultant public dissatisfaction. Huang was also hurt by Jaw Shaw-kong's candidacy for mayor on the CNP ticket. Jaw's high visibility on corruption and government efficiency issues undoubtedly attracted voters who would have normally voted for Huang, although Jaw did not do as well as CNP supporters thought he would. Chen received 44% of the vote, Jaw 30%, and Huang 26%. The CNP and the DPP did well in picking up Taipei City Council seats. Although the KMT won 20 seats, it was not enough to claim a majority as the DPP won 18 seats and the CNP won 11.[28] The Taipei mayor's race and the city council race were significant losses for the KMT. Despite this, party leaders seemed relieved to have done well in the other key races.

Run-up to the Presidential Elections

With December elections behind them, KMT leaders began looking ahead to the 1995 legislative yuan elections and the 1996 election for president. The elections for the legislative yuan would be a proving ground for Lee's policies. Lee wasted no time in trying to bring a focus to his political program. In mid-December he announced a cabinet reshuffle that coincided with changes made earlier in the central standing committee. Several figures, including Wu Poh-hsiung were moved to cabinet positions to help formulate Lee's campaign strategy. By early 1995, Lee took advantage of the DPP's continued division over the independence clause of its political platform, and Chen Shui-pien's problems in appointing a coalition cabinet in the Taipei mayor's office, to capture the national spotlight again.

Lee's cabinet released more details on how Taiwan would serve as a regional economic hub to Asia. They were united in their desire to increase trade with the mainland and downplay political differences.[29] Trade would dictate the terms of contact with the mainland rather than some of the more explosive issues of government representation and formal talks of unification. They detailed sea, air, and communications facilities to make Taiwan an attractive center of trade, especially for Southeast Asia. They announced plans for new manufacturing centers, and modern industrial parks to attract national and international investors. Media facilities were to be improved to offer new options in domestic and international television programming and high-tech communications.[30]

Lee realized trade and economic promise would not be enough to soften the subethnic conflict that had become such a volatile issue in the previous fall's campaigns. The KMT had to distance itself even more from the KMT of Chiang Kai-shek and Chiang Ching-kuo. In March Lee Teng-hui formally apologized for the 2-28 incident. He pledged to open the books on the affair. For the first time, the government officially acknowledged that 18,000 to 28,000 people died at the hands of government troops. There was additional evidence linking the Chiang family to specific executions.[31] Lee's chore was to convince voters that under his leadership, the new KMT was not in any way connected to these deeds and was fully devoted to Taiwan's interests first.

But more than any other issue, details of the 1994 corruption scandals continued to threaten the credibility of Lee's efforts. The Ministry of Justice reported the linkage between criminal elements and elected officials in Taiwan were shamefully close. Investigators estimated that one-third of the 858 city and county councilors in Taiwan had criminal records, and 60% of the representatives on these councils had direct connections to organized crime.[32] They speculated there were over 1,200 gangs in Taiwan involved in official graft, some committing violent acts including murder. The ministry was investigating over 4,000 cases of corruption. 2,100 indictments had already come from 856 cases in 18 months. Of those indicted, 25% were senior government officials or top corporate executives, and 40% of all local officials and hundreds of their supporters. The sheer volume of cases caused investigators to focus on catching individuals, even if they could not be convicted, in the hope it would deter future cases of corruption.

The momentum of Lee's strategy helped channel attention towards the future of Taiwan, even though the scandals that had marred the image of the KMT a year earlier continued to haunt the party. People also seemed to distinguish between local criminal elements and Lee Teng-hui, even though local factions were considered loyal to Lee. The quality of Lee's leadership had to be high in order to maintain support in and out of the party leading up to the 15th party congress when the party would select its official candidate for president. There was no doubt non-mainstream candidates would push for alternatives to Lee. As in the months prior to the 14th party congress of 1993, once again rumors were heard of splinter parties forming on or before the August congress. But Lee's position seemed secure given that only 13% of the party were mainlanders and because Lee had managed to maintain a high public approval rating of his job performance.

Taiwan's First Presidential Campaign and Election

There were many important political issues competing for attention in 1995 and into the Spring of 1996. All these matters added to the excitement of the first fully democratic campaign and election for president. Foreign affairs, the 15th National Party Congress of the Kuomintang, year-end elections to the legislature, and upcoming elections to the national assembly all became part and parcel of the presidential campaign.

Lee Teng-hui's Diplomatic Mine Field

Since the question of Taiwan's national identity had become such a heated issue with the emergence of democracy, candidates running for public office had the difficult chore of trying to explain what role they believed Taiwan should play in the community of nations. This was especially true for presidential candidates. For several years, Lee Teng-hui regularly reminded Taiwan's voters that Taiwan was defacto independent of the mainland. At the same time he maintained that reunification was a long-term goal. He hoped the tentativeness of his message would not offend pro-independence supporters nor alienate those committed to reunification. He saw the drive for UN membership as a way of strengthening his position because membership would be positively received by nearly all supporters and critics of reunification. Lee argued a UN seat for Taiwan was legitimized by Taiwan's democratization (a goal fostered by the UN), the fact that the Taipei and Beijing regimes were defacto independent of one another, the reality of the PRC-ROC division that had existed since 1949, and Taiwan's membership in other international organizations.[33] His position as president gave him the ability to use the media to convince Taiwan voters of his diplomatic skill. This was evident in his campaign for UN membership (which Lee acknowledged would be supported by the people of Taiwan even if it was a long-shot), and in his efforts to reach out to Asian neighbors and countries in other parts of the world.

In late January 1995, General Secretary Zhiang Zemin of the communist party, issued an eight-point proposal to rekindle talk of reunification between the mainland and Taiwan. Zhiang's efforts were clearly a response to Lee's UN initiatives, and his official and unofficial diplomatic missions to Asia and elsewhere. Zhiang was also thinking of his own political future. If he could demonstrate that he could rein-in Taiwan's ambitions for independence prior to the death of Deng Xiaoping, it could strengthen his political position vis-a-vis others at Deng's departure. Zhiang wanted to show he had the political skills to keep Taiwan in the Chinese realm without having to resort to force. This was apparent in the language of his proposal--the most important aspect being Zhiang's desire to encourage negotiation over conflict and offer protection for Taiwan businesses operating on the mainland. President Lee's response was essentially a restatement of Taiwan's goals for national reunification formulated in 1991--Taiwan and mainland China were separate political entities, and Taipei was interested in increased exchanges between China and Taiwan. True reunification could only come about with a successful democratic transition occurring on the mainland.[34] Lee also added that Taiwan deserved to be a member of the United Nations like other divided states such as North and South Korea, and East and West Germany prior to reunification. Lee's sharp response to Zhiang's proposal did not rule out talks, however. Taiwan authorities continued to meet with their mainland counterparts until June. There was even agreement in Taipei that improved economic links between Taiwan and China would necessitate Taiwan making talks between the two more official by improving government-to-government contact.[35] But talks were suspended by Beijing when Lee received permission to visit the United States.

Lee Teng-hui had asked for permission to visit the United States before his June 1995 visit. The state department rejected Lee's requests, stating that such a visit would create undesirable political consequences between the U.S. and China. In May, the state department granted Lee a visit to speak at an Alumni gathering at his alma mater at Cornell University. Members of congress had pressured President Clinton and the state department to grant the visa, arguing Taiwan's democratization and China's dismal record on human rights warranted Washington extending the courtesy to Lee. Congressional critics further accused the state department of welcoming known terrorists to the United States, namely Gerry Adams of the Irish Republican Army and Yassir Arafat of the Palestine Liberation Organization, but had repeatedly rejected the request of the leader of democratic Taiwan from visiting.[36]

Beijing's protests were vociferous and took many in Washington by surprise. China threatened to step-up its military readiness to take Taiwan by force. They accused the U.S. of violating the Chinese-American agreement over Taiwan's status.[37] Suddenly the hope generated by Zhiang's eight-point proposal on reunification was lost. Washington tried to downplay the significance of the visit by claiming Lee was coming in the capacity of a citizen, and that his visa had been granted on humanitarian, not diplomatic grounds. Officially, Taipei described Lee's visit as personal, though they admitted the visit could enhance U.S.-Taiwan ties.[38] Lee clearly saw the Cornell visit as a way to wear-down Taiwan's diplomatic isolation. His visit was strongly supported by Taiwan's people. This in turn gave him an immediate boost in popularity. Nearly 85% of those polled in Taiwan felt Lee's visit would improve Taiwan's diplomatic standing.[39] Lee had succeeded in convincing Taiwan's people that Taipei could gain diplomatic respect in spite of the two China problem. This was exactly the goal Lee had sought and it seemed to bode well for him leading into the presidential campaign.[40]

Lee Teng-hui expected there to be an emotional response from China. His efforts to earn Taiwan a UN seat, his shuttle diplomacy, and the Cornell visit would no doubt invite strong rhetoric from Beijing. But by July it became apparent that Beijing's response would be more than rhetoric. The People's Liberation Army began missile tests in July. Other military exercises were promised. Lee and his advisers took note of the situation and reasserted that the Kuomintang supported a one-China policy. The military threats continued into August as the Kuomintang met for its 15th party congress.

And as Taiwan continued its push for a UN seat in the Autumn, the PRC made every effort to block Taiwan's entry. Taiwan lost its UN bid, but promised to continue the fight each succeeding year, believing its chances would improve with time.

Military threat and Lee's diplomatic efforts fueled the reunification debate. Candidates for the legislative yuan stated their position on the issue. As the elections neared, Beijing renewed their willingness to take Taiwan by force if independence candidates won election and made an attempt to make Taiwan an independent republic.

The issue of Taiwan's national identity and the mainland's military threats increased the drama and intensity of Taiwan's presidential campaign as the March 1996 election came closer. By February, mainland authorities had announced their intention to hold war games in waters off the Northern and Southern coasts of Taiwan. As the Chinese fired missiles and conducted naval maneuvers, Taiwan's population nervously went to the polls and made their choice. Instead of feeling intimidated, however, most Taiwan voters felt a strong resolve to give Beijing the message that they would not bend to China's threats. In fact, Beijing's war games brought strong international condemnation against China and a U.S. show of force, as President Clinton ordered two carrier battle groups into position near the Taiwan straits. Though there was no explicit American promise to defend Taiwan, the Chinese saw the move as a direct threat and violation of previous agreements between Washington and Beijing on Taiwan's political status. As soon as the election was over, Beijing ended its war games, threatening to return again in the summer. Lee Teng-hui acknowledged Beijing's threats by stating his diplomatic efforts to win a UN seat would continue. He also said Taiwan would seek to improve ties with other countries, though not with the same intensity as earlier. Lee's willingness cut-back on his unofficial diplomatic visits was an acknowledgement that he had gone too far in seeking to improve Taiwan's international status. He reiterated the long-standing intention of the KMT to reunify Taiwan and China, though many doubted the sincerity of his remarks.[41]

The 1995 Legislative Yuan Elections

The 1994 Taipei and Kaohsiung city elections, and elections for the provincial governor and assembly gave no clear indication of how the three main parties would do in the 1995 elections for the legislature. The CNP's strength had been established in the Taipei metropolitan area, but there was strong, traditional support for the DPP and KMT there as well. The KMT needed a strong showing in the upcoming election for its candidates not only to win a majority in the legislature, but to sure-up Lee's presidential bid as well.

Issues of national identity and security were important in the legislative race. This was especially so towards the end of the campaign. The people tended to accept Taiwan's independent status and its possible future reunification with the mainland, if only for security reasons. This was what Lee Teng-hui and senior party leaders in the party mainstream had hoped for. But there were plenty of traditional issues that interested voters as well. The DPP and CNP continued to campaign against the corruption of the KMT mainstream. Some KMT candidates also made clear attempts to distance themselves from fellow party members who were associated with graft. DPP candidates pointed to other abuses of the KMT machine, and pledged to protect the weak and those unhappy with KMT policies. They also campaigned against CNP candidates whom they viewed as mainland sympathizers.

The DPP and CNP had developed policies of their own, but they still had much in common with the majority KMT party when it came to economic development strategies. This was especially true for the CNP. It was believed that the CNP was beginning to lose ground vis-a-vis the other parties because of internal problems among its leadership and because of poor policy development. Some party leaders accused recent recruits of being members of the party in name only. These leaders alleged that the recruits joined the party because of the CNP's popularity in districts where they had an interest in running for public office, not because they necessarily believed in the party's platform. Once elections were over, loyalty to the party was withdrawn.[42]

KMT party central worried about the party's loosing its majority in the elections. They took some risky steps to bolster their position. One of these measures was to run Vincent Siew, head of the Council for Economic Planning and Development (a cabinet level post), and run him against popular DPP legislator Tsai Tung-jung in Siew's hometown of Chia-yi, a city in South-central Taiwan. If Siew won the legislative seat he would be assured of three years on the legislature. If he were to lose the seat, he would hold no government post.[43] The Kuomintang also made greater efforts to focus support on specific candidates who could in turn campaign for Lee Teng-hui. The party was able to achieve greater unity between the center and local districts than it had in the 1992 election. Vote buying was still evident. Prior to the election, Justice Minister Ma Ying-jeou personally went to schools in a public relations campaign to ask children to persuade their parents not to engage in election graft.[44]

As in the 1992 election, Taiwan's people voted for candidates that addressed the issues of greatest importance to local regions. While honesty in politics and national security were important, economic growth and stability proved to be most important to voters.⁴⁵ The Kuomintang won a majority in the election (85 out of 164 seats), with the CNP and DPP vowing to work together to fight against the KMT's narrow majority. KMT efforts to get Vincent Siew elected paid off as he defeated the incumbent DPP candidate. The DPP won four more seats than they won in the 1992 elections (54), and the CNP won two more than they had won as New KMT Alliance candidates in the previous elections for the legislative yuan (21). The CNP continued to struggle outside of the Taipei metropolitan area. Despite winning a majority, the KMT saw their percentage of the vote slip to 46% of the total votes cast from 53% in the 1992 elections.⁴⁶ Party central was still relieved the party held on to its majority and could now focus its attention on the presidential race.

The Presidential Candidates, Campaign, and Election

All three of the parties had difficulties in selecting their presidential candidates. Lin Yang-kang made his intentions known in March 1995 that regardless of the nomination outcome at the Kuomintang's 15th party congress, he would be a candidate for president.⁴⁷ Hsu Hsin-liang and Peng Ming-min both announced their intentions to run as the DPP's candidate for president. The CNP had difficulty finding a candidate to run for president. Jaw Shao-kang was at one time interested in running as was Wang Chien-hsien. But internal problems within the party and past electoral performance seemed to indicate neither man could do well against Lee Teng-hui. The CDRA continued to make overtures to the CNP to join forces in supporting the same candidates for president. The CNP rejected such offers. In their attempt to distance themselves from members of the CDRA, CNP party leaders openly admitted that the CDRA was too right-wing for their taste. They believed the CDRA to be dominated by an older generation of leaders in Taiwan who no longer had anything to offer Taiwan's people.⁴⁸ But the CNP was finding it difficult, in spite of their attempts to correct the perception of their being a mainlander political party, to make inroads into areas where the KMT and DPP remained strong.

Much was at stake for Lee Teng-hui in the 13th and 14th party congresses of the KMT. In the 13th party congress Lee was able to consolidate his power within the party ranks and move ahead with the political initiative in Taiwan. At the 14th party congress Lee won a sizable majority of support for continuing as party chairman in spite of the fact that the old KMT apparatus was beginning to unravel quickly. By the 15th party congress, few paid attention to the membership of the central committee and central standing committee. In fact, the most anticipated activity of the 15th party congress was the party's nomination of its presidential candidate. While few doubted

Lee's ability to win that nomination, many wondered what kind of effort would be required to keep the party rank-and-file unified enough to give Lee the support he desired to hold off candidates from the other parties. At the party congress, only Lee Teng-hui and Lin Yang-kang's names appeared on the party's primary ballot. Not surprisingly, the KMT gave Lee 91% of the party delegate votes. He selected Premier Lien Chan as his running mate. Lien was popular and had worked effectively with the legislature during the democratization process.

Even though Lee became the official candidate of the KMT, Lin Yang-kang vowed to continue his bid for the presidency as an independent candidate. CNP officials and members of the CDRA were interested in Lin's bid for the presidency. In addition, Chen Li-an, president of the control yuan, resigned his membership in the Kuomintang and announced his intention to run as an independent candidate for president as well. Some speculated Chen may have wanted endorsement by the CNP.[49] He was viewed as an honest public figure and had a reputation as a hard worker. Thus the 15th party congress ended with three people having declared their intentions to run for president, but only Lee Teng-hui had the party's blessing.

Lee Teng-hui savored the role of incumbent. He and Lien Chan emphasized their experience and achievements in helping to create Taiwan's "economic miracle" and "quiet revolution of democracy." There was early speculation that Lin Yang-kang and Chen Li-an might join together as presidential and vice presidential candidates. But there were sharp differences that kept the two apart. Lin Yang-kang and Hau Pei-tsun joined forces to help CNP candidates in the legislative yuan elections, and then counted on the CNP for endorsement as running mates in the race. As a vice presidential candidate, Hau was seen as closely associated with Taiwan's authoritarian past, but the Lin-Hau ticket received the support of both the CNP and the CDRA. They were deeply opposed to Lee Teng-hui personally and tried to focus on clean politics. They accused Lee of bringing Taiwan to the brink of war with China as a result of his cavalier efforts at diplomacy. Their candidacy and the assistance they gave the CNP resulted in their being expelled by the party shortly after the legislative yuan elections. Chen Li-an chose Wang Ching-feng as his running mate. As the only woman in the race, Wang originally announced her intention to run as a presidential candidate. But Chen's name recognition and support was attractive to Wang as a newcomer to Taiwan politics. The Chen-Wang team stressed traditional values and cross-straits peace if elected. The DPP eventually came to nominate Peng Ming-min and Frank Hsieh as its presidential and vice presidential candidates. Peng and Hsieh focused much of their attention on KMT abuses of the past and the need for Taiwan to emerge from the shadow of mainland China. The message was controversial as most in Taiwan opposed an open break with the mainland for security reasons.[50]

Elections to the national assembly were to be held on the same day as the presidential election. The KMT wanted to hold on to their majority in the assembly so they could pass an amendment to the constitution that would require elections in the legislative yuan, national assembly, and presidency to be held at the same time. The DPP wanted a majority on the national assembly so they could amend the constitution and abolish the national assembly, and then give powers of constitutional review to the legislature. The CNP wanted to bring back tenets of the original constitution of the ROC. They believed the KMT had gone too far in recent assembly sessions in changing much of the original constitutional structure introduced by Sun Yat-sen. All three of these positions were debated freely in the presidential race. The national assembly had managed to make constitutional reforms in recent sessions, though many believed the outcome of the election would make it impossible for the assembly to continue constitutional reform if there was no clear majority winner.

Recent constitutional reforms and Taiwan's new election law established some useful campaign procedures. The election of the chief executive was formally put in the hands of the people. This removed the national assembly's role in electing the president. Citizens residing overseas could only vote for president if they returned to Taiwan to vote. The government would pay for television time for the candidates. This provided the voters with a first-hand look at the candidates without the three main government T.V. stations offering their take of the candidates positions. There was an expenditure sealing put on the presidential race to prevent moneyed interests from having an unfair advantage in advertising.[51]

As the presidential election neared, the conflict in the Taiwan Straits was debated openly in the campaign. Lin and Hau accused Lee Teng-hui of bringing the country to the brink of war. Similar accusations were made by Chen Li-an. Peng Ming-min believed Taiwan should stand firm and press forward for a future break with the mainland. Lee's position was that the conflict was that war was not likely and that the mainland's frustration was with Taiwan's democratization, not with Lee Teng-hui.[52] Lee's position was not only convincing to Taiwan's people, it was also true. Democratization had created a different political culture in Taiwan than existed on the mainland. No amount of bargaining or compromise could change the differences that had become apparent between the two political entities, though Lee had aggravated the situation with his independent diplomatic efforts in the year prior to the election.

On March 23, Taiwan's people elected Lee Teng-hui president and Lien Chan vice president. Peng and Hsieh were a distant second, Lin and Hau third, and Chen and Wang finished last. As indicated in Table 7.3, Lee and Lien won in every city and county except Nantou County. Lin Yang-kang was

Table 7.3 Election Results, 1996 Race for President/Vice President

Team	Total Votes	% of Vote	City/Counties Won
Chen/Wang	1,074,044	10	0
Lee/Lien	5,813,699	54	24
Lin/Hau	1,603,790	15	1
Peng/Hsieh	2,274,586	21	0

Source: Central Election Commission, Government Information Office, March 25, 1996.

born in Nantou and remained popular there throughout his career, thus ensuring his and Hau's victory in Nantou by a comfortable margin.

Elections for the national assembly gave the KMT a slight majority. It captured 49.7% of the vote, to the DPP's 30%, and the CNP's 14%.[53] The slight majority for the KMT made constitutional reform seem remote. No party had enough support to root out redundancies in elected bodies and government yuans, nor was there hope for streamlining election processes because it would be nearly impossible to get the cross-party support needed to amend the constitution.

The long awaited presidential election in Taiwan was over. In declaring victory, Lee announced his intentions to move ahead with reforms of the judicial system, fight corruption, and work on reunification with the mainland. In spite of the threat from the mainland that had plagued the presidential election, there was a calm over Taiwan. Former candidates vowed to take-up their fight in future campaigns. In the election's aftermath, attention was refocused on the new legislature, new media outlets, and the problems of overlapping responsibilities in the legislative yuan, provincial assembly, and national assembly. For the first time, the people of Taiwan were able to elect a president in a truly democratic fashion. The most important authoritarian element of the old Kuomintang had fallen. The KMT's victory in the presidential race was more than simply having its candidate win. The Kuomintang emerged from the race a partner in bringing democracy to Taiwan.

Conclusion

One of the most important aspects of change in the presidential election process has been the ending of KMT special privileges in the government. Like parties in any democratic state, the KMT had no guarantee its candidate would win the presidency nor could it block the election of an opposition candidate. Furthermore, the KMT hierarchy lost its ability to select a candidate acceptable only to them. With each step the Kuomintang took in the direction of democracy, the KMT organization and inner-party policies became increasingly anachronistic.

1-Leadership

Lee Teng-hui accepted the inevitability of democracy. He used democratic reforms to his political advantage. His support for popular elections in choosing the president was important not only for the sake of democracy, but as a way of distancing himself from his mainlander critics. Party hardliners have proven to be a tougher challenge to Lee than the DPP because of their resistance to his position as party leader, president, and his support for reforms. As in European and Latin American cases, the more party hardliners criticized Lee and other softliners, the more people perceived the hardliners as enemies in the democratization process.[54] Older mainlanders could no longer rely on strong party leaders to maintain the orthodoxy of the past and hold the party together. Leaders had become increasingly dependent on the support of party members and the people of Taiwan. Because conservatives were a minority, their influence mattered less as time went by.

It is doubtful any party chairman could have done a better job in maintaining party unity than Lee Teng-hui has. The shift from mainlander to Taiwanese rule of the party, coupled with increased democratization would cause organizational problems that any party leader would find frustrating. Another party chairman could have destroyed the KMT and possibly the democratization of Taiwan, had he attempted to maintain party dominance over an increasingly liberal political system and a party that had come to rely on Taiwanese leaders to run party positions left vacant by mainlanders. In many respects, Lee Teng-hui was the ideal leader for the transitional period. He was chosen by Chiang Ching-kuo, thereby demanding early mainlander acquiescence, and was Taiwanese by birth, thus winning support of the party majority.

In other respects, political liberalization in Taiwan has shed light on the qualities needed for democratic leadership. Lee made use of traditional disciplinary measures to assure the votes he needed in party meetings prior to the 1993 party congress. These methods were not needed and slowed reform within the Kuomintang. Had Lee allowed democratic elections for party chairman, he would have taken ammunition away from his critics and still been able to secure the top party spot. In addition, he could have furthered democracy in Taiwan by sticking to his original pledge to not seek reelection to the presidency in 1996. This would have allowed for a successful transition to take place and sealed Taiwan's democratic fate. Lee would not step aside because of personal ambition and because the mainstream of the party came to see Lee as the most effective person to go against popular non-mainstream candidates. Li Huan attempted to undermine Lee's power by introducing democratic reforms that would have limited the powers of the presidency. Yet despite wrapping themselves in the banners of democracy, prominent non-mainstream faction leaders have been erstwhile defenders of party privilege and critics of liberalization. They are believers in the Kuomintang's earlier goals of mainland recovery. They resent the Taiwanese majority. Their goals are best preserved by a Leninist party structure. For this reason, they are out of sync with the political realities of Taiwan and will become increasingly irrelevant in political debates. The focus of political power has shifted from KMT party chairman to the presidency. The campaign for the presidency surpassed all other elections in importance. This was evident during the 15th party congress. The most significant item on the agenda was the presidential primary. Hardly a word was uttered about KMT vice chairmen and membership on the central committee and central standing committee by party delegates or the press. The strength of the presidency vis-a-vis other institutions of democratic power is a matter of concern, however, because of the newness of Taiwan's democratic experience.

Many local faction leaders of the party's mainstream are just beginning to learn that political corruption has limits in a democratic system. One of the greatest concerns to Taiwan's voters in recent years has been local leaders' involvement in political graft. Local leaders need to wage clean election battles not only to advance their party's image, but to champion democracy as well.

2-Organization

Calls for reform within the party and the development of Taiwan's representative bodies have changed the KMT. The years of party domination by mainlanders has come to an end. As long as the party and political system could be run by a strong leader through the Kuomintang's Leninist structure, Taiwanese party members would have only marginal influence in the party. Natural attrition has taken significant numbers of KMT senior leaders from the scene. Taiwanese party members selected by Chiang Kai-shek and his son who served in administrative party and government posts have been pushed aside by younger party members who have a keener sense of electoral politics. For the new generation KMT leaders, power comes from the ballot box, not central directives from the party chairman under threat of party discipline. This realization has prompted local KMT factions to challenge the wisdom of party leaders and to reject mainlander views, especially those of the CDRA and Chinese New Party. As factional differences grew into major rifts, leaders were unable to stop the diminution of power from the center, and the growing influence of local factions. Factional infighting led to multiple party vice chairmen and a more diverse central committee and central standing committee, thus weakening the largely singular role of party chairmen like Chiang Kai-shek and Chiang Ching-kuo. By the 15th party congress, even the central committee and central standing committee had lost the importance they held in the past. Power had shifted almost completely to the elected bodies.

With the passing of time, the position of party chairman will continue to decline as the principles embraced by the KMT are swept away by democracy. Already the party is primarily a Taiwanese party. The Kuomintang is interested in China mainly for reasons of security and economics.

In some respects, the party organization in Taipei has become only a hollow shell to local party organizations. Local cadres have increased regional interests and see Taipei as a sometime ally, sometime enemy, and generally an increasingly irrelevant voice. As political perspectives change within the party because of Taiwan's rapidly evolving political landscape, many in the party mainstream may abandon the KMT in favor of another political organization, or formally remake the Kuomintang into a party of local political interests. As one analyst puts it, the ability of former Leninist parties to adapt

> depends on whether the leadership at the moment of the transition is comprised primarily of political pragmatists who are willing to dump the ideological baggage of the past and present the party as a credible alternative in order to take advantage of new political opportunities.[55]

The KMT has adapted well so far and seems to be well poised to hold power in the near future.

3-Ideology

Most people in Taiwan believe democracy is superior to authoritarianism. Most believe the changes Taiwan has experienced are good. But there has been disappointment expressed at the proliferation of corruption and petty fighting between politicians. Taiwan needs democratic ideals to stand as a bulwark against its authoritarian past and to give guidance for the future. Leaders frequently use democratic rhetoric, but Taiwan's leaders have failed to articulate what democratic virtues they believe in. Democratic virtues are necessary to improve the moral and intellectual conditions of Taiwan's political culture.[56] They are essential to the maintenance of democracy. It is an area where the KMT, DPP, and CNP have all fallen short. Democratic ideology is essential for laying the foundations to a democratic culture and a civil society.[57]

What has become of the *San Min Chu I*? Mainstream national KMT leaders still mention the *San Min Chu I*, though they are careful to refer to its concepts superficially. If a theoretical discussion of the *San Min Chu I* captured island-wide attention it could be to the detriment of the KMT. This is because the *San Min Chu I* was used to deny political rights and exclude the people of Taiwan from political participation in the decades prior to Taiwan's political liberalization. Officially, the KMT claims it went through the military and tutelage phases of national reconstruction and is now in the constitutional phase on Taiwan. Along the way, the tenets of the *San Min Chu I*, nationalism, livelihood, and democracy have been realized on Taiwan and must now be extended to the mainland. But the KMT does not offer much in terms of how these tenets will be attempted on the mainland in the future.

Non-mainstream party members have continued to pledge their allegiance to the *San Min Chu I*. But their claims that Lee Teng-hui was the first to abandon these precepts is not accurate, given the almost total disregard for the political doctrines of Sun Yat-sen by Chiang Kai-shek and Chiang Ching-kuo. Taiwan's path to democracy did not follow the plan articulated by Sun, it was the result of a political give-and-take between KMT leaders and critics of the KMT party-state.

The Kuomintang needs a political platform that specifically addresses the political situation in Taiwan. While interest in mainland reunification has declined, the party's pledge to consider Taiwan first in all matters needs a solid theoretical foundation. This can only come about after considering what democracy is supposed to mean on Taiwan and how the party supports this goal. Such considerations will give guidance to local KMT factions and provide a common ideology to rally behind at a time when the party is threatened nationally and locally by factionalization. The development of a new ideological focus containing democratic tenets will further erode the party's prospects as an all-China party. As democracy grows in Taiwan, popular demands will need to be met by the KMT, which will drive the party further from its lingering interests on mainland China, and in turn, alarm Beijing even more than it already has.

4-Agenda Setting

The KMT lost the reform agenda a year or so after the death of Chiang Ching-kuo. By this time, reforms championed by the opposition took on a life of their own. Representative bodies were democratized leading the way for an opening in nearly every corner of the political system. This is not, however, to say that the KMT was irrelevant in the process. Once the KMT committed itself to reform, the party understood it could only harm the political system and its own vitality by reining-in reforms. Realizing reform was in its own interest, the party did its best to smooth the way. Sometimes the party resisted, as they did in early meetings of the national assembly where delegates discussed how to select the president of the republic. But party leaders managed to do a good job of satisfying demands at the right time.

The Kuomintang failed to seriously consider the roles of the president and the premier. Although a 1994 amendment to the constitution eliminated the premier's power to countersign legislation, redundancies in duties remain. Similarly, the problem of overlapping responsibility in the government yuans remains unsolved. It could be that this task will fall on the new national assembly elected in 1996, or a future government not dominated by KMT interests.

As the Taiwan economy matures, the Kuomintang will need to develop new policies in an increasingly complicated economic world. Policies that worked in the past will not be as effective in the future and the party will have to provide a reasonable plan if it wants to succeed. The Kuomintang has always provided a strong vision of economic goals. It will not be as easy in the future because Taiwan will soon be to the point when it is no longer catching-up with developed countries. If the leading economies of the world are adequate indicators, long-term plans are not easy to formulate or follow. Taiwan's people have come to expect results. Any political party is going to find it tough to meet high expectations.

5-Quality of Governance

The speed of reforms on Taiwan has been breathtaking. The lifting of press restrictions, repeal of the Sedition Act, dissolving of the garrison command, and strengthening of the judicial system have greatly increased respect for political rights in Taiwan. The extension of universal elections for selecting officials in the legislative yuan, national assembly, and all mayoral offices and the presidency of the republic, is also encouraging. Taiwan's transition has been remarkably stable. Yet there are lingering concerns.[58]

The presence of political corruption is not surprising, though its prominence is alarming. Because corruption has long-term effects and can threaten people's faith in the system, it is necessary for the KMT and all political parties to do their best to eradicate illegal practices. One of the best ways to do so is to teach democratic virtues in rhetoric and by example. The watering-down of the Sunshine Law by KMT lawmakers has weakened public confidence in their leaders, and by extension, the democratic system. Democratic development for Taiwan has established democratic processes, but democratic virtues continue to be lacking both within the KMT, and within the political system. As a result, civil society has not developed fully enough.[59] But people recognize that criticism of the government is not the same as criticizing democracy as a regime.[60] This is an important step and one that suggests democratic consolidation is underway.

6-Party-Government Relations

The separation of party and government functions improved government services on Taiwan. Government agencies have become largely responsible for their own performance and no longer expect the party to dominate all aspects of public policy. The addition of new ministries designed to address quality of life issues, the empowerment of real representative bodies that demand better performance from government agencies, and the ending of surveillance activities by the garrison command and other official agencies, have improved public administration in Taiwan. Bureaucrats have gradually come to realize they are responsible to elected leaders and the public, not to a particular political party. Some controversy remains, especially in regard to the presence of loyal KMT party members who hold significant positions in government agencies. This is a long-term problem, however, and one that will decline with the establishment of further reforms and administrative retirements.

Notes

1. Tsiang Yen-si, interview, June 8, 1993.
2. Alexander Ya-li Lu, interview, May 19, 1993.
3. Lien Chan, "The Republic of China Belongs in the United Nations," *Orbis* (Fall 1993).
4. *China News*, July 13, 1993.
5. *Shih-jie Ryh-pao*, July 30, 1993.
6. *Lien-ho Pao* (United Daily News), July 13, 1993.
7. *Shih-jie Ryh-pao*, August 4, 1993.
8. It should be noted that Lin Yang-kang is Taiwanese but has always favored policies of the non-mainstream faction.
9. *Shih-jie Ryh-pao*, August 18, 1993.
10. Ibid., August 19, 1993.
11. Ibid., August 25, 1993.
12. Ibid., August 7, 1993.
13. Ibid., September 8. 1993.
14. Ibid., August 19, 1993.
15. *Chung-kuo Shih-pao*, September 9, 1993.

16. *Shih-jie Ryh-pao*, September 17, 1993.
17. See for example the comparison of party platforms in the *Lien-ho Pao*, September 11, 1993.
18. *Chung-kuo Shih-pao*, October 1, 1993.
19. *Shih-jie Ryh-pao*, September 16, 1993.
20. *China Post*, September 18, 1993.
21. *China News*, September 20, 1993.
22. *Chung-kuo Shih-pao*, November 29, 1993.
23. Ibid., November 28, 1993.
24. Ibid., November 29, 1993.
25. *Free China Journal*, February 4, 1994.
26. Ibid., April 15, 1994.
27. Yu-shan Wu, "Taiwan in 1994: Managing a Critical Relationship," *Asian Survey*, January 1995, p. 65.
28. *Free China Journal*, December 9, 1994.
29. *FEER*, January 5, 1995.
30. *Free China Journal*, March 31, 1995.
31. *FEER*, March 23, 1995.
32. Ibid.
33. See text of Lee's UN Communique in the *Free China Journal*, June 30, 1995.
34. National Unification Council and the Executive Yuan, "Guidelines for National Reunification," March 14, 1991.
35. *FEER*, June 15, 1995.
36. *FEER*, June 1, 1995.
37. Xinhua, May 22, 1995. FBIS *Daily Report*, China, May 23, 1995.
38. CNA, May 23, 1995. FBIS *Daily Report*, China, May 23, 1995.
39. *Free China Journal*, June 16, 1995.
40. *Tzuli Wanpao*, June 12, 1995. FBIS *Daily Report*, China, August 331, 1995.
41. Government Information Office, Post-Election News Summary, March 25, 1996.
42. *Hsin Hsin Wen*, January 7, 1995. FBIS *Daily Report*, China, March 24, 1995.
43. *FEER*, November 23, 1995.
44. *Free China Journal*, November 10, 1995.
45. *Lien-ho Pao*, December 3, 1995.
46. Statistics provided by the Central Election Commission of the Republic of China, December 3, 1995.
47. CNA, March 18, 1995. FBIS *Daily Report*, China, March 20, 1995.
48. *Heipai Hsinwen* (Taiwan Weekly), May 14, 1995. FBIS *Daily Report*, China, August 2, 1995.
49. CNA, August 29, 1996. FBIS *Daily Report*, China, August 29, 1996.
50. Government Information Office, "Biographies and Platforms of the Candidates for President and Vice President," March 15, 1996.
51. "Presidential Election Law of the Republic of China," transcript provided by the Central Election Commission and the Government Information Office, January 19, 1996.
52. Presidential News Conference, February 23, 1996. Transcript made available by the Government Information Office, February 24, 1996.

53. Central Election Commission, "Results of the Vote for the National Assembly," March 24, 1996.
54. O'Donnell and Schmitter, *Tentative Conclusions*, p. 24.
55. John T. Ishimaya, "Communist Parties in Transition: Structures, Leaders, and Processes of Democratization in Eastern Europe," *Comparative Politics* (January 1995), p. 148.
56. Tocqueville, *Democracy In America*, Volume I, p. 299.
57. Fukuyama, "Democracy's Future," p. 9.
58. Meaney, "Liberalization, Democratization, and the Role of the KMT," pp. 114-115.
59. Larry Diamond, "Rethinking Civil Society: Toward Democratic Consolidation," *Journal of Democracy*, July 1994, pp. 7-11.
60. Diamond and Linz, "Politics, Society, and Democracy in Latin America," p. 13.

8

Concluding Analysis: The Kuomintang and Political Development on Taiwan

While the Kuomintang has undergone and continues to undergo rapid change, several questions arise. What are the lessons of KMT rule on Taiwan? Are KMT leaders responsible for the emergence of democracy on Taiwan? What will the KMT have to do to maintain popular support on Taiwan? What will the KMT look like in several years now that the forces of democratization are at work inside the party apparatus? While these questions have been addressed in this book, it is necessary to offer a final summary and analysis in this chapter.

As stated in the introduction, there are several general conclusions of this study. KMT leaders have played a key role in the democratization process. This is not to underestimate the role of the opposition. Opposition forces were the real catalyst of political change in Taiwan. The opposition was driven by subethnic rivalry and tempered by viable KMT development schemes. Thus, prerequisites to democracy such as economic growth, culture, education, and foreign pressure were all stabilizing factors in the liberalization process.

While the KMT's Leninist structure created a stable economic and political environment, it was also an obstacle to democracy. Finally, the quality of democracy in Taiwan depends on the acceptance of more democratic virtues, and the KMT's future depends on the party's ability to reform itself into a conventional democratic political party. The final analysis and these conclusions are best presented within the context of our framework.

The Kuomintang Record on Taiwan

1-Leadership

One of the principle reasons for the reorganization of the Kuomintang in 1924 was to streamline the party apparatus and give Sun Yat-sen the power he believed he needed to make his revolution work. And while Sun did not want to be remembered as an authoritarian, his political theories called for a strong leader who would be unchallenged in his efforts in building a powerful, modern state prior to the establishment of constitutional democracy.

The 1950 reorganization committee tried to revive that formula and strengthen the role of the party chairman. Chiang Kai-shek's rhetoric often referred to Sun's tenets of political tutelage, but he showed little devotion to it. Reorganization was successful in giving Chiang better control over a more streamlined party. He increasingly came to rely on party officials trained in economics, agriculture, industry, and other expert skills. While Chiang's desire to ruthlessly root-out his critics continued, he nevertheless allowed greater inclusion in the party, especially by the late 1960s. Taiwanese came to fill important posts as technocrats both within the party and the government. Chiang Ching-kuo was responsible for bringing many Taiwanese in during his father's later years, but the younger Chiang continued this trend during his reign, both as a way to gain legitimacy, but also out of necessity. Many mainlander KMT leaders either lacked the skills and know-how to push Taiwan's ambitious economic plans, or were leaving party and government service because of age and death. This began the Taiwanization of the KMT, and the beginning of the end to mainlander-domination of the party.

In his first years as chairman, Chiang Ching-kuo's control over the party was nearly as absolute as his father's. But there were developments that strengthened the role of other party leaders. The loss of U.S. recognition, financial scandals, and rumors of KMT-supported murders forced the party to become more public minded. Many younger party members advocated reaching out to the public to sure-up their image. Conservatives feared younger Taiwanese party members did not appreciate the role of the KMT as a party dedicated to mainland recovery. They believed the party would lose sight of that mission if it became too responsive to public demands. Chiang believed the position taken by the younger party members to be most important in the short run. He therefore strengthened their hand by anointing Lee Teng-hui to succeed him as party chairman and president of the republic.

Lee's battle with party conservatives began immediately following Chiang's death. Even though he was closely aligned with the mainstream Taiwanese wing of the party that favored reform, he used many of the tactics used by previous party chairmen to secure his position as party chairman. These included the denial of secret ballots in his nomination to be party chairman and president, and threats to demote party members for not going along with his policies. But in the new political climate of Taiwan, public criticism of the Kuomintang and Lee began to grow, first outside and then inside the party. Local leaders ignored directives from party central. Left out of the political circle for so long, cadres in local areas developed networks of their own that facilitated the exchange of political favors and monetary rewards. At the national level, rifts grew into full-blown factional fights. Lee and other party leaders feared the party was headed for self-destruction. By the time of the 14th party congress, Lee found it necessary to keep the party from splitting apart by allowing for the creation of multiple vice chairmen slots. Instead of unifying the party, however, open political debates continued, as rival factional leaders sought new forums to criticize Lee and one another.

In Western political parties, most party leaders are selected on the basis of their abilities to formulate a party agenda based on the collective interests of the party's principle power centers and electoral demands. The Leninist concept of democratic centralism allowed Kuomintang chairmen to send their policies through the party apparatus without interference. As the government of Taiwan became increasingly democratic, the legitimacy of party chairmen as Leninist leaders began to erode. This has not resulted in KMT party leaders taking a role similar to leaders in Western political parties, however. The power of the party chairman will continue to decline, and the role of factions will become increasingly important. In the meantime, little will be done to improve the quality of party leadership in local organs, thereby distancing the rank-and-file membership from party central even further.

The most significant characteristics of KMT leaders has been their metamorphosis from authoritarians to reluctant democrats. This transformation occurred not simply because of outside pressure, but because they saw it to be in their interest to allow gradual liberalization to occur. This process occurred in distinct steps over several decades:

1. The reorganization of the KMT from an ineffective party into a hierarchically organized party dominated by Chiang Kai-shek.

2. Chiang determines greater attention must be made to socio-economic development. This necessitates introducing experts into the development process.

3. Chiang Ching-kuo finds it necessary to give the party and government greater legitimacy by bringing in more technocrats and Taiwanese into the system.

4. Opposition leaders take advantage of Chiang Ching-kuo's policies and demand more openness. Initially Chiang represses such demands, but eventually allows measured political reforms.

5. Public expectations rise, causing Chiang to meet demands with further reform. He eventually acknowledges the need to democratize the system and publicly commits the party to that end.

6. Lee Teng-hui continues Chiang's pledge to extend reforms. The opposition and Kuomintang begins to adjust to democratic realities. Democratic elections for president are held, and the process of democratic consolidation begins.

The role of elites both within the opposition and thee KMT have been the most important players in the democratization process. Taiwan's democratization mirrors the experience of countries in Latin America and Southern Europe in this respect. A unique aspect has been the successful, albeit long-term transition of a Leninist regime to democracy. This aspect will be discussed in greater detail below.

2-Organization

As a Leninist party the KMT was able to maintain sharp discipline within the ranks. The party hierarchy determined the rules in the system and did not have to pay attention to the expansion of political rights as long as they could justify authoritarian rule. It has been popular to claim the party became authoritarian when Chiang Kai-shek took over the top leadership position. This was not the case. Sun Yat-sen wanted to control the party's decision making process. For this reason, he embraced a Leninist structure for the party. But he still held democracy to be the ultimate goal. There is no doubt much of the ideology of Sun Yat-sen was lost in Chiang Kai-shek's drive to consolidate and maintain power. Chiang failed to understand that the party organization was weakened by his personal leadership style. While his reorganization efforts of 1950 finally gave him a tightly-controlled, well-disciplined party, the regime proved more loyal to authoritarianism than to the principles of political tutelage espoused by Sun Yat-sen.

The introduction of Taiwanese technocrats into the KMT and government organizations during the 1960's began to change the Kuomintang. At first the changes were barely noticed, but as time went on, the "Taiwanization" of the party became a necessity. Improved skills were needed to reach the ambitious economic development plans undertaken by the KMT and to replace aging mainlanders. Broader inclusion in the party and government bureaucracy brought increased pressure to decentralize some decision making power.

Taiwanization was only a first step in the party's transformation process. Other voices began to call for increased representation on governing bodies and greater public input in policy formation. The KMT fought to contain these demands, at first allowing only token elections, but gradually opening the system to greater participation. By the early 1970's the press was allowed to cast judgment on some government policies. This increased the public's desire to have greater freedoms extended. Diplomatic setbacks, a softer rhetorical line from Beijing, and several KMT scandals in the late '70s and mid '80s brought increased attention to anachronistic KMT authoritarianism. All of these developments led to demonstrations and a less-passive population demanding an end to martial law and one-party rule. Chiang Ching-kuo's reluctance to open the system gave way to an acknowledgement that the KMT had to include others or risk economic and political catastrophe.

When Lee Teng-hui took over the party, he inherited Chiang's pledge to democratize. As membership on the representative bodies were replaced according to democratic rules, and as other extraconstitutional limitations on political participation were eliminated, the KMT found that many of the calls for democratization were made by its own party members who felt excluded from the decision making process. Local KMT politicians rebelled against party central during campaigns and refused to go along with the party's legislative agenda. They used their new found influence to broker political deals and chase after businessmen anxious to buy influence in the new political climate.

The political power of the legislative yuan grew. Sensing that the old days of party control were slipping away, several mainlander-dominated factions tried to take control of the party to save the KMT from turning into a Taiwan-based political party and to keep the dream of recapturing the mainland alive. When the party met for its 14th party congress in August 1993, party leaders saw their organization fall into temporary disarray as competing camps fought to dominate the congress agenda. The election of four vice-chairmen, and a more independent central committee and central standing committee, were all indications that the power of the party chairman had peaked and would be diminished in the years to come.

The KMT's staying power can be attributed to its Leninist organization. If the KMT had been a more conventional authoritarian party, it may not have outlived its founder. The party is fundamentally different now than it was under Sun Yat-sen and Chiang Kai-shek. Because of democratization, the conditions needed to support a Leninist party have disappeared. It is too difficult for the party to maintain tight hierarchical discipline in the midst of a system having truly representative elected bodies and open political debates.

Lee Teng-hui's willingness to compromise in allowing for multiple vice-chairmen and a more diverse central standing committee is an acknowledgement that the party is losing its authoritarian structure. While the KMT is far less democratic than most Western political parties, it is still significantly different from the party whose chairman used to be able to determine nearly every aspect of political life by sending down directives through the party apparatus. Local party organs are freer to determine how best to meet the needs of their constituencies. National KMT politicians are given more room to voice opposition to established party policies. Party central has come to view other political parties as legitimate contenders for power that have their own popular following. This has resulted in the KMT becoming more public-minded in its approach to politics.

In short, each one of these factors has undermined the legitimacy of the Leninist organization and set the KMT on a course of reform. It will fundamentally change the way the party formulates policy and makes demands on its members. This evolution will be to the Kuomintang's advantage. Research has shown that center-right parties have much greater success in winning the acceptance of the people. It has a positive effect on the growth of democratic values and the rejection of extreme parties and groups.[1]

Some scholars and members of the press speculate the KMT will become or at least would like to become more like the Liberal Democratic Party (LDP) of Japan.[2] While there are similarities between the two parties, they are mostly superficial. Both the LDP and the KMT are broad-based parties, and both have major factions that fight for control of the political agenda. But the KMT continues to have a strong role for the party chairman, whereas the party president of the LDP is much more beholden to factional leaders for his support. While it is true Lee Teng-hui has had to compromise more than he would like, as KMT chairman and president of the republic, Lee is still the most significant voice in Taiwan politics. Japanese prime ministers seldom enjoy anything beyond modest success in carrying-out their own political agendas because of the strength of party factions.[3]

A key to understanding the dominance of the LDP in Japanese politics has been to consider the way voting districts have been gerrymandered and how multi-member districting schemes have ensured electoral success. While Taiwan also has multi-member district representation in the legislative yuan, it has not been as controversial or viewed as beneficial to the KMT as in the LDP case in Japan.[4] Although corruption has harmed the image of both parties, the KMT rank-and-file is more likely to be involved in money schemes at the local level, while the LDP's money ties are both locally and nationally based.

The primary differences between the LDP and KMT is the focus of political power. In Taiwan the legislature continues to grow as a focus of political power. As it does, it weakens the Kuomintang organization. For this reason, the legislature in Taiwan has more real decision making power than the parliament in Japan, which is dominated by party policy committees that constantly have to broker factional interests within the LDP and among the bureaucracies. The KMT's factions in the legislature tend not to be as rigid and dominated by key personalities as those in the LDP, making it easier to compromise on various issues.

Finally, the LDP's decline since 1989 in Japan can in part be attributed to excesses the party has taken to maintain power. Local KMT organs and factions are generally stronger than those of the LDP. Politics, therefore, has more of a local flavor in Taiwan than it does in Japan. The Taiwan electorate is more likely to vote for individual candidates and than by party slate as in Japan.[5] In this regard, the KMT is a closer proximity to some of the other major democratic parties of East Asia than the LDP.[6]

It is striking how the Kuomintang and the Democratic Progressive Party mirror each other. The DPP's party structure is quite similar to the KMT's. Democratization is having the same kind of influence on both parties. The DPP leadership would like to have a freer hand in setting party policy and in controlling the political agenda, but it has found the role of individuals to be too great to enjoy that luxury. To be sure, the party hierarchy of the KMT plays a larger role than the DPP hierarchy because of the KMT's financial base and because of the dominant role party leaders have had in the past. But Taiwan's growing democratic culture will continue to erode consensus within the KMT and cause the party to split into smaller parties defined along specific interests, or become a catch-all party held together by general principles. It is possible the KMT could even change its name and formally reorganize, although the substantial financial assets held by the party are valuable resources that for now keeps the party together in waging future campaigns.

3-Ideology

Sun Yat-sen called for a plan that addressed three things the Chinese needed: a national identity, economic prosperity, and a vibrant political system. His ideas were modern in the sense that nationalism, contemporary notions of economic development, and constitutional democracy stood in sharp contrast to the corruption of the Ch'ing regime and the conservative tenets of Confucianism. While there is little doubt his prescriptions for developing a sense of nationalism were vital to the creation of a modern state, the other two tenets of the *San Min Chu I* were rather vague. One of the major reasons for this is Sun's failure to allow others to criticize and help develop his economic and political ideas. Another reason was Sun's piecemeal knowledge of Western economic and political systems.

Despite these shortcomings, Sun was visionary. He knew where China stood in the community of nations and understood that to be a great nation in the twentieth century, China would have to have a profound sense of national identity, be able promote the economic welfare of its people, and become a democratic nation like the great powers of the West. He desperately wanted this vision to become the guiding ideology of the Kuomintang, even though his personal leadership style often kept party members from understanding the full impact of this dream.

Unlike Sun Yat-sen, Chiang Kai-shek's political vision was limited. Like Sun, he was fond of quoting classic texts and stories to make political points about governance and ways to organize society. But Chiang said and did little to show that he desired the establishment of democracy in China. He seems to have garnered some Weberian notions of the modern state characterized by the centralization of power in the hands of the state, an efficient and highly developed government bureaucracy, and a powerful role for political leaders. This would have satisfied both his classical interest in governance and his belief that effective control over the state and society would restore China's prestige in the community of nations.

Party reorganization on Taiwan established organizational stability the KMT never had on the mainland. But there was no ideological purpose for the KMT other than the repetition of the vague notions contained in the *San Min Chu I*. Chiang made few attempts to energize the party with new political ideas. The party machine was used to squelch independent political thinking.

Chiang Ching-kuo did not develop any new political ideas either. Though not as consumed with security and control as his father, Chiang's interest was in economic development and continued KMT control. For this reason he turned to technocracy. But technocracy results in far more than economic specialization and industrialization. It leads to contending ideas of development and the emergence of pluralism both in and out of party circles. It became apparent to Chiang that political liberalization was needed to help the Taiwan economy mature and to prevent a collapse of KMT legitimacy. Like his predecessor, Lee Teng-hui could not hold back the democratic tide, and therefore fought to keep pace with political reforms. The official line of the party is that the *San Min Chu I* succeeded on Taiwan, as Taiwan passed from political tutelage into constitutional rule. But Taiwan's road to democracy was not a product of Kuomintang guidance, but a result of leaders responding to the twin pressures of broad-based development and a desire of Taiwan's people to bring an end to political repression. In this regard, Taiwan's transition is similar to the route taken by other countries who had no ideology based on a *San Min Chu I*. The steps in Taiwan's ideological transition include the following:

1. The Taiwanization of the KMT and government ended mainlander dominance in the party. This brought economic development to Taiwan through the introduction of Taiwanese specialists trained in economics and industry, and introduced more voices into the development process generally. The party eventually had to rely more on specialists and less on party cadres to maintain the rapid economic growth that provided the KMT legitimacy in the absence of specific political liberties.

2. The creation of a middle class provided economic stability helping to provide a calm environment for political reform. It also helped the people of Taiwan develop a sense of bourgeois values necessary to sustain political reforms. The party found it necessary to accommodate expressions of political dissatisfaction. Intellectuals found new freedom to point to successes and failures in the system. At the same time, the relative passivity of Taiwan's people stabilized the transition process. Though leaders had to bring the middle class up to pace with new reforms from time to time, this allowed political elites to stay ahead of middle class demands. In time, democratic mores began to take hold and the people of Taiwan began to take democratization as a given. This helped focus debates to the center of the political spectrum and gave democratizers a mandate.

3. The KMT's political opposition included few political radicals that could have polarized the system. While some terror tactics were attempted, most political opponents tried to appeal to the sensibilities of the KMT and the general population rather than through violent threats. The Tang-wai pledged itself to uphold social stability. This gave it greater legitimacy in its fight to be recognized as a political party. After becoming a political party, the DPP devoted itself to defeating the KMT at the ballot box thus recognizing the Kuomintang as a legitimate political rival. At the same time it promised to maintain a strong military for national defense. The KMT's recognition of the DPP as a legal political contender also kept the opposition from taking drastic measures to win political inclusion. In the long run, this process also gave the KMT a new identity as a political party in a multiparty system. The KMT's future success became dependent

not on controlling all avenues of political participation, but in seeking public approval.

4. Token elections for some seats on representative bodies and for local offices raised expectations that real electoral choice was necessary and should become the norm on Taiwan. Over the course of two decades, the KMT gradually allowed more opposition candidates to run and more seats to be contested. Taiwan's people came to expect greater candidate choice in routine elections scheduled well in advance. They believed their votes had a direct bearing on the way Taiwan is governed.

5. The strengthening of legislative bodies and constitutional reforms changed the role of the Kuomintang in society. Legislative debates increased the growth of factions and cliques and forced the KMT to be more accountable for its policies. It also forced the party to liberalize by reducing the powers of the party chairman and the party's leading organs.

6. With the growth of democracy in the 1980s and '90s, other countries, especially the Unites States, put pressure on the KMT to democratize. Congressman Stephen Solarz became well known in Taiwan for his criticism of KMT political privilege and the absence of democracy in Taiwan. This was bolstered by his even-handed criticism of authoritarian rule in other countries, notably mainland China. For this reason, the KMT could not complain that Solarz was unfairly singling-out the party.

7. The KMT did not want a repeat of its darkest days. To turn back the tide of democracy would have reestablished the party as the bully it was on the mainland. Economic success would have been compromised, and the KMT's long-standing pledge to establish democracy would have proven to be a lie. The party's pledge to democratize gave it a safety valve the Leninist systems of the communist world did not have. By 1989, the people and the government came to the mutual understanding that democratization was necessary, desirable, and inevitable, thereby allowing the transition to occur at a measured pace.

Democracy as a regime is widely accepted in Taiwan. Authoritarianism is viewed as vulgar, backward, and beneath Taiwan's standards. Modernization in Taiwan has been accompanied by an intellectual and cultural acceptance of democracy--essential components for long-term stability.[7]

The seven points described above makes it difficult for the KMT to claim that the guiding ideology of the *San Min Chu I* resulted in the realization of democracy on Taiwan. But this is not to suggest that the KMT has not had a significant role in the development of Taiwan economically, or in accommodating the processes of liberalization. The KMT's shortcomings in developing better political ideas have hurt the quality of Taiwan's democracy, however. Western systems have tended to embrace democratic ideology and institutions prior to becoming democratic cultures.[8] East Asian states have developed democratic cultures first, and found the consolidation process difficult because of a lack of an ideological base. Had party chairmen and other significant party leaders familiarized themselves with democratic theory, the Taiwan system may have been able to move beyond the issues of democratic process (regular elections, electoral competition, etc.), and focus more on the virtues of democratic thought as espoused in the writings of many Western political philosophers.

This is a specific weakness of the "Asian-style democracy" theories sometimes forwarded by scholars.[9] Regimes based too much on patron-client relations, personalism, a strong state, and the authority of dominant one-party systems, are not suitable examples of democratic regimes. As shown by Robert Putnam in his work on civic traditions in Italy, the acceptance of liberal virtues plays a large role in determining whether or not a system truly develops democratically.[10] Civic mindedness and the creation of a regime that is universally respected for its quality are important to the vitality of a regime. If Kuomintang leaders can begin to think in these terms, they will have a better chance in winning the admiration of Taiwan's people, and in time, help Taiwan mature into a democracy characterized by civility and virtue, rather than by the minimalist standards of democratic process.

4-Agenda Setting

The Kuomintang's retreat to Taiwan underscored the importance of basic reforms in agriculture and in governance. The party oversaw a successful land reform program and a vast improvement in government services. Chiang wanted a more efficient state, though he did not believe democracy was a necessary condition for the establishment of such a state. Industrial development plans were laid out, and the KMT began to draft multi-year economic plans to modernize the island. At the same time, the party's reorganization introduced professionalism into the KMT. The goal of mainland recovery remained the major objective of the Kuomintang, though economic growth was seen as a tool in that endeavor. Despite the creation of a feared secret police force, Chiang Kai-shek's policies reflected greater balance in his approach, suggesting that he had learned from his mistakes on the mainland.

At Chiang Ching-kuo's urging, the elder Chiang allowed for the inclusion of Taiwanese technocrats in the government and party to facilitate economic growth. When Chiang Ching-kuo formally took the reins of power, this trend continued in greater earnestness. The younger Chiang believed the party had to be more responsive to public opinion in order to maintain support. He focused on the party's accomplishments and created a sense of confidence in the KMT's drive to modernize the country. He tended to downplay mainland recovery more than his father did, realizing the party's legitimacy had come from policy success on Taiwan, not on a distant goal that for most people seemed impossible to realize.

In time, greater specialization in the party and government bureaucracies, and reliance on outside experts within society to help in Taiwan's modernization, brought inevitable calls for democratization. Chiang knew continued economic success and shrinking hopes of realizing the party's goal to rule all of China, meant the party would have to allow the system to liberalize. Chiang agreed to end martial law, and to begin discussions surrounding the selection of officials sitting on representative bodies. The policy agenda shifted from a primary emphasis on economic development to political development.

The people of Taiwan reacted nearly as cautiously to the prospects of democratization as the party did. But once the KMT's special privileges began to fall, liberalization began at a rapid pace. Chiang Ching-kuo's death sped-up the demand for reform. Lee Teng-hui was immediately swept-up by the challenge to democratize and simultaneously consolidate his power. As the spirit of democracy began to reach the people, the political agenda became broad-based. The KMT had become a key player among several in the democratization process. It was able to maintain its position as the most popular party. Newer parties failed to distinguish themselves in a meaningful way from the Kuomintang, other than on the issue of Taiwan independence-- an issue the people were ambivalent about.

In spite of electoral success, the KMT needs a new policy agenda. Table 8.1 indicates a modest but steady decline in support for the KMT in nearly every election. This decline in support is likely to continue as parties become more differentiated and look for innovative ways to solve problems. The efforts of the party to win Taiwan a seat on the United Nations, and its efforts to increase the island's representation on other international organizations is significant, but not enough to warrant continued support in the future.

The issue of Taiwan independence is only partially dependent on events on China's mainland. Taiwan has developed a political culture that is unique from the mainland's. German reunification benefitted from a giant, robust

Table 8.1 Political Parties and Percentage of Electoral Support

Year	Race	KMT	DPP	CNP	Other
1989	LegYuan	60	29	-	11
1991	N. Assembly	68	23	-	7
1992	LegYuan	53	31	-	15
1993	City/County Chiefs	48	40	4	8
1994	Prov.Assm/ City Councl	49	32	6	14
1994	Governor/ Mayoral	52	39	8	1
1995	LegYuan	46	33	13	8

Source: Central Election Commission, *Lien-ho Pao*, December 3, 1995.

economy in free Germany at the time of reunification. While Taiwan's economy is dynamic and promising, it is dwarfed by the potential problems of the mainland's economy. At the same time, Taiwan's people have do not have as many familial attachments to the mainland as they used to. This factor has been exacerbated by Taiwanese-mainlander tensions on the island. At some point, Taiwan's people will have to have a role in deciding the future relationship of Taiwan to the mainland. The Kuomintang will need to do more to accommodate this decision.

Taiwan's economic catch-up is within sight. As the economy matures, matters such as political corruption, environmental degradation, and other quality of life issues are going to grow in importance. The Kuomintang has benefitted from its opposition having poor policy development. But it will have to take the lead in policy development if it is going to remain the party of choice in future elections.[11] Much of this is dependent on the KMT rethinking its ideological purpose. Once the Kuomintang formulates an insightful ideological foundation, it will be easier to create a new policy agenda.

5-Quality of Governance

If looked at in terms of its one-hundred year history, life under Kuomintang rule has not been easy. In fact, it has only been in the last five years that one can point to the emergence of democracy on Taiwan even though Sun Yat-sen pledged to bring democracy to China over eighty years ago. But real changes began in 1949.

The KMT's admission that the mainland had been lost because of its neglect of social problems brought about greater resolve to meet the people's needs on Taiwan. It was a far easier task for the Kuomintang. Taiwan was not as large, and with the huge party and government organizations transplanted on the island, Chiang could reorganize both the party and the state apparatus to meet these needs. In addition, the KMT defeat on the mainland had been so convincing, party leaders knew they had to succeed on Taiwan or loose all political power. Taiwan's land reform was a tremendous success. Industrialization also took hold, giving the KMT legitimacy it never enjoyed on the mainland. Unlike many developing countries, income growth was real and steady. Health care improved, as did literacy, and opportunities for higher education. While many of the party's repressive measures continued, economic growth gave the Kuomintang new life.

Chiang Ching-kuo's desire to establish laws to protect business and his willingness to accept some dissent, had a positive effect. Under the younger Chiang's rule, there was less arbitrary use of power, and more reliance on rules and accepted norms for formulating policy. Non party specialists from higher education and from abroad were invited to voice their opinions on Taiwan's development strategies as a way to maintain economic growth. By the mid 1980s, political beatings, murders, and other illegal activities seemed completely out of sync with the growing sense of economic maturity and the political expectations of Taiwan's people. Realizing economic success was no longer enough, the KMT began to yield to the demands of its critics and open the system to opposition parties.

Under Lee Teng-hui, the people of Taiwan have seen the formal end of most extraconstitutional rules and have witnessed the growth of real democratic institutions. Courts continue to gain independence from the executive branch of government, elections occur regularly, and policies and leaders may be critically scrutinized by the people without fear of reprisal. Quality of life issues such as environmental protection, anti-corruption laws, health care, care for the elderly, and education have been put on the political agenda by the people of Taiwan who complain the government has neglected these issues for too long. In spite of these popular changes, the quality of Taiwan's democracy remains seriously limited by unparliamentary tactics in the island's elected bodies, and by the unwillingness of competing groups to compromise on some issues in the spirit of liberalism. Taiwan remains focused on the processes of democracy rather than on questions of whether or not the system of government can approach a semblance of greatness that political thinkers have traditionally believed democracy could attain. The existence of widespread corruption weakens the public's image of politicians and the institutions they represent. Part of the Kuomintang's future success depends on whether or not it will be able to develop political ideas that reflect democratic virtues. This will be difficult given the high stakes game the KMT fights everyday to maintain power. But providing a vision of a high quality democratic system is the key to long-term political success.

6-Party-Government Relations

The KMT reorganization on Taiwan and a commitment by party leaders to not repeat their mainland mistakes strengthened the KMT-government relationship. Ministries were better developed, and training became a high priority. The party brought greater talent into the government and party. Party leaders saw the need to bring in specialists who could assure the greatest chances for policy success. This led to greater specialization in government. By the 1970s, party membership was no longer as expedient to hold significant government posts. Bureaucracies began to be filled with experts who developed a sense of government service increasingly independent of the party. In time, democratic forces were sufficient to support the reform of representative institutions, making them a focus of political power.

By the time Lee Teng-hui took the reins of power, the party had already begun to lose some of its power to the government. Political liberalization was affecting every level of government. Formal censorship practices came to an end and news organizations began to do more investigative reporting. Women's, youth, school, and industrial groups that had been co-opted under the party-state system became depoliticized in the new political climate. The role of the KMT began to change rapidly. The position of KMT chairman as president of the republic was no longer a certainty. The government bureaucracies resisted taking blame for the extraconstitutional privileges claimed by the KMT. They felt freer to criticize certain aspects of Kuomintang rule. As the focus of power shifted to representative bodies, raucous debates rocked the legislature and national assembly. The tensions in these organs spilled over into inner Kuomintang debates, thus weakening the party even further.

While the separation of party and government affairs has become a reality, it is not yet complete. The KMT continues to hold informal and formal power over some government activities either through personal loyalties, or through official government contracts with KMT enterprises. The defeat of KMT candidates in popular elections for the legislative yuan and the presidency would have an alarming impact on the KMT. Many enterprises are already in financial trouble, and the lack of government funding by contract would greatly hurt the party. The party has already had difficulty finding jobs for its own party members who have had to leave full time party employment because of financial downscaling. Reorganizing and selling unprofitable KMT firms would increase the ranks of the KMT unemployed.

As separation becomes more certain, many of the KMT's atrocities of the past, especially those committed in the first two decades of party rule on Taiwan, will be exposed. The fact that many of the leaders who oversaw the work of the security apparatus are dead will help younger KMT leaders distance themselves from the actions of their predecessors. Media coverage has focused on political tortures and deaths at the hands of the security apparatus, which they have attributed to KMT leaders, not the government.

The Kuomintang and Political Development

Most observers agree Taiwan has had a bona fide economic miracle. Has there been a corresponding political miracle? This study suggests there has not. The forces that have given rise to democracy on Taiwan are similar to ones identified in other case studies documenting the transition to democracy albeit more institutional and long-term. Economic development, a markedly patient yet persistent opposition, high education levels, foreign pressure from liberal regimes, and a recognition of the inevitability of democracy to cool political hostility, are all important factors in Taiwan's democratization.

Taiwan's case is important for several reasons. The Kuomintang has shown that a Leninist regime can evolve into a democratic regime without the ruling party losing control. But if a Leninist regime has been plagued with an ideology that tries to fundamentally transform society into a fascist or communist state, the chances of its finding success as a democratic party decreases dramatically. The KMT pledged to establish democracy and maintain a free economic system. It also allowed for other freedoms that totalitarian systems do not. These qualitative differences are essential in understanding the prospects of Leninist regimes becoming democratic regimes.

Does the KMT experience on Taiwan suggest a model of democratic transition for other authoritarian regimes to follow? If authoritarian regimes follow the KMT example of building a middle class, listening to the encouragement of democratic governments, improving education levels, seeing compromise with the opposition as an inevitable good where all parties benefit--then the Kuomintang model is a fine example to follow. It has been mentioned several times in this study that Taiwan reaffirms the conclusions of scholars like Schmitter and O'Donnell in the transitions literature. Elites make democratic decisions by compromising at crucial political points. Nevertheless, this study also suggests the democratic prerequisites literature that has been criticized in recent years (indeed by O'Donnell and Schmitter) is still relevant for studying transitions to democracy.[12] But it must be stated again that the Kuomintang's overarching purpose was not to democratize. It was a party dominated by Leninist leaders for most of its history. Leninist organizations are dangerous. The purpose of the party is to consolidate power in the hands of a party elite, and use party organs to extend power. The party has staying power that other authoritarian parties do not have. It is more effective than conventional one-party states at squelching political criticism and neutralizing opponents in and out of the party.

Effective economic development programs are rarely associated with Leninist parties. Taiwan's economic miracle was not dependent on the KMT's Leninist organization. In fact, economic development in Taiwan occurred in spite of the Kuomintang's devotion to Leninist politics. While other Leninist states attempted to centrally plan and organize every aspect of their economies, economists in Taiwan employed a variety of economic schemes enroute to making Taiwan an economic powerhouse. Even the much heralded economic achievements in mainland China have limits. By the late 1980s, scholars only gave Beijing a slight chance of success in their reform program.[13] In fact, economic reforms have aggravated factional infighting within the communist party of China, threatening reforms altogether. By contrast, Taiwan's economic reforms gave the KMT popular support throughout the democratization process.[14]

Authoritarians, therefore, should note the particulars of Taiwan's democratization. First of all, full economic development is usually complimented by democratization.[15] Even though there are liberal political regimes that have relatively non-liberal economic systems, economies are more responsive to public demands in democratic countries than in authoritarian countries. The existence of a democratic government usually helps stabilize the economy and gives greater promise for expansion. In general, authoritarian regimes that liberalize their economies are more successful because they increase the prospects for broad-based economic growth. But at some point they must also liberalize the political system. The failure to do so invites political turmoil that destroys the foundation of successful economic policies. This realization became more apparent to KMT leaders with each successful economic policy implemented on Taiwan. It is an important lesson for mainland China to keep in mind. Beijing's desire to reach economic maturity in the absence of democratic development is a feat that has not been accomplished by a single contemporary nation-state.

Authoritarians also need to pay particular attention to the limits of political repression. People living under authoritarian regimes will often tolerate harsh political treatment as long as there is real progress in other areas, such as in economic development, or in meeting basic human needs. But such toleration is temporary. Success must be continuous and eventually lead to the liberalization of political life if leaders expect to outlast leaders in other regimes who continue to snuff out broad-based political participation.[16] Authoritarian leaders who lack meaningful political agendas and fail to make real attempts to improve people's lives risk challenges to their power from fellow elites. If the regime demonstrates a real concern for the social well being of its people, and develops policies to address these needs, it is possible to limit violent challenges to power from critics within the regime and from the general populace. But sooner or later, regime leaders will have to elicit help and support from other members of the regime who at one time were not part of the decision making group. There will be a need to rely on outside experts, and eventually, a necessity to address the demands of the political opposition.

KMT leaders were influenced by a related theme. More authoritarians are worrying about their reputations and place in history. They would rather be remembered as reformers than tyrants. It is becoming increasingly difficult for authoritarian leaders to win aid monies and carry-on trade with democratic states without being roundly criticized for their repressive policies by international organizations, foreign governments, and the international press.[17] The current wave of democratization has helped the reputations of leaders like those in Taiwan because they liberalized. At the same time, the reluctance to liberalize has villainized the non-progressive, antidemocratic leaders in authoritarian states like China, Burma, and numerous countries throughout the Middle East and North Africa. If leaders in these countries will come to see that their only chances for political survival are in presiding over the processes of liberalization and democratization, reform would not be viewed with the same degree of loathing. The KMT has proven it is possible for a Leninist party to survive the collapse of Leninist rule and emerge a democratic party. But in doing so, leaders came to agree that a fundamentally new political system had to replace their exclusive regime, and the would have to risk their own political survival in the process. There are no guarantees for reform-minded leaders.

The experience of the Kuomintang points to the relevance of all of these lessons. The Kuomintang was fortunate to survive its debacle on mainland China. Most authoritarian regimes, especially Leninist ones, do not get second chances. A final assessment of the party's successes and failures on Taiwan must wait for the question of Taiwan's political identity vis-a-vis mainland China to be resolved and for democratic forces to mature. But there is reason for optimism. The spirit of democracy is sweeping the international community. Tocqueville was one of the first to note the significance of this phenomena:

> If the men of our time should be convinced, by the attentive observations and sincere reflection, that the gradual and progressive development of social equality is at once the past and future of their history, this discovery alone would confer upon the change the sacred character of a divine decree. To attempt to check democracy would be

in that case to resist the will of God; and the nations would then be constrained to make the best of the social lot awarded them by Providence.[18]

While many will disagree with Tocqueville over the influence of divinity in democratic development, few can deny the overwhelming victory of democracy over authoritarianism.

Whether or not the Kuomintang can survive as a democratic party is a question that becomes less important with each passing day. After one-hundred years of KMT rule, democratic principles are finally taking center stage in this marathon political drama. And while the KMT has done much to thwart democracy during this century, it has finally seen the necessity and desirability of yielding to democratic forces. It is the party's greatest political accomplishment to date.

Notes

1. Robert R. Kaufman, "Liberalization and Democratization in South America," p. 105; Jose Maria Maravall and Julian Santamaria, "Political Change in Spain and the Prospects for Democracy," *Transitions from Authoritarian Rule: Southern Europe*, pp. 104, 106-7.

2. Edwin A. Winckler, "Taiwan Transition," p. 253.

3. Kenji Hayao, *The Japanese Prime Minister and Public Policy* (Pittsburgh: University of Pittsburgh Press, 1993).

4. Gary W. Cox and Emerson Niou, "Seat Bonuses Under the Single Non-transferable Vote System: Evidence from Japan and Taiwan," *Comparative Politics* (January 1994), pp. 221-236. See also Andrew J. Nathan, "The Legislative Yuan Elections In Taiwan: Consequences of the Electoral System," *Asian Survey* (April 1993), p. 434.

5. Ronald J. Hrebenar, *The Japanese Party System*, Second Edition (Boulder: Westview Press, 1992).

6. Haruhiro Fukui, *Political Parties of Asia and the Pacific*, Vol. 1 (Westport, CT: Greenwood Press, 1985), 8.

7. Tocqueville, *Democracy In America*, Volume I, p. 299; Volume II, p. 107.

8. Fukuyama, "Democracy's Future," pp. 7-14.

9. Neher, "Asian Style Democracy," pp. 949-961.

10. Robert B. Putnam, *Making Democracy Work: Civic Traditions in Modern Italy* (Princeton: Princeton University Press, 1993).

11. Terry Lynn Karl, "Dilemmas of Democratization in Latin America," pp. 12-13.

12. O'Donnell and Schmitter, *Transitions from Authoritarian Rule*. Huntington is still a defender of much of the findings in the prerequisites tradition. See his *The Third World*.

13. Michael Oksenberg and Kenneth Lieberthal, "Forecasting China's Future," *The National Interest* (Fall 1986), pp. 18-27. See also Harry Harding's *A Fragile Relationship: The United States and China Since 1972* (Washington: The Brookings Institution, 1992), pp. 138-206.
14. Steven J. Hood, "Reform and Factional Strife in China," *Asian Thought and Society* (May-August 1994), pp. 124-135.
15. Schmitter and Karl, "What Democracy Is...And Is Not," p. 85.
16. Martins, "The Liberalization of Authoritarian Rule in Brazil," pp. 79-81.
17. Huntington, *The Third Wave*, pp. 45-6.
18. Tocqueville, *Democracy In America*, Volume One, p. 7.

Acronyms

CAC = Central Advisory Council
CC = Central Committee
CEC = Central Executive Committee
CSC = Central Standing Committee
CDRA = Chinese Democratic Reformers Alliance
CNP = Chinese New Party
DPP = Democratic Progressive Party
FEER = Far Eastern Economic Review
KMT = Kuomintang (Nationalist Party of China)
PRC = People's Republic of China (mainland China)
ROC = Republic of China (on Taiwan)
TW = Tang-wai
UN = United Nations
U.S. = United States

Bibliography

Books

Arendt, Hannah. *Totalitarianism: Part Three of the Origins of Totalitarianism.* New York: Harcourt, Brace, Jovanovich, 1951.

Aristotle. *The Politics.* Translated and edited by Carnes Lord. Chicago: Chicago University Press, 1984.

Ballantyne, Joseph W. *Formosa: A Problem for United States Foreign Policy.* Washington: Brookings Institution, 1952.

Bendix, Richard. *Kings or People?* Berkeley: University of California Press, 1978.

Central Committee, Kuomintang. *Ke-min Wen-hsien* (Documents of the Revolution). Taipei: Kuomintang Central Committee, 1966.

Chang, Carsun. "Chiang Kai-shek and Kuomintang Dictatorship." In Pinchon P.U. Loh's *The Kuomintang Debacle of 1949: Conquest or Collapse?* Boston: D.C. Heath, 1965.

Chang Ch'i-yun. *Chang Ch'i-yun Hsien-sheng Wen Chi* (The Writings of Mr. Chang Ch'i-yun). Volume XIV. Taipei: Chinese Culture University, 1989.

Ch'en Ch'eng. *Land Reform in Taiwan.* Taipei: China Publishing, 1961.

Cheng Tun-jen and Haggard, Stephan, eds. *Political Change in Taiwan.* Boulder: Lynne Reinner, 1992.

Chiang Kai-shek. *Soviet Russia in China: A Summing Up at Seventy.* Taipei: China Publishing, 1969.

Chiang Yung-chin. *Pai-nien Lau Tien: Kuomintang Ts'an-sang Shih* (One Hundred Year-Old Store: The Kuomintang's Turbulent History). Taipei: Chu'an Chi Wen Hsueh Ch'u-pan She, 1993.

Chu Yun-han. *Crafting Democracy in Taiwan.* Taipei: Institute for National Policy Research, 1992.

Clough, Ralph. *Island China.* Cambridge: Harvard University Press, 1978.

Dahl, Robert A. *Polyarchy: Participation and Opposition.* New Haven: Yale University Press, 1971.

Diamond, Larry, and Linz, Juan J. *Democracy in Developing Countries.* Four volumes. Boulder: Lynne Reinner, 1989.

Feng Yu-lan. *A History of Chinese Philosophy.* Translated by Derk Bodde. Princeton: Princeton University Press, 1953.

Fukui Haruhiro. *Political Parties of Asia and the Pacific*. Westport: Greenwood Press, 1985.
Gold, Thomas. *State and Society in the Taiwan Miracle*. Armonk: M.E. Sharpe, 1986.
Halbeisen, Herman. "In Search of a New Political Order? Political Reform in Taiwan." In Steve Tsang's *In the Shadow of China: Political Developments in Taiwan Since 1949*. Honolulu: University of Hawaii Press, 1993.
Han Lih-wu. *Taiwan Today*. Taipei: Hwa Kuo Publishing, 1951.
Harding, Harry. *A Fragile Relationship: The United States and China Since 1972*. Washington: Brookings Institution, 1992.
Hayao, Kenji. *The Japanese Prime Minister and Public Policy*. Pittsburgh: University of Pittsburgh Press, 1993.
Hrebenar, Ronald J. *The Japanese Party System*. Boulder: Westview Press, 1993.
Huang, Mab. *Intellectual Ferment for Political Reforms in Taiwan, 1971-1973*. Ann Arbor: Michigan Papers in Chinese Studies, no. 28, 1976.
Huntington, Samuel P. *Political Order in Changing Societies*. New Haven: Yale University Press, 1968.
_____. *The Third Wave: Democratization in the Late Twentieth Century*. Norman, Oklahoma: University of Oklahoma Press, 1991.
Hwang, Y. Dolly. *The Rise of a New World Economic Power: Postwar Taiwan*. Westport: Greenwood, 1991.
Israel, John. "Politics on Formosa." In Mark Mancall, ed. *Formosa Today*. New York: Praeger, 1964.
Jacoby, Neil H. *U.S. Aid to Taiwan: A Study of Foreign Aid*. New York: Praeger, 1966.
Kaplan, John. *The Court-Martial of the Kaohsiung Defendants*. Berkeley: Institute of East Asian Studies, University of California Press, 1981.
Kerby, William C. *Germany and Republican China*. Stanford: Stanford University Press, 1984.
Kingdon, John W. *Agendas, Alternatives, and Public Policies*. Boston: Little, Brown, 1984.
Kuo Ping-chia. *China: New Age and New Outlook*. New York: Alfred A. Knopf, 1956.
Kuo, Shirley W.Y. *The Taiwan Economy in Transition*. Boulder: Westview Press, 1983.
LaPalombara, Joseph, and Weiner, Myron, eds. *Political Parties and Political Development*. Princeton: Princeton University Press, 1966.
Lenin, Vladimir. *What Is To Be Done?: Burning Questions of Our Movement*. In *The Collected Works of V.I. Lenin, Volume II*. New York: International Publishers, 1934.
Lerner, Arthur J. *Taiwan's Politics: The Provincial Assemblyman's World*. Washington: University Press of America, 1978.
Li Chien-nung. *The Political History of China*. Translated and edited by Teng Ssu-yu and Jeremy Ingalls. Stanford: Stanford University Press, 1956.
Linz, Juan J., and Stepan, Alfred, eds. *The Breakdown of Democratic Regimes, Part I: Crisis, Breakdown, and Reequilibration*. Baltimore: Johns Hopkins University Press, 1978.

Bibliography

_____. "Totalitarian and Authoritarian Regimes." Edited by Fred Greenstein and Nelson Polsby. Reading, Massachusetts: Addison Wesley, 1975.

Liu, Alan P.L. *Phoenix and the Lame Lion: Modernization in Taiwan and Mainland China, 1950-1980*. Stanford: Hoover Institution Press, 1987.

Mei Wen-li. "The Intellectuals on Formosa." In Mark Mancall, ed. *Formosa Today*. New York: Praeger, 1964.

Mendel, Douglas. *The Politics of Formosan Nationalism*. Berkeley: University of California Press, 1970.

Metzger, Thomas A. *Escape from Predicament: Neo-Confucianism and China's Evolving Political Culture*. New York: Columbia University Press, 1977.

Montesquieu. *The Spirit of the Laws*. Translated and edited by Anne Cohler, Basia Miller and Harold Stone. Cambridge: Cambridge University Press, 1989.

Moody, Peter R., Jr. *Political Change in Taiwan: A Study of Ruling Party Adaptability*. New York: Praeger, 1992.

Moore, Clement. "The Single Party as Source of Legitimacy." In Samuel P. Huntington and Clement Moore, eds., *Authoritarian Politics in Modern Society: The Dynamics of Established One-Party Systems*. New York: Basic Books, 1970.

Nathan, Andrew J. and Ho, Helena V.S. "Chiang Ching-kuo's Decision for Political Reform." In *Chiang Ching-kuo's Leadership in the Development of the Republic of China on Taiwan*, Shao-chuan Leng, ed. Lanham, Maryland: University Press of America, 1993.

_____. *China's Crisis: Dilemmas of Reform and Prospects for Democracy*. New York: Columbia University Press, 1990.

O'Donnell, Guillermo and Schmitter, Philippe C., and Whitehead, Laurence. *Transitions from Authoritarian Rule*. Volume I, *Comparative Perspectives*; Volume II, *Southern Europe*; Volume III, *Latin America*; Volume IV *Comparative Perspectives*; Volume V, *Tentative Conclusions about Uncertain Democracies*. Baltimore: Johns Hopkins University Press, 1986.

_____. *Modernization and Bureaucratic-Authoritarianism: Studies in South American Politics*. Berkeley: Institute of International Studies, 1979.

Putnam, Robert B. *Making Democracy Work: Civic Traditions in Modern Italy*. Princeton: Princeton University Press, 1993.

Pye, Lucian. *Asian Power and Politics: The Cultural Dimensions of Authority*. Cambridge: Belknap Press of Harvard University Press, 1985.

Ra Jyh-pin. "The Introduction of American and European Constitutionalism to China." In Ray S. Cline and Hungdah Chiu's *The U.S. Constitution and the Development of Constitutionalism in China*. Washington: United States Global Strategy Council, 1988.

Rubenstein, Murray A. *The Other Taiwan: 1945 to the Present*. Armonk: M.E. Sharpe, 1994.

Schumpeter, Joseph A. *Capitalism, Socialism, and Democracy*. New York: Harper and Row, 1942.

Shieh, Milton J. T., editor and translator. *The Kuomintang: Selected Historical Documents, 1894-1969*. New York: St. John's University Press, 1970.

Sun Yat-sen. *Fundamentals of National Reconstruction for the Nationalist Government of China*. China: 1924.

_____. *San Min Chu I* (The Three Principles of the People). Chungking: Ministry of Information of the Republic of China, 1943.

Tai Hung-chao. *Land Reform and Politics: A Comparative Analysis*. Berkeley: University of California Press, 1974.

Tang Tsou. *America's Failure in China, 1941-1950*. Chicago: University of Chicago Press, 1963.

Tien Hung-mao. *Government and Politics in Kuomintang China, 1927-1937*. Stanford: Stanford University Press, 1972.

_____, ed. *The Great Transition: Political and Social Change in the Republic of China*. Stanford: Hoover Institution Press, 1989.

_____, ed. *Taiwan's Electoral Politics and Democratic Transition: Riding the Third Wave*. Armonk: M.E. Sharpe, 1996.

Tocqueville, Alexis de. *Democracy in America*. Translated and edited by Henry Reeve. New York: Alfred A. Knopf, 1980.

Ts'ao Chun-han. "Su-tsao Chung-kuo Kuomintang Wei Kung-kung Cheng-tse Cheng-tang Tse-yi" (Molding China's Kuomintang into a Responsive Public Party). In Yang T'ai Shuenn, ed. *Cheng-tang Cheng-chih yu Taiwan Min-chu Hua*.

Tucker, Robert C., ed. *The Lenin Anthology*. New York: W.W. Norton, 1975.

Verba, Sidney. "Sequences and Development." In James S. Coleman, Joseph LaPalombara, Lucian Pye, Sidney Verba and Myron Weiner, *Crises and Sequences in Political Development*. Princeton: Princeton University Press, 1971.

Wachman, Alan. *Taiwan: National Identity and Democratization*. Armonk: M.E. Sharpe, 1994.

Wu Joseph Jaushieh. *Taiwan's Democratization: Forces Behind the New Momentum*. Oxford: Oxford University Press, 1995.

Yang T'ai-shuenn. *Cheng-tang Cheng-chih yu Taiwan Min-chu Hua* (Party Politics and Taiwan's Democratic Culture). Taipei: Democracy Foundation, 1991.

Government Sources

Central Election Commission, Republic of China. "Legislative Yuan Election Returns, 1995." Taipei: December 3, 1995.

_____. "Presidential Election Law of the Republic of China." Taipei: January 19, 1996.

_____. "Results of the Vote for the National Assembly." Taipei: March 24, 1996.

Executive Yuan, Republic of China. "Guidelines for National Reunification." Taipei: March 14, 1991.

Department of Commerce, Foreign Broadcast Information Service. *Daily Report*. Far East and the Pacific, and China Reports. Washington, D.C.

Government Information Office, Republic of China. "Biographies and Platforms of the Candidates for President and Vice President." Taipei: March 15, 1996.

_____. "Post Election News Summary, March 25, 1996." Taipei: March 25, 1996.

_____. "Transcript of Presidential News Conference." Taipei: February 24, 1996.

Ministry of Information, Republic of China. *China Handbook, 1951*. Taipei: China Publishing, 1951.

Subcommittee on Asian and Pacific Affairs, Committee on Foreign Relations, U.S. House of Representatives. *Taiwan: The National Affairs Council and Implications for Democracy*. Hearing, October 11, 1990. Washington: U.S. Government Printing Office, November 1990.

Interviews and Oral Histories

Chinese Oral History Project, Rare Books and Manuscripts Division, Columbia University Library, New York. Oral Histories Used:
"The Reminiscences of Li Han-Hun."
"The Reminiscences of Chen Li-fu."
"The Reminiscences of Wu Kuo-cheng."
Chang Ch'un-nan (Antonio Chang). Interview, May 19, 1993. Taipei, Taiwan.
Chien Han-sheng (Hansen). Interview, June 14, 1993. Taipei, Taiwan.
Chu Yun-han. Interview, May 19, 1993. Taipei, Taiwan.
Chung Jih-hong. Interview, July 20, 1993. Taipei, Taiwan.
Feng Hu-Hsiang. Interview, July 22, 1993. Taipei, Taiwan.
Hu Fo. Interview, May 28, 1993. Taipei, Taiwan.
Ilan County Party Cadres. Interview, June 15, 1993. Ilan, Taiwan.
Ku Feng-Hsiang. Interview, August 17, 1988. San Jose, California.
Lin Chia-lung. Interview, July 22, 1993.
Lu Ya-li. Interview, May 19, 1993. Taipei, Taiwan.
Sheng, Chien-nan (Johnny Jen-nan Sand). Interview, May 28, 1993. Taipei, Taiwan.
Taoyuan County Party Cadres. Interview, June 22, 1993. Taoyuan, Taiwan.
Tsiang Yen-si. Interview, June 8, 1993. Taipei, Taiwan.
Yang T'ai-shuenn. Interview, May 24, 1993. Taipei, Taiwan.
Ye Chu-lan. Interview, July 1, 1993. Taipei, Taiwan.

Scholarly Journals

Appleton, Sheldon. "Taiwan: Portents of Change." *Asian Survey* (January 1971).
Bermeo, Nancy. "Democracy and the Lessons of Dictatorship." *Comparative Politics* (April 1992).
_____. "Rethinking Regime Change." *Comparative Politics* (April 1990).
Chang, Parris. "Taiwan in 1982: Diplomatic Setback Abroad and Demand for Reforms at Home." *Asian Survey* (January 1983).
Cheng, Peter P. "Taiwan 1975: A Year of Transition." *Asian Survey* (January 1976).
Cheng, Tun-jen. "Democratizing the Quasi-Leninist Regimes in Taiwan." *World Politics* (July 1989).
Chou Yangsun, and Nathan, Andrew J. "Democratizing Transition in Taiwan." *Asian Survey* (March 1987).
Copper, John. "Taiwan in 1981: In a Holding Pattern." *Asian Survey* (January 1982).

Cox, Gary W., and Niou, Emerson. "Seat Bonuses Under the Single Nontransferable Vote System: Evidence from Japan and Taiwan." *Comparative Politics* (January 1994).

Diamond, Larry. "Rethinking Civil Society: Toward Democratic Consolidation." *Journal of Democracy* (July 1994).

Dickson, Bruce. "The Lessons of Defeat: The Reorganization of the Kuomintang on Taiwan." *China Quarterly* (March 1993).

Domes, Jurgen. "Taiwan in 1991: Searching for Political Consensus." *Asian Survey* (January 1992).

Fukuyama, Francis. "Democracy's Future: The Primacy of Culture." *Journal of Democracy* (January 1995).

Hood, Steven J. "Political Change in Taiwan and the Rise of Kuomintang Factions." *Asian Survey* (May 1996).

———. "Reform and Factional Strife in China." *Asian Thought and Society* (May-August 1994).

Huntington, Samuel P. "Will More Countries Become Democratic?" *Political Science Quarterly* (Summer 1984).

Ishimaya, John T. "Communist Parties in Transition: Structures, Leaders, and Processes of Democratization in Eastern Europe." *Comparative Politics* (January 1995).

Jacobs, J. Bruce. "Taiwan 1972: Political System." *Asian Survey* (January 1973).

Karl, Terry Lynn. "Dilemmas of Democratization in Latin America." *Comparative Politics* (October 1990).

Lawson, Stephanie. "Conceptual Issues in the Comparative Study of Regime Change and Democratization." *Comparative Politics* (January 1993).

Li Cheng and White, Lynn. "Elite Transformation and Modern Change in Mainland China and Taiwan: Empirical Data and the Theory of Technocracy." *China Quarterly* March 1990.

Lien Chan. "The Republic of China Belongs in the United Nations." *Orbis* (Fall 1993.)

Lijphart, Arend. "Consociational Democracy." *World Politics* (January 1969).

Ts'ai Ling and Myers, Ramon H. "Surviving the Rough-and-Tumble of Presidential Politics in an Emerging Democracy: The 1990 Elections in the Republic of China." *China Quarterly* (March 1992).

Lu Ya-li (Alexander). "Future Domestic Developments in the Republic of China." *Asian Survey* (November 1985).

McBeath, Gerald. "Taiwan in 1977: Holding the Reins." *Asian Survey* (January 1978).

Nathan, Andrew J. "The Legislative Yuan Elections in Taiwan: Consequences of the Electoral System." *Asian Survey* (April 1993).

Neher, Clark D. "Asian-Style Democracy." *Asian Survey* (November 1994): 949-961.

O'Donnell, Guillermo. "Delegative Democracy." *Journal of Democracy* January 1994).

Oksenberg, Michael, and Lieberthal, Kenneth. "Forecasting China's Future." *The National Interest* (Fall 1986).

Plummer, Mark. "Taiwan: The New Look in Government." *Asian Survey* (January 1969).

Rustow, Dankwart A. "Transitions to Democracy: Toward a Dynamic Model." *Comparative Politics* (April 1970).
Schmitter, Philippe C. and Karl, Terry Lynn. "What Democracy Is...And Is Not." *Journal of Democracy* (Summer 1991).
____. "Danger and Dilemmas of Democracy." *Journal of Democracy* (April 1994).
Seymour, James D. "Taiwan in 1988: No More Bandits." *Asian Survey* (January 1989).
Shin Doh Chull. "On the Third Wave of Democratization: A Synthesis and Evaluation of Recent Theory and Research." *World Politics* (October 1984).
Snyder, Richard. "Explaining Transitions from Neopatrimonial Dictatorships," *Comparative Politics* (July 1992).
Wang Gung-hsing. "Nationalist Government Policies, 1949-1951." *The Annals of the American Academy of Political and Social Science* (September 1951).
Wilson, Richard A. "A Comparison of Political Attitudes of Taiwanese Children and Mainlander Children on Taiwan." *Asian Survey* (December 1968).
Winckler, Edwin A. "Institutionalization and Participation on Taiwan: From Hard to Soft Authoritarianism." *China Quarterly* (September 1984).
Wu Yu-shan. "Taiwan in 1994: Managing a Critical Relationship." *Asian Survey* (January 1995).

Magazines and Newspapers

China Post, Taipei.
China News, Taipei.
Chung-Kuo Shih-Pao (China Times), Taipei.
Chung-yang Jyh-pao (Central Daily), Taipei.
Far Eastern Economic Review, Hong Kong.
Free China Journal, Taipei.
Hong Kong Standard, Hong Kong.
Kuo-shih P'ing-lun (China Forum), Taipei.
Lien-ho Pao (United Daily), Taipei.
New York Times
Shih-jie Ryh-pao (World Journal Newspaper), Taipei, for world distribution.
Ts'ai Hsun (Wealth Magazine), Taipei.
Tse-li Pao (Independent Daily), Taipei.
Tzu-li Wanpao (Indpendent Evening Daily), Taipei.
Washington Post

Index

2-28 incident, 30, 69-70, 132-133

Bamboo Gang, 77

Carter, Jimmy, 64-65
CC Clique, 21
Chang, Carson, 21
Chang Chi-yun, 33
Ch'en Ch'eng, 30
Chen Li-an, 59, 139
Chen Li-fu, 21
Chen Wen-cheng, 69
Chen Yi, 30
Chiang Ching-kuo (chapters 4 and 5), 9, 35, 46
  assumes power, 48-49
  decision to democratize, 79
  head of security system, 35, 49
  political ideas, 61, 79-80, 83-85
  leadership style, 85-86
  legacy, 132
Chiang Kai-shek (chapters 2 and 3) 32-33
  adversion to democracy, 151
  cultification of, 36, 43, 46-47, 49
  legacy, 132
  political ideas, 50-53
Chiang, Madame, 94
Chiang Wei-kuo, 77
Chien, Frederick, 59
China Forum, 114
Chinese Democratic Reformers Alliance (CDRA), 114, 122, 138
  See Also Kuomintang, non-mainstream
Chinese New Party (CNP), 119, 126-28, 137-38
  See also Kuomintang, non-mainstream; and New Kuomintang Alliance
Chung-li incident, 63

Confucianism, 16, 33
Constitution, 21, 32, 101-102, 133, 140-146
Control Yuan, 28
  overlapping responsibilities, 101-102

Democracy, 31, 84, 87-88, 141, 159-160
Democratic consolidation, 10, 141, 144-145, 165-168
Democratic Progressive Party (DPP), 80-82, 99-100, 106, 121, 128-129, 131-132, 136-138
  similarities to KMT organization, 156
  See also Political opposition; Tang-Wai
Democratization, 4, 7-8, 16-17, 79-80, 83-84, 99-100, chapter 7, 141, 145, 147, 158-160, 165-167
  See also Liberalization
Deng Xiao-ping, 64-65

Economics, 29-31, 49, 61, 145-46
  APEC membership, 120
  development policies, 42-43, 146, 160-161
  GATT membership, 120
Eighties, 66
Elections, 34, 74, 161-162
  control yuan, 47-48
  legislative yuan, 47-48, 62-63, 65, 73-74, 98, 105-108, 136-138
  local, 34, 127, 129
  mayoral, 94, 127-130
  national assembly, 140
  presidency, 97-100
  provincial assembly, 37
  risks of, 9-10
Executive Yuan, 164-165
  overlapping responsibilities, 101-102

Fei Hsi-ping, 62
Formosan, 66
Free China Fortnightly, 44
Fundamentals of National Reconstruction, 6-7

Garrison command, 35, 49, 53, 59, 69, 77, 106
See also Martial Law

Hau Pei-tsun, 96, 99-100, 114, 123, 139
Hsieh, Frank, 139
Hsieh Tung-min, 62
Hsu Shui-te, 107
Hu Shih, 37
Huang Hsin-shieh, 62, 66

Independence movement, 65-68, 80-82, 103-106, 120, 134
See also United Nations

Japan
New Party, 126-127
Liberal Democratic Party, 155-156
Jaw Shao-kang, 83, 129

Kaohsiung incident, 66-68
Kuan Chung, 83
Kuansyi, 75
Kung, H.H., 21,
Kuomintang (KMT), 1, 6
agenda, 14, 53, 88, 146
chairman, 59
community programs, 116
congresses, 36, 42, 47, 68-69, 95-97, 120-127
contradictory goals, 10-11, 26-28, 95
corruption, 63-64, 128-130, 132-33
county chiefs, 34, 110-111
finances, 44, 128
factions, 108-117
ideology, 13-14, 52-53, 87-88, 156-160
inner-party democracy, 95-96
leaders, 8-9
leadership structure, 8, 12-13, 51, 63
leadership quality, 151-153
local organs, 28, 34
organization, 13, 23-29, 51-52, 86-87, 124-125, 143-144, 153-156
mainstream, 109-115
non-mainstream, 115-119
political development, 165-67
public opinion, 107
relation to government, 15, 55, 89-90, 164-65
reorganization, 21-29
Taiwanese majority, 96, 104-111, 122, 125-126
See also Taiwanization
vice chairmen, 123-124

Land reform, 30-31, 93
Lee Ching-hua, 113
Lee Teng-hui, (chapters 6 and 7)
conservative opposition to, 84
gains chairmanship, 93-97
leadership, 142-43, 150-56
presidential candidate, 136-141
visits U.S., 135-36
Legislative Yuan
first open elections, 105-107
KMT narrow majority, 161-162
limited elections, 47-48
overlapping responsibilities, 101-103
under Chiang Kai-shek, 22-23
Lei Chen, 44-46
Leninism, 6-8, 23, 28-29, 99-100
and democracy, 16-17, 165-167
and economic development, 166
Li Huan, 47, 58, 94, 96, 98-100
Li Tsung-jen, 21
Liberalization, 4, 9-10, 16-17, 59-60, 65-66, 74-76, 103-106, 121, 141-143
See also Democratization
Lien Chan, 59, 107, 139, 141
Lin Yang-kang, 99, 114, 123, 139,
Liu, Henry, 77
Liu, Tzu-ying, 44

Ma Ying-jeou, 122, 137
Mainland China,
academic exchanges, 96
family contacts, 82
journalists travel to, 96

recovery, 10, 65, 105-108
trade with, 103
war games, 135-136
Martial law, 22, 47, 75, 77, 105
  See also Garrison command; National Security Law; Press restrictions; Political opposition; Political prisoners
Military
  retirements, 47
  spending, 97-98

National Assembly
  constitutional reform, 101-102, 105, 130
  election of president, 43-44
  elections, 140
  overlapping responsibilities, 101-102
National Security Law, 82-83
  See also Constitution; Garrison commmand; Martial law
New Kuomintang Alliance, 106, 113-114, 122
  See also Chinese New Party

Organized crime elements, 130-131
  See also KMT, corruption
Overseas Chinese, 37-38, 102-102, 130-131

Peng Ming-min 46, 138-141
Platforms of candidates for president, 138-140
Political elites, 9, 11-13, 16
Political moments, 12
Political opposition, 3, 9, 43, 45-46, 53, 66
  and liberalization, 8-11
  survival, 10
  See also Democratic Progressive Party; Martial law; Tang Wai
Political prisoners, 30, 44, 47, 59, 69-70, 132-133
  See also Garrison command; Martial law
Political support, 79-80
Political torture, 30, 35-36, 69

fatigue bombings, 66-68
Political tutelage, 5-7
Prerequisites to democracy, 7-8, 16
Press restrictions, 38-, 45, 49, 59, 66
  See also Garrison commmand; Martial law
Prime minister's office, 105-106
Private institutions, 82-83
Provincial assembly
  first elections, 37
  graft, 130

San Min Chu I, 5-7, 36, 87-88, 119, 145
  See also Kuomintang, ideology; Sun Yat-sen
Shih Ming-teh, 62, 66
Siew, Vincent, 137, 139
Soong, James, 107, 113, 131-132
Soong, T.V., 21
Sun Fo, 21
Sun Yat-sen, 5-7, 36
Sunshine Law, 122-123
  See also Kuomintang, corruption

Taiwan Political Review, 66
Taiwan Straits, 43, 136
Taiwanization, 44, 46, 59-60, 74-76, 89
Tang-wai, 62-63, 66, 70, 73-74
  See also Democratic Progressive Party; Independence movement
Tenth Credit Corporation scandal, 77-78
Tocqueville, Alexis, 168
T'ung Meng Hui, 114-116

United Independent Front, 58
United Nations (UN)
  expells ROC, 48-49
  membership efforts 103, 120, 134-135
United States (U.S.), 21, 31
  foreign aid, 45
  human rights concerns, 77
  severs diplomatic ties, 64

Wang Chien-shien, 113
Wang Ching-feng, 139
Wang Ching-wei, 115
Wisdom Club, 112

Wong Hsi-ling, 77
Wu Kuo-cheng (K.C. Wu), 35-36
Wu Po-Hsiung, 59

Yao Chia-wen, 62

Yen, C.K., 47
Yok Mu-ming, 113
Yu Kuo-hwa, 94, 96, 99, 114

Zhiang Zemin, 134

About the Book and Author

Is the Nationalist party of China (Kuomintang, or KMT) the villain it is sometimes portrayed to be? Or is the embodiment of the political and moral good that partisans have claimed it to be? The KMT has managed an incredible feat of economic modernization in Taiwan and has become a proponent of democracy, yet its reputation has been marred by ineptitude and by brutal acts of repression.

Focusing on the role of KMT party elites in the democratization process, Steven Hood considers the KMT's evolution from a Leninist state party to a fractious party in a competitive political system. Many contemporary studies suggest that democratization is the product of decisions, compromises, and accidents—the result of relatively short-term confrontations between elites in the opposition and between softliners and hardliners within authoritarian regimes. Although these factors are important, the democratization of Taiwan has been a long-term process of elites wrestling within the confines of existing political institutions. Taiwan's case study reminds us that we need to revisit the prerequisites that must underline a true democracy—factors that are too often ignored or dismissed by scholars studying the democratization process.

Steven J. Hood is associate professor of politics and international relations at Ursinus College.

Printed and bound by CPI Group (UK) Ltd, Croydon, CR0 4YY
08/10/2024
01042434-0002